FOR ORGANS, PIANOS & ELECTRONIC KEYBOARDS

E-Z PLAY TODAY

346

BIG BOOK OF CHRISTMAS SONGS 2ND EDITION

ISBN-13: 978-0-7935-1481-6
ISBN-10: 0-7935-1481-9

HAL•LEONARD
CORPORATION

7777 W. BLUEMOUND RD. P.O. BOX 13819 MILWAUKEE, WI 53213

In Australia Contact:
Hal Leonard Australia Pty. Ltd.
4 Lentara Court
Cheltenham, Victoria, 3192 Australia
Email: ausadmin@halleonard.com

Visit Hal Leonard Online at
www.halleonard.com

CONTENTS

All My Heart This Night Rejoices

Registration 4
Rhythm: March

Words and Music by Johann Ebeling
and Catherine Winkworth

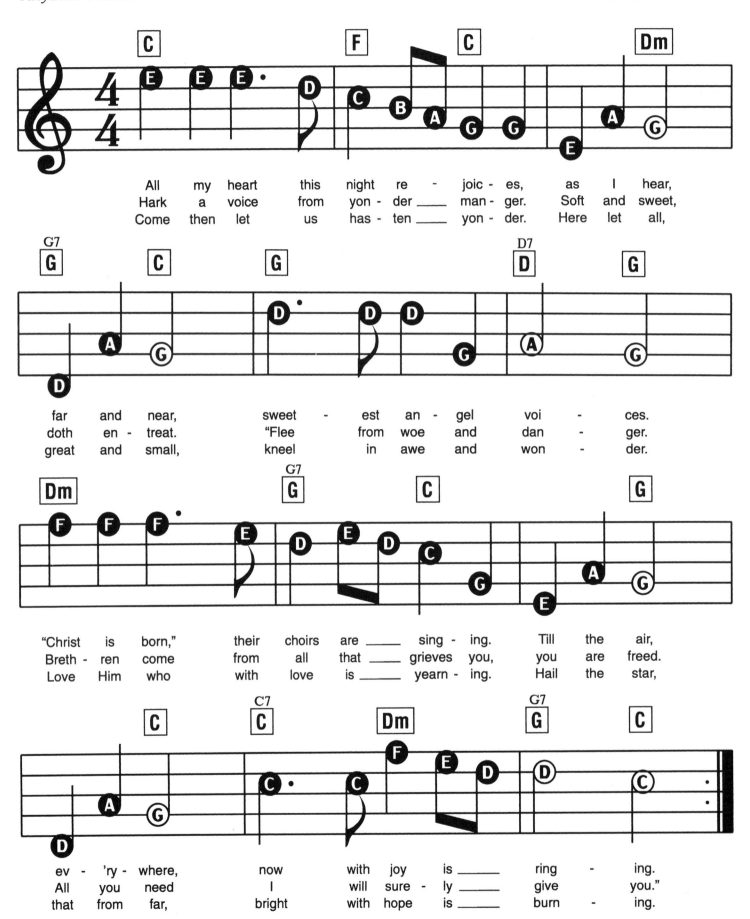

All Through the Night

Registration 8
Rhythm: None

Welsh Folksong

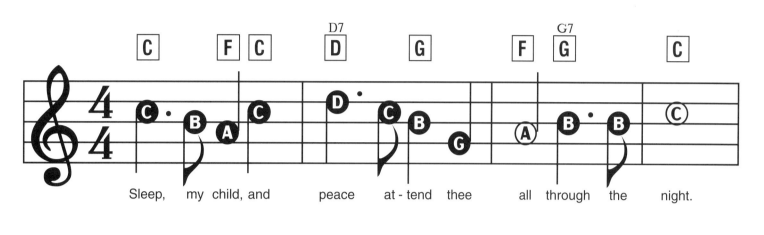

Sleep, my child, and peace at-tend thee all through the night.

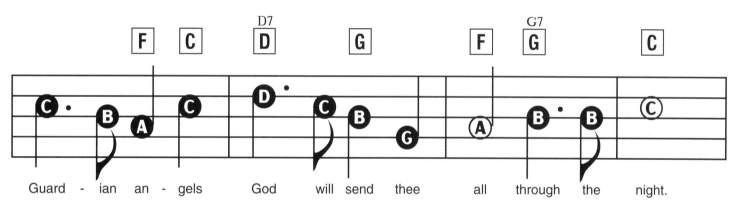

Guard - ian an - gels God will send thee all through the night.

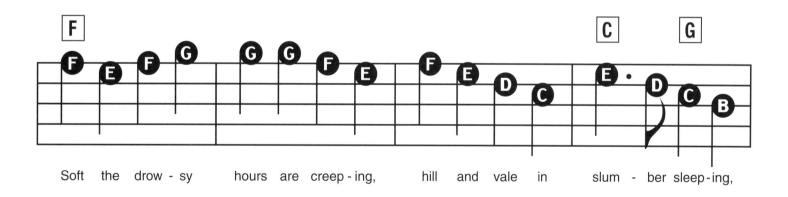

Soft the drow - sy hours are creep - ing, hill and vale in slum - ber sleep-ing,

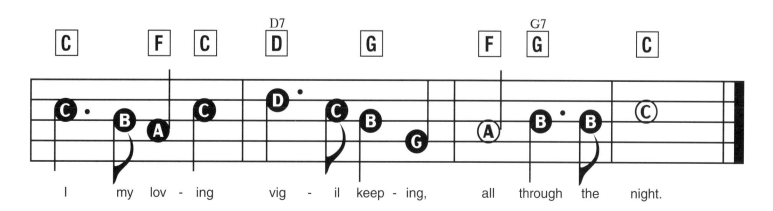

I my lov - ing vig - il keep-ing, all through the night.

Angels from Heaven

Registration 8
Rhythm: Swing or Shuffle

Traditional Hungarian

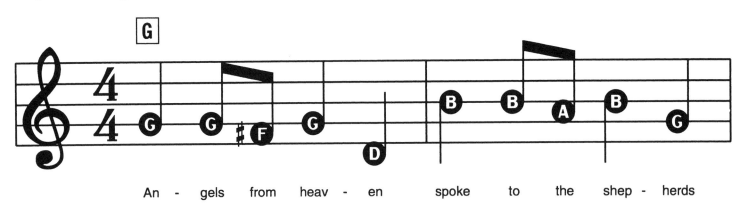

An - gels from heav - en spoke to the shep - herds

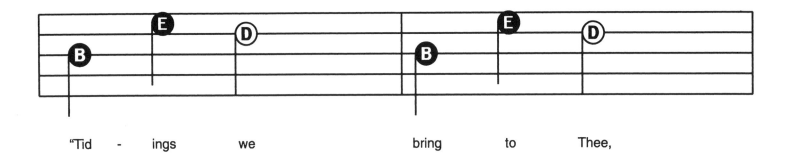

"Tid - ings we bring to Thee,

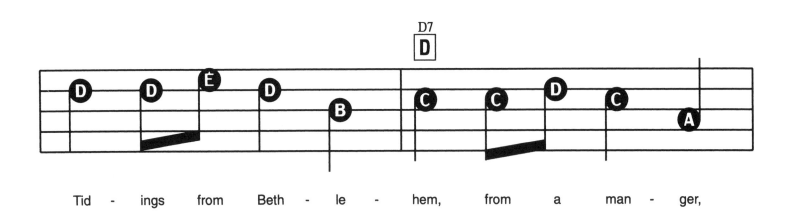

Tid - ings from Beth - le - hem, from a man - ger,

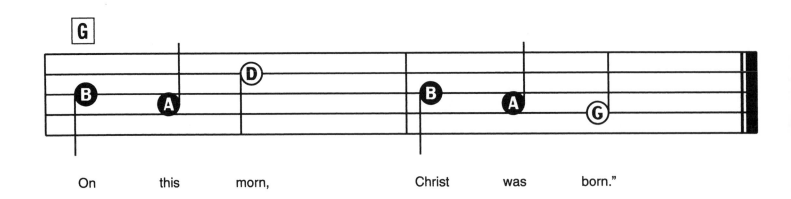

On this morn, Christ was born."

Angels from the Realms of Glory

Registration 2
Rhythm: March

Words by James Montgomery
Music by Henry T. Smart

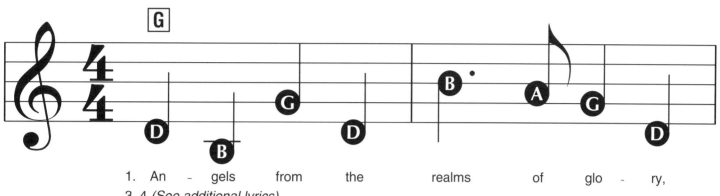

1. An - gels from the realms of glo - ry,
3.,4 *(See additional lyrics)*

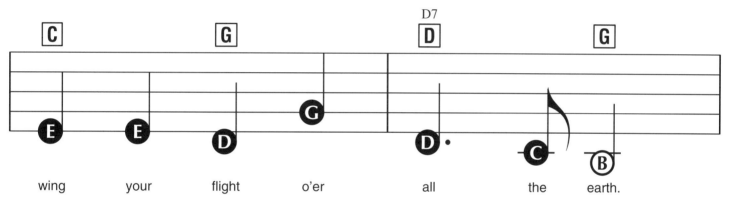

wing   your   flight   o'er   all   the   earth.

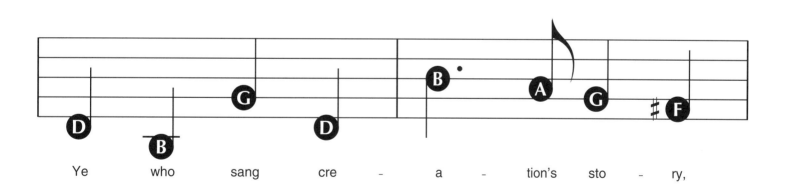

Ye   who   sang   cre - a - tion's   sto -   ry,

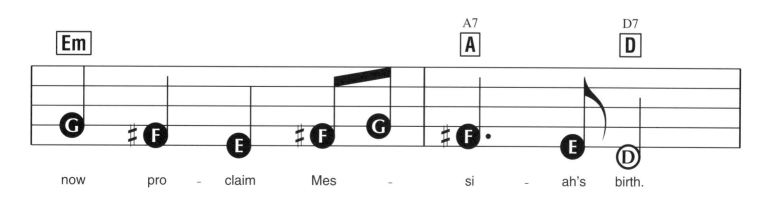

now   pro - claim   Mes -   si -   ah's   birth.

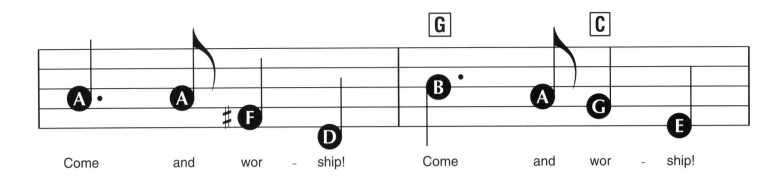

Come and wor – ship! Come and wor – ship!

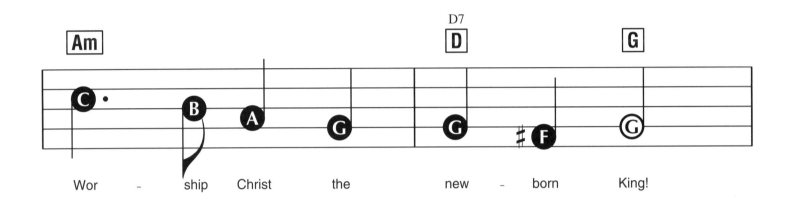

Wor – ship Christ the new – born King!

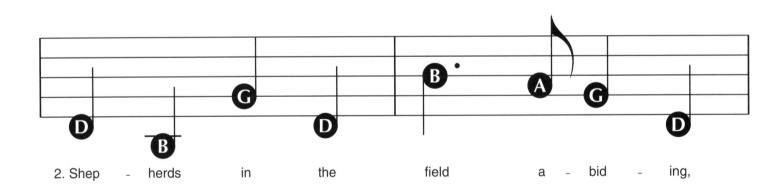

2. Shep – herds in the field a – bid – ing,

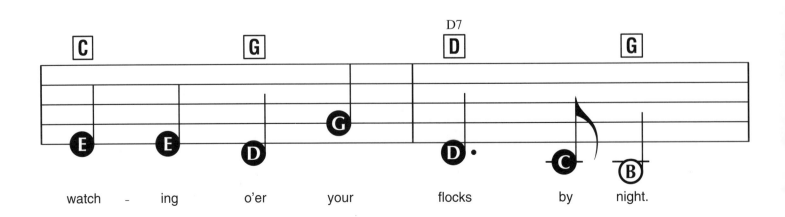

watch – ing o'er your flocks by night.

9

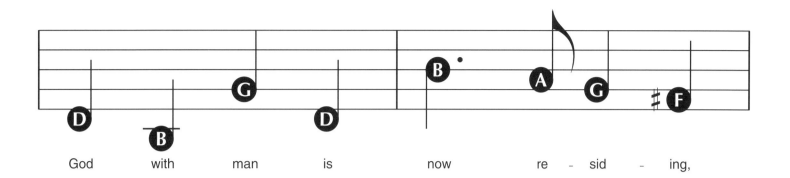

God with man is now re - sid - ing,

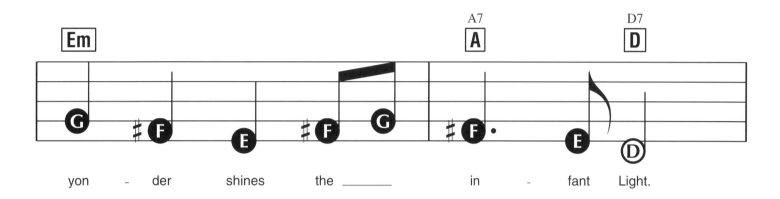

yon - der shines the _____ in - fant Light.

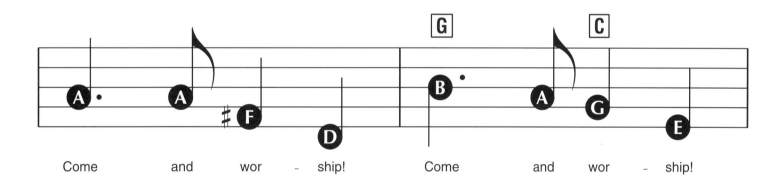

Come and wor - ship! Come and wor - ship!

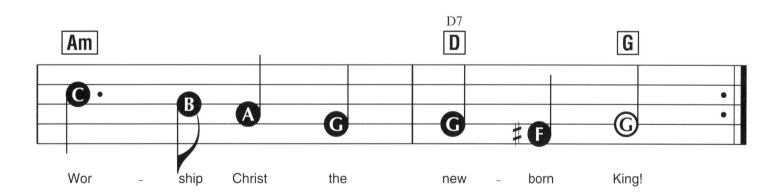

Wor - ship Christ the new - born King!

Additional Lyrics

3. Sages, leave your contemplations,
   brighter visions beam afar.
   Seek the great Desire of Nations.
   Ye have seen His natal star.

   Come and worship!
   Come and worship!
   Worship Christ the newborn King!

4. Saints before the altar bending,
   watching long in hope and fear.
   Suddenly the Lord, descending,
   in His temple shall appear.

   Come and worship!
   Come and worship!
   Worship Christ, the newborn King!

Angels We Have Heard on High

Registration 3
Rhythm: None

Traditional French Carol
Translated by James Chadwick

1. An - gels we have heard on high,
2.-4. *(See additional lyrics)*

sweet - ly sing - ing o'er the plains,

and the moun - tains in re - ply

ech - o - ing their joy - ous strains.

11

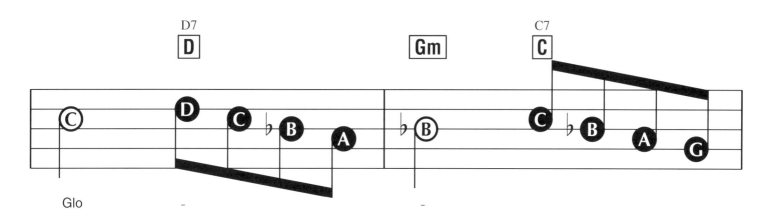

Glo -   -

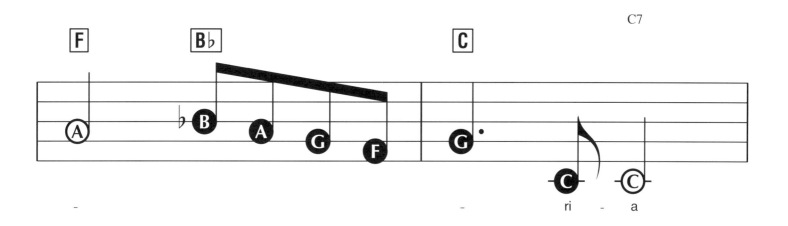

-                        -   ri - a

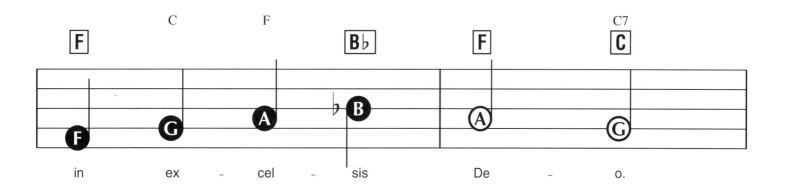

in   ex - cel - sis   De   -   o.

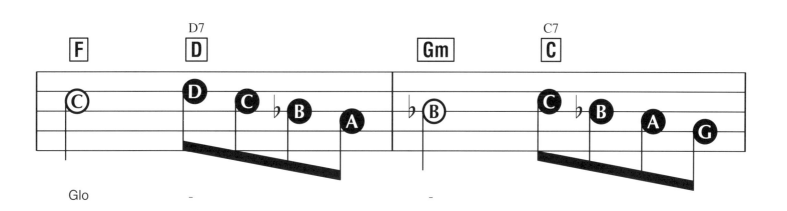

Glo -   -

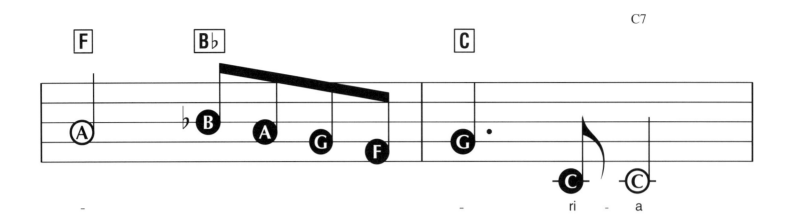

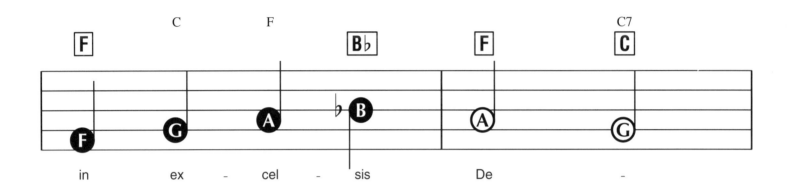

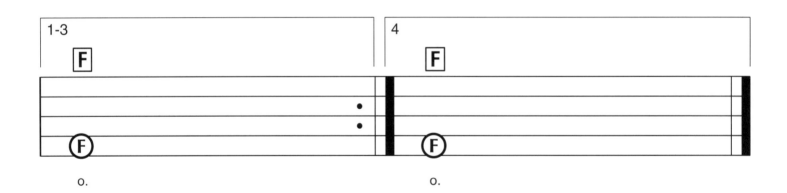

Additional Lyrics

2. Shepherds, why this jubilee?
   Why your joyous strains prolong?
   Say what may the tidings be
   Which inspire your heavenly song?

   Gloria in excelsis Deo,
   Gloria in excelsis Deo,

3. Come to Bethlehem and see
   Him whose birth the angels sing.
   Come, adore on bended knee,
   Christ the Lord, the newborn King!

   Gloria in excelsis Deo,
   Gloria in excelsis Deo.

4. See Him in a manger laid
   Whom the choirs of angels praise;
   Mary, Joseph, lend your aid,
   While our hearts in love we raise.

   Gloria in excelsis Deo,
   Gloria in excelsis Deo.

As Each Happy Christmas

Registration 4
Rhythm: March

Traditional

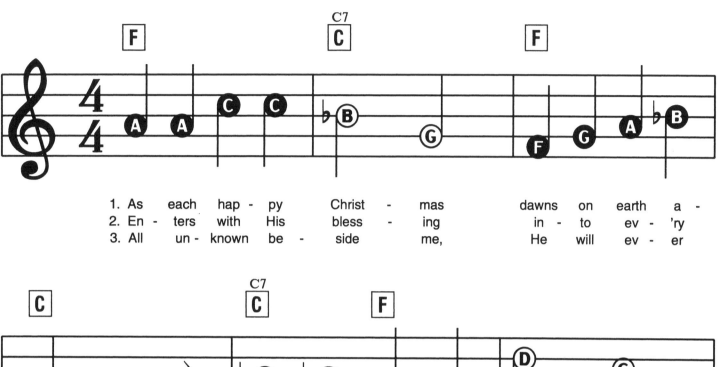

1. As each hap - py Christ - mas dawns on earth a -
2. En - ters with His bless - ing in - to ev - 'ry
3. All un - known be - side me, He will ev - er

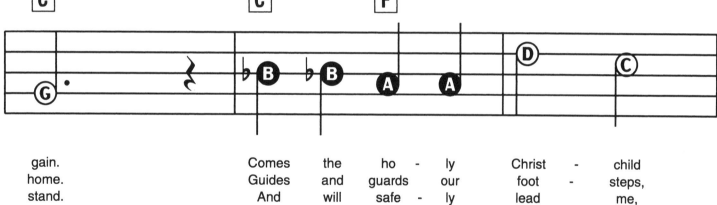

gain. Comes the ho - ly Christ - child
home. Guides and guards our foot - steps,
stand. And will safe - ly lead me,

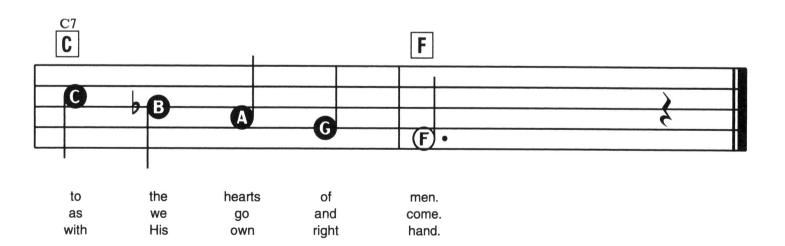

to the hearts of men.
as we go and come.
with His own and right hand.

As Lately We Watched

Registration 1
Rhythm: None

19th Century Austrian Carol

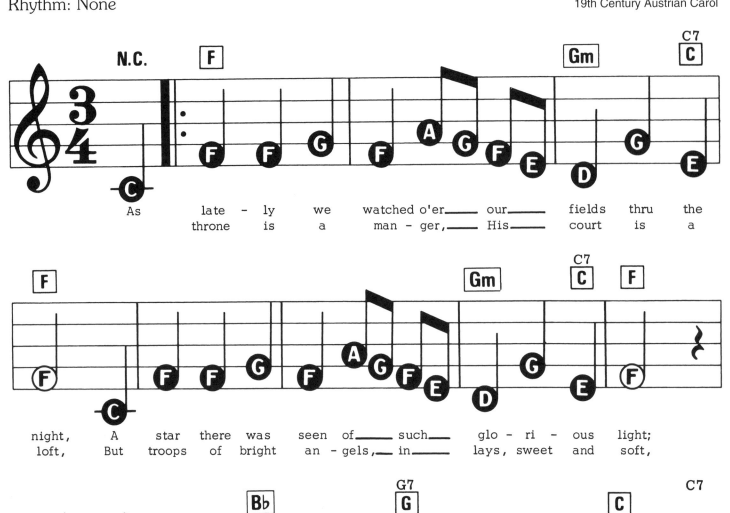

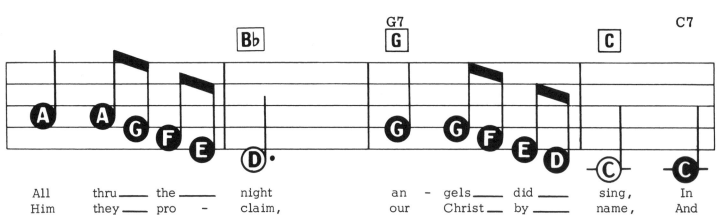

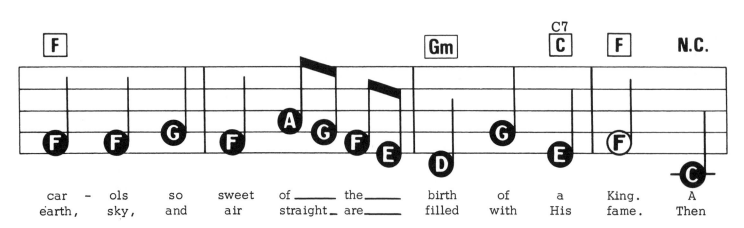

15

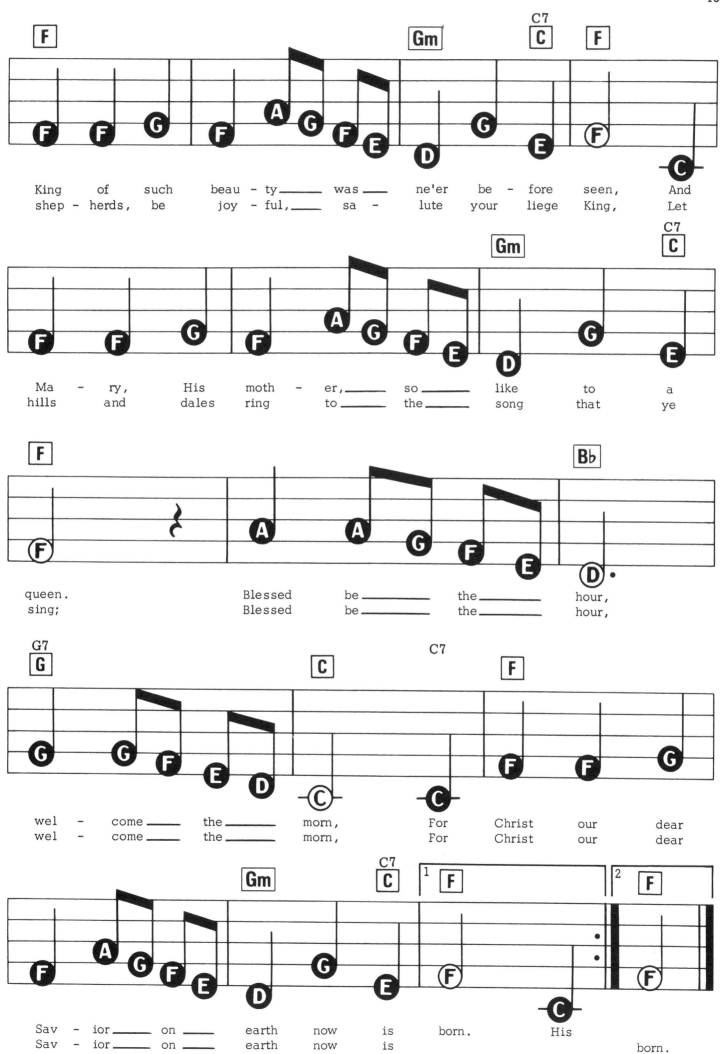

As with Gladness Men of Old

Registration 10
Rhythm: None

Words by William Chatterton Dix
Music by Conrad Kocher

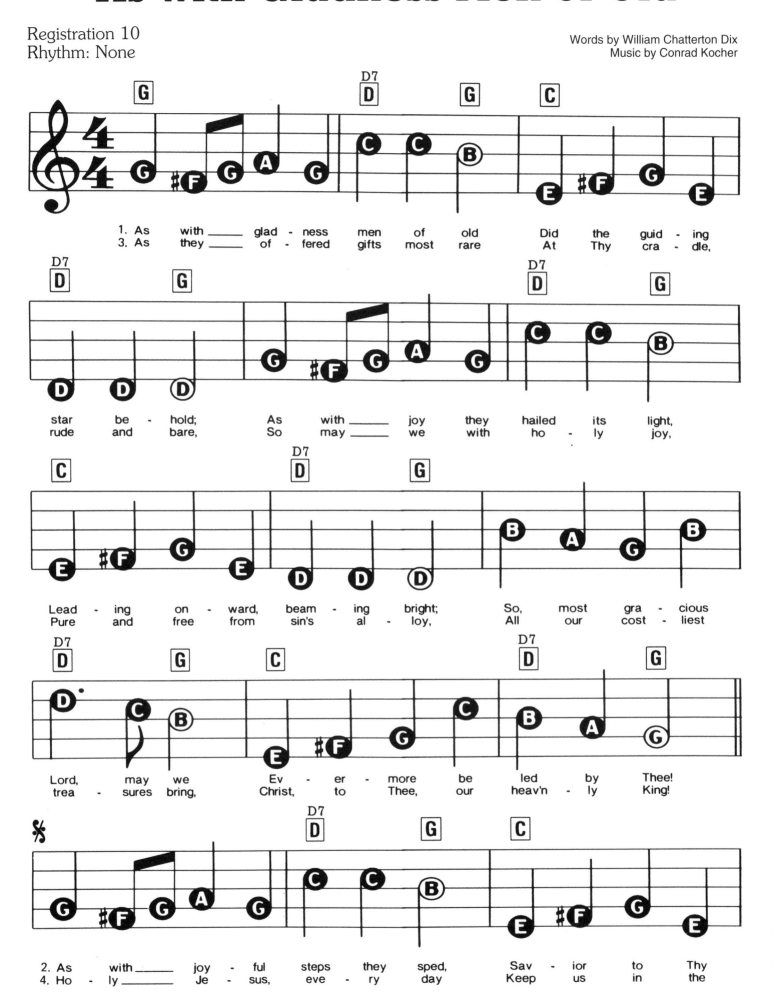

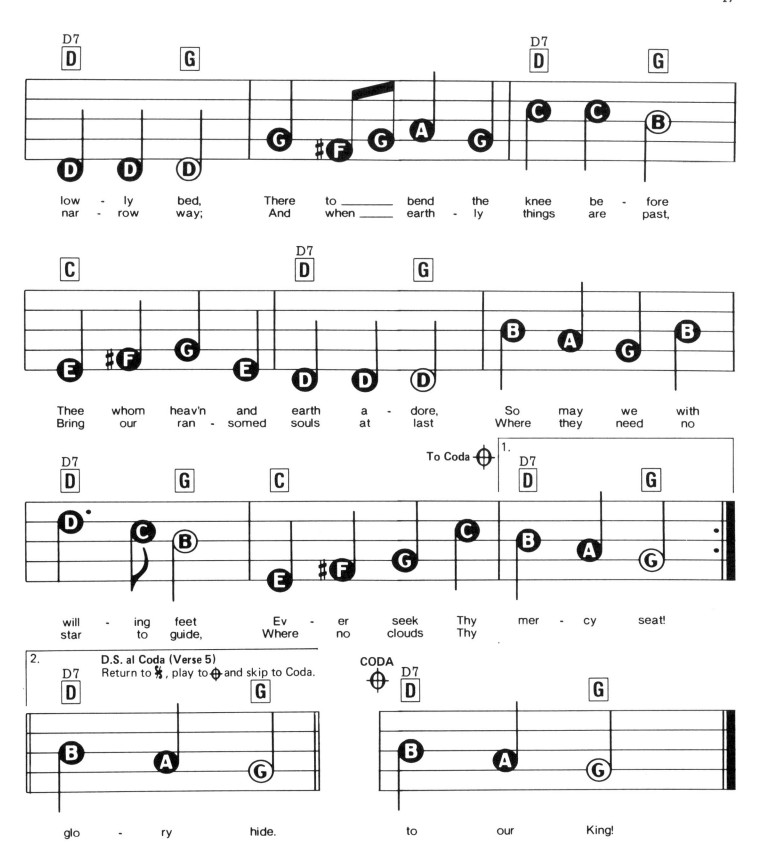

5. In the heavenly country bright
   Need they no created light;
   Thou its Light, its Joy, its Crown,
   Thou its Sun which goes not down.
   There forever may we sing
   Alleluias to our King!

At the Hour of Midnight

Registration 7
Rhythm: March

Traditional

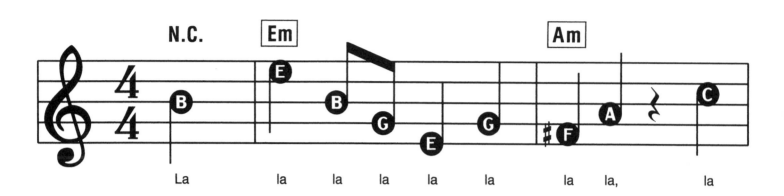

La la la la la la la la, la

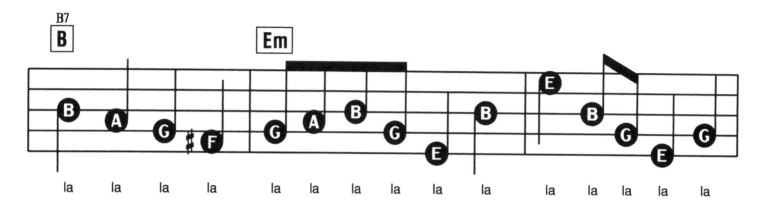

la la la la la la la la la la la la la la la

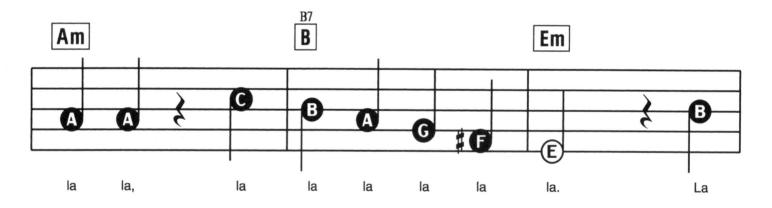

la la, la la la la la la. La

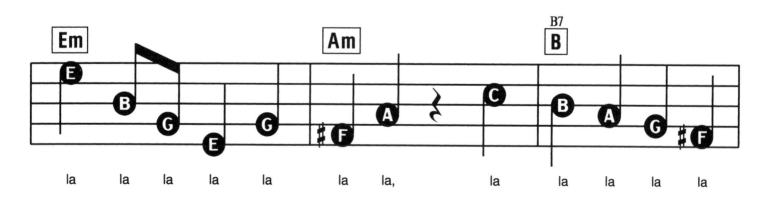

la la la la la la la, la la la la la la

19

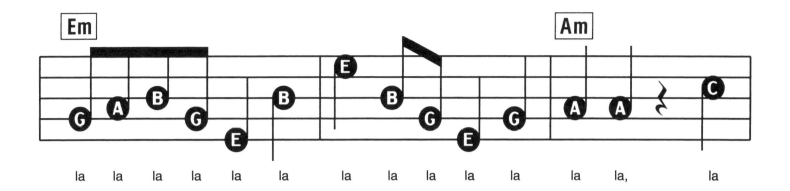

la la la la la la la la la la la la la, la

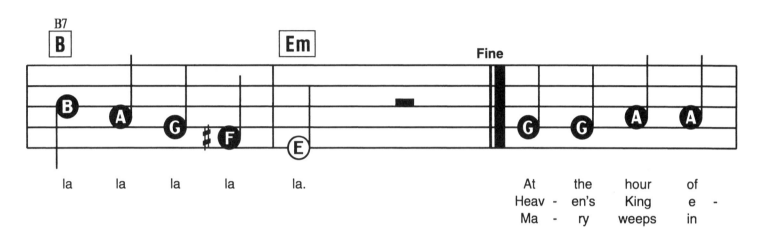

la la la la la.

At the hour of
Heav - en's King e -
Ma - ry weeps in

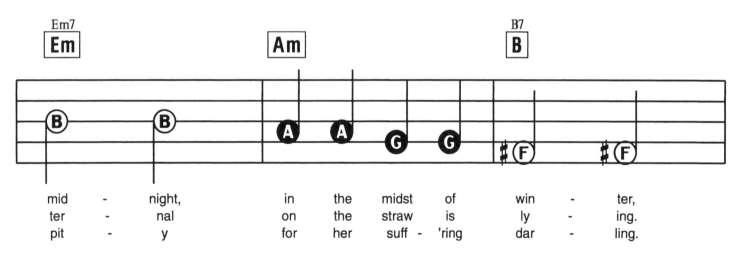

mid - night, in the midst of win - ter,
ter - nal on the straw is ly - ing.
pit - y for her suff - 'ring dar - ling.

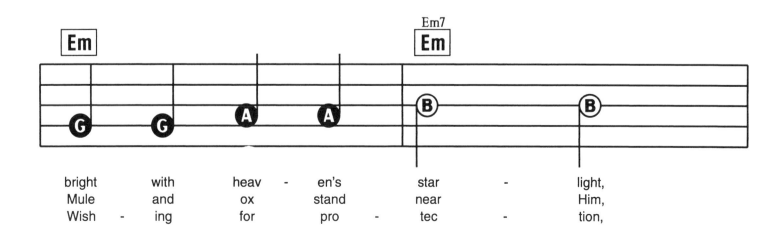

bright with heav - en's star - light,
Mule and ox stand near Him,
Wish - ing for pro - tec - tion,

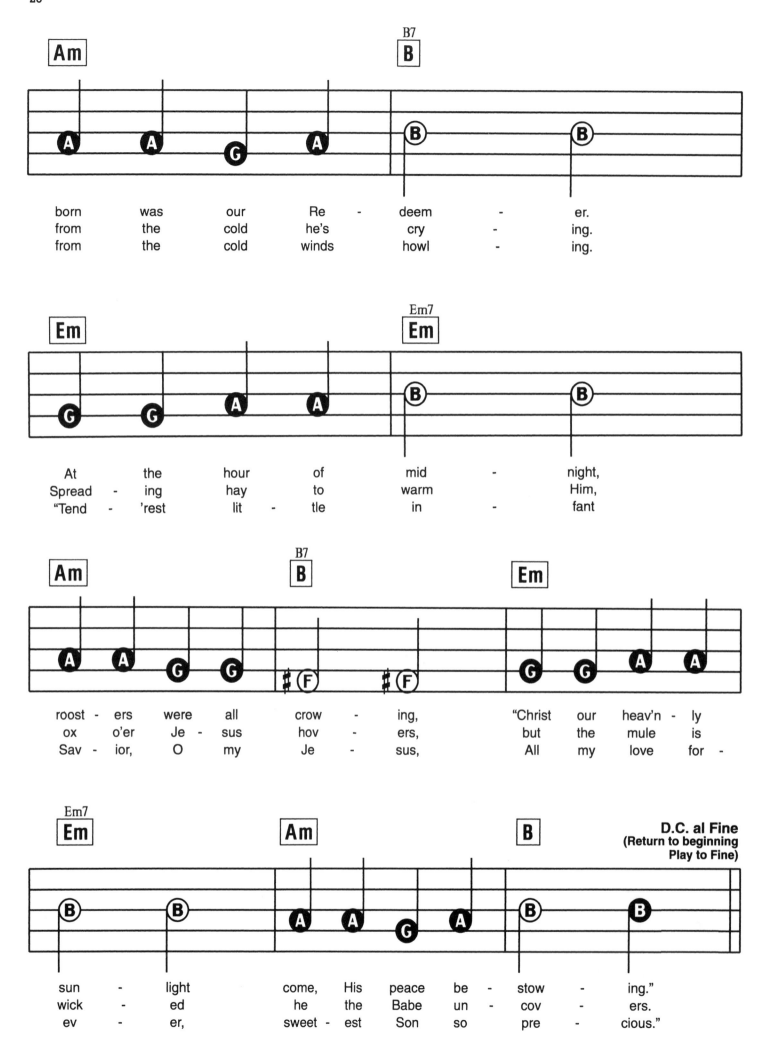

Bells Over Bethlehem

Registration 6
Rhythm: None

Traditional Andalusian Carol

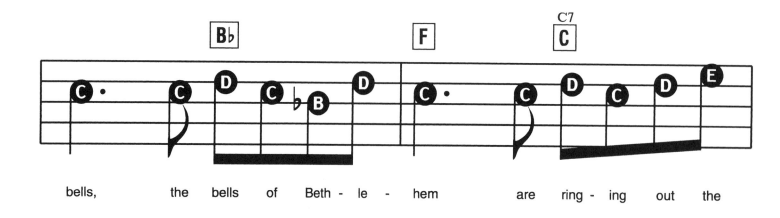

bells, the bells of Beth - le - hem are ring - ing out the

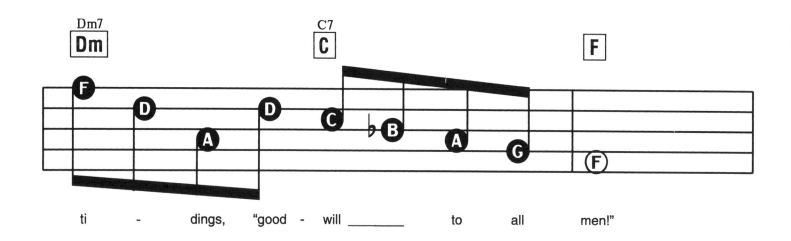

ti - dings, "good - will _____ to all men!"

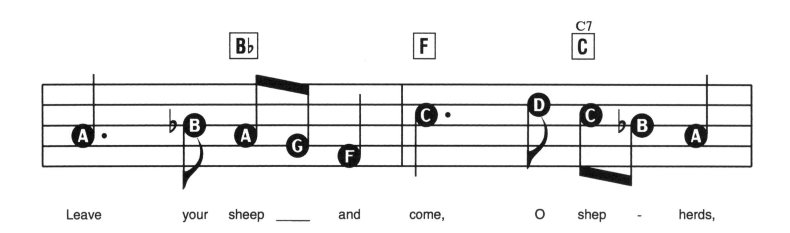

Leave your sheep ____ and come, O shep - herds,

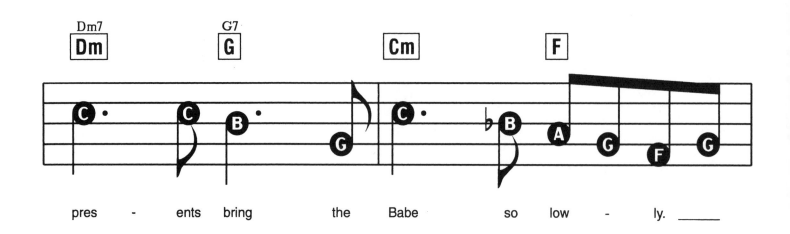

pres - ents bring the Babe so low - ly. _____

23

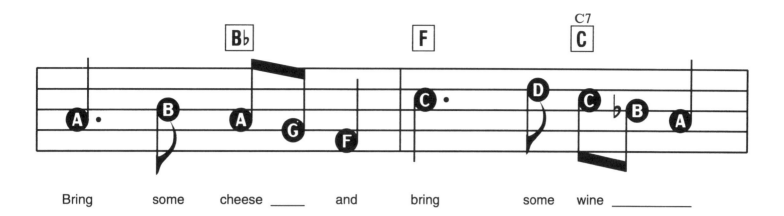

Bring some cheese _____ and bring some wine _____

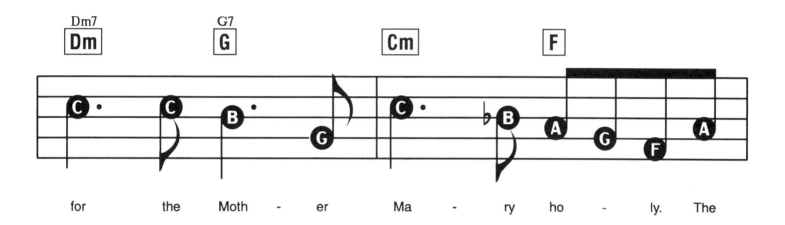

for the Moth - er Ma - ry ho - ly. The

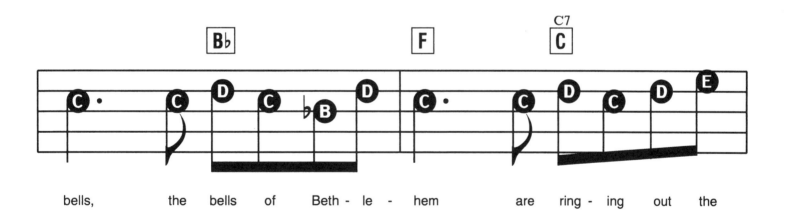

bells, the bells of Beth - le - hem are ring - ing out the

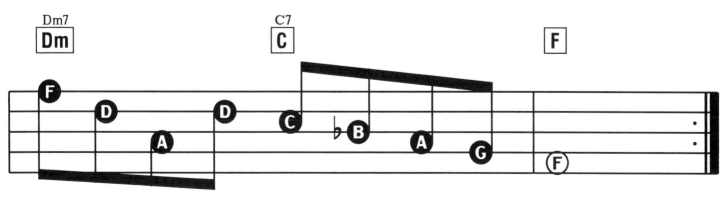

ti - dings, "good - will _____ to all men!"

Auld Lang Syne

Registration 2
Rhythm: None

Words by Robert Burns
Traditional Scottish Melody

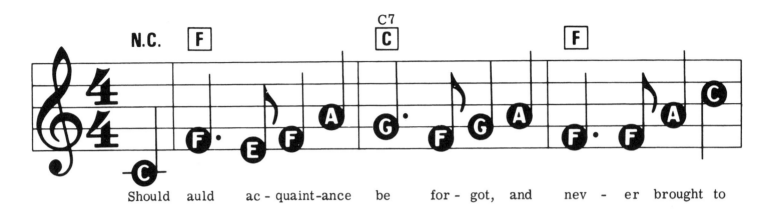

Should auld ac - quaint-ance be for - got, and nev - er brought to

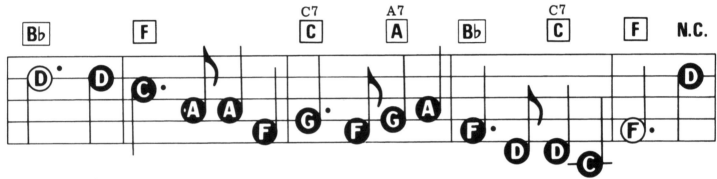

mind? Should auld ac- quaint-ance be for - got and days of Auld Lang Syne? For

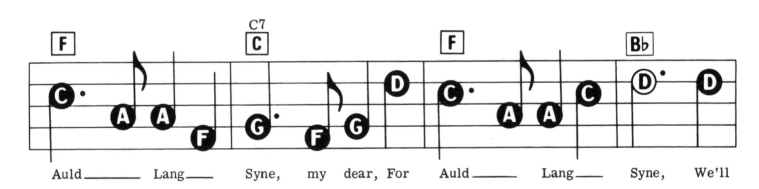

Auld_____ Lang____ Syne, my dear, For Auld_____ Lang____ Syne, We'll

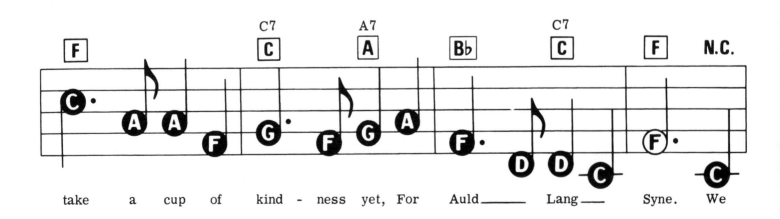

take a cup of kind - ness yet, For Auld_____ Lang____ Syne. We

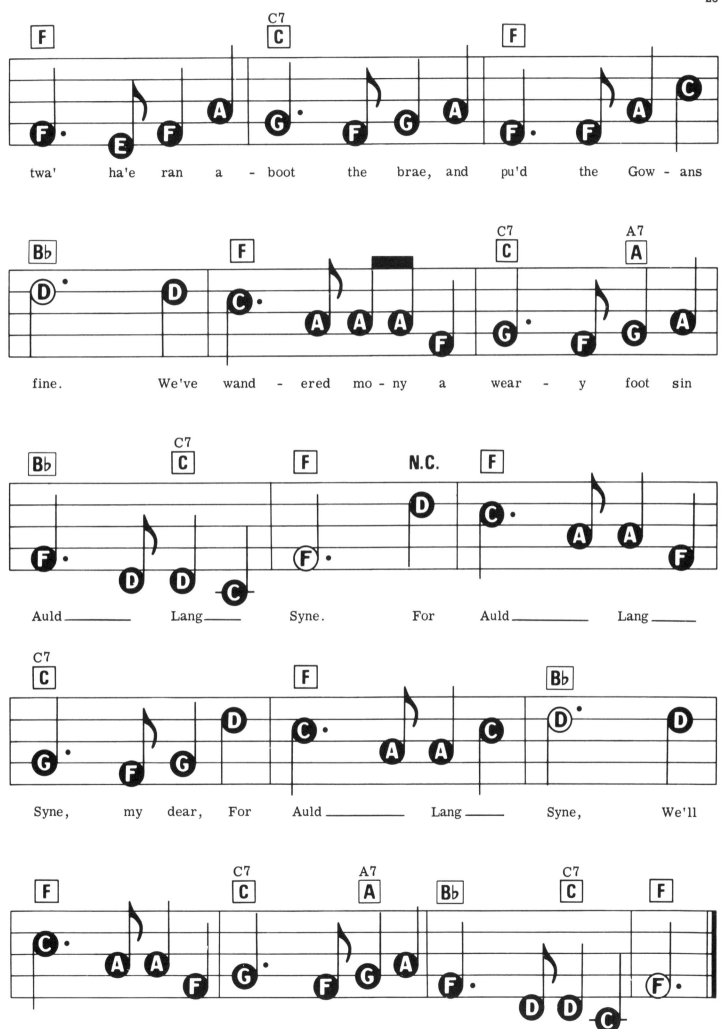

Away in a Manger

Registration 2
Rhythm: Waltz

Traditional
Words by John T. McFarland (v.3)
Music by William J. Kirkpatrick

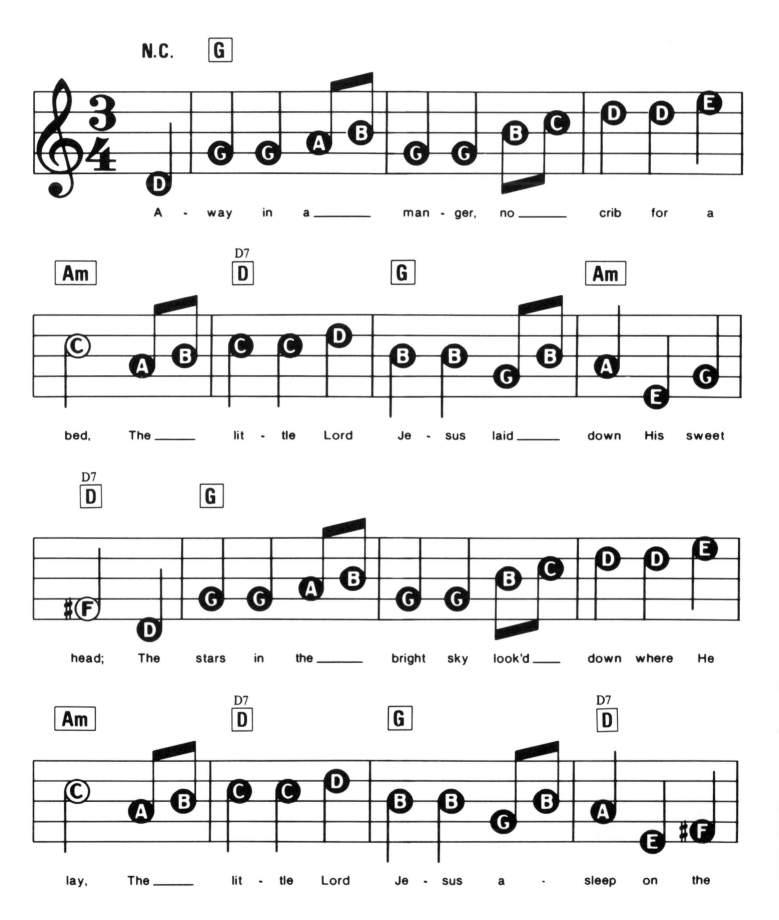

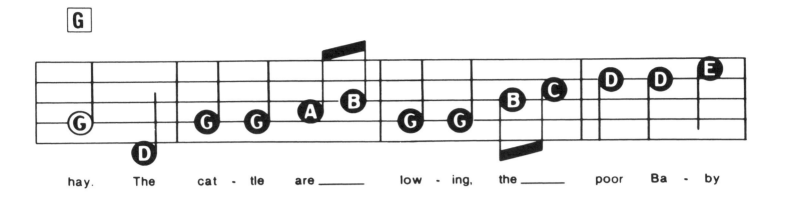

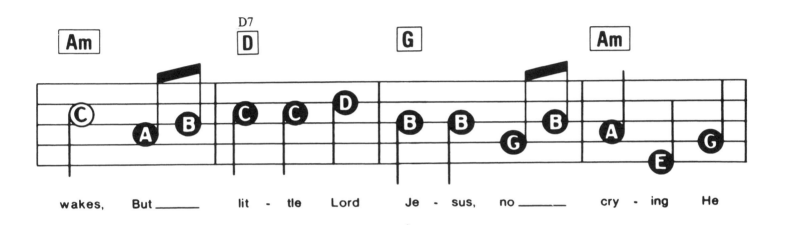

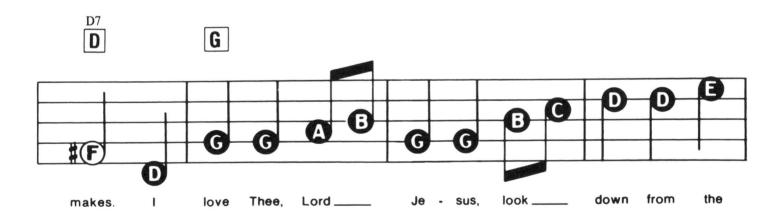

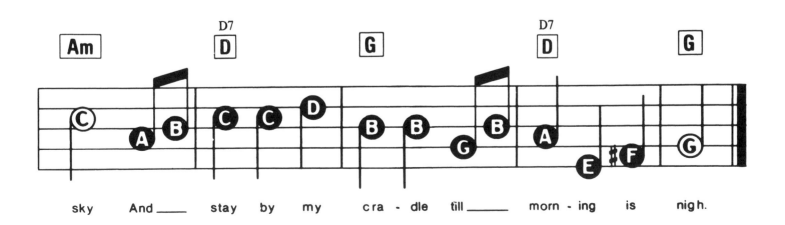

Away in a Manger

Registration 1
Rhythm: Waltz

Traditional
Words by John T. McFarland (v.3)
Music by James R. Murray

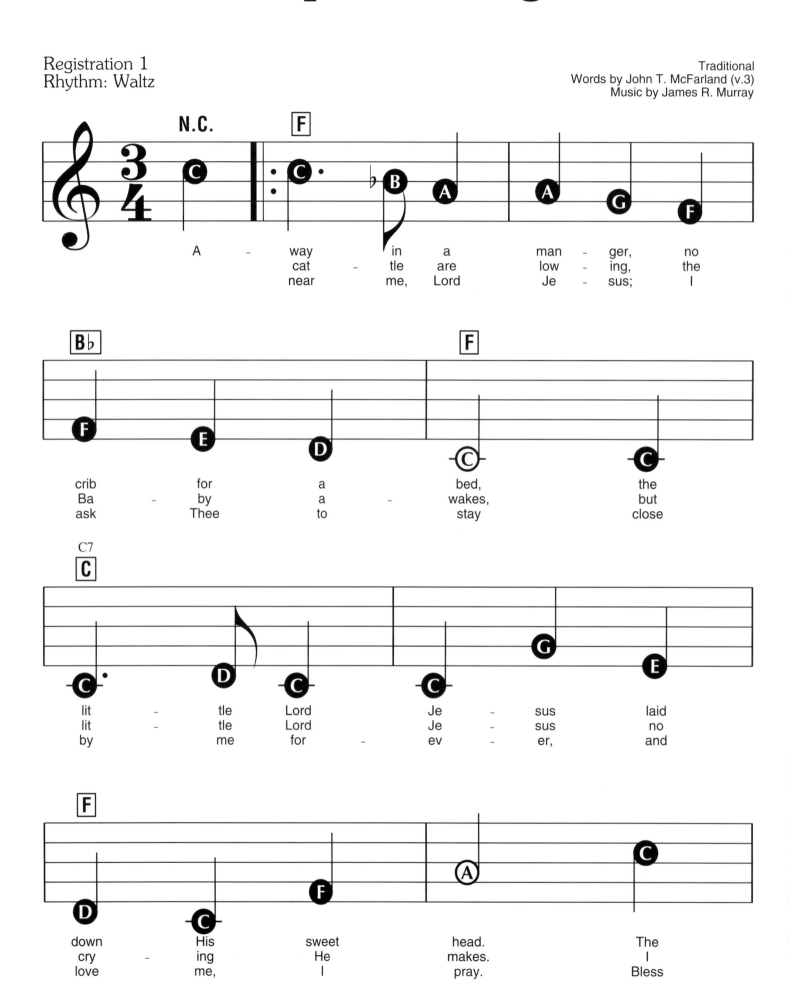

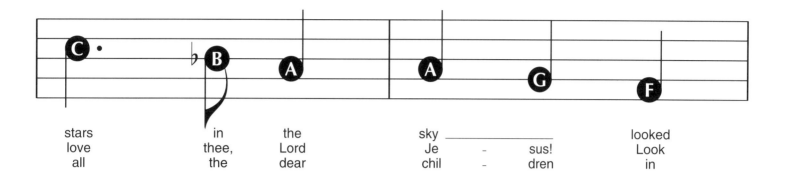

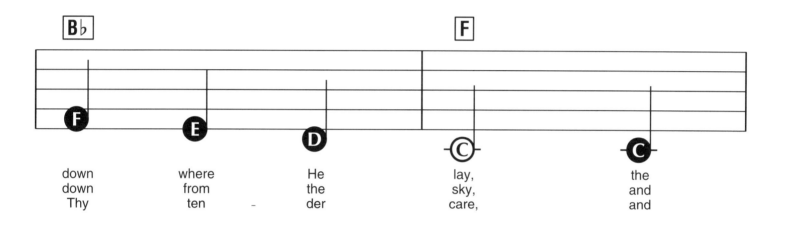

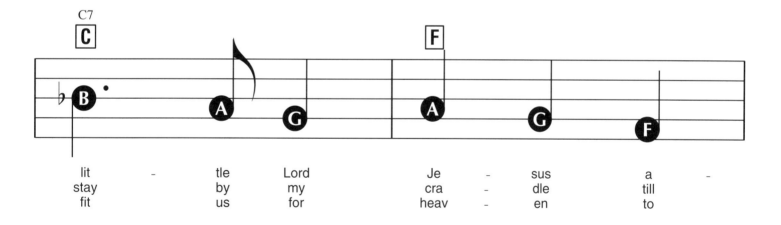

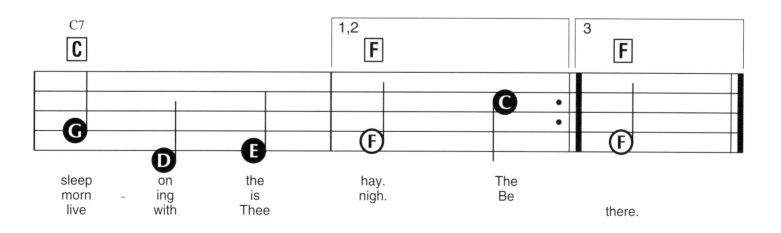

The Babe of Bethlehem

Registration 4
Rhythm: None

Traditional

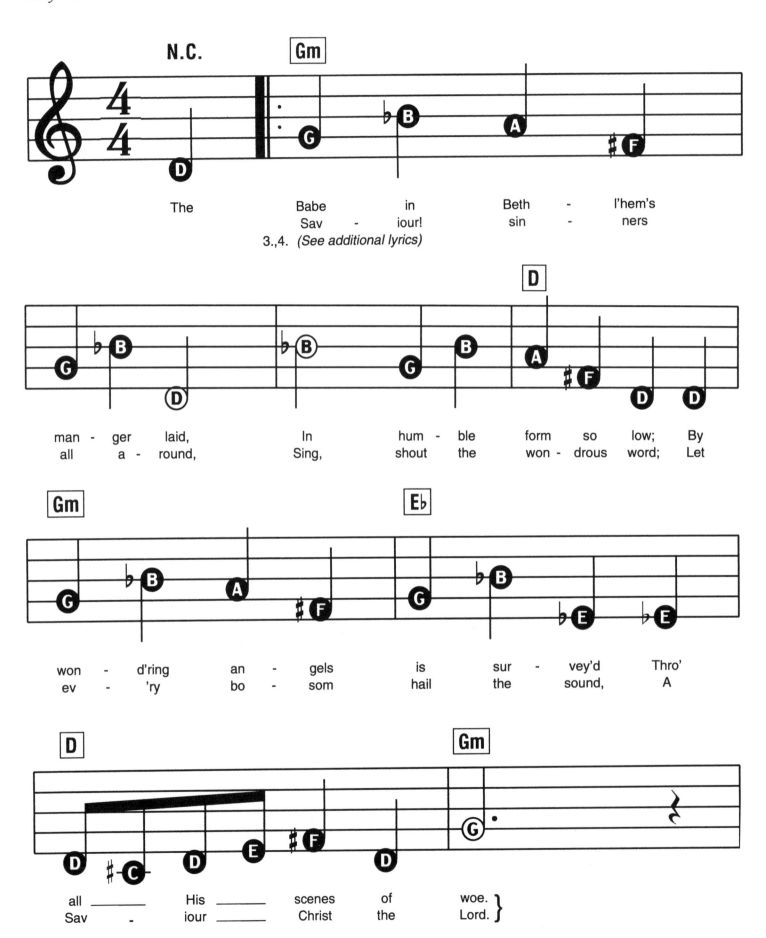

31

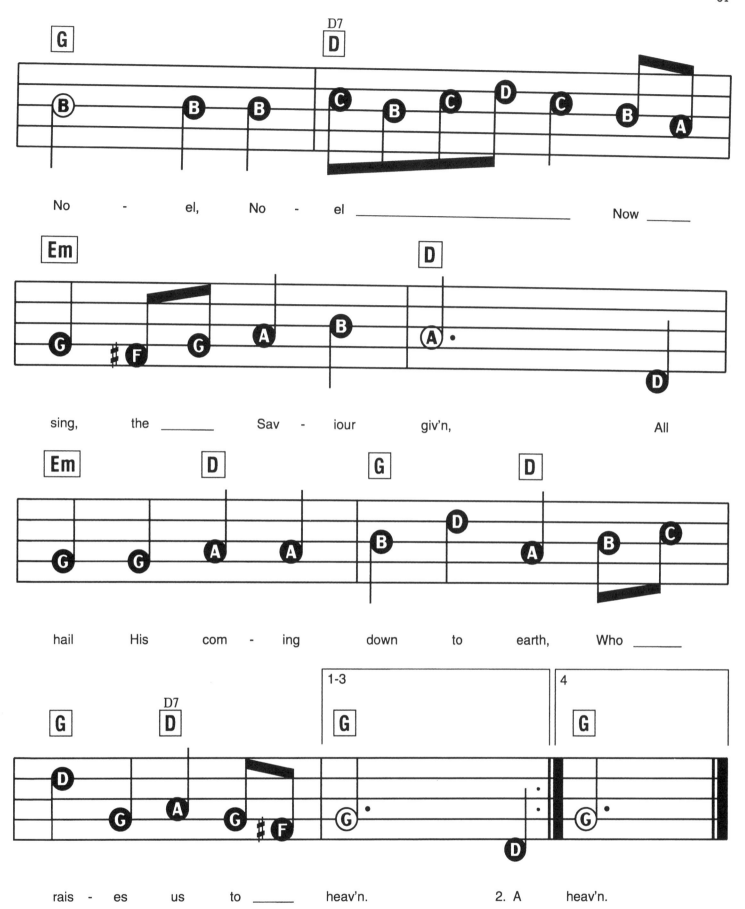

Additional Lyrics

3. Not for to sit on David's throne
   With worldly pomp and joy,
   He came for sinners to atone
   And Satan to destroy.
   Chorus

4. Well may we sing a Saviour's birth,
   Who need the grace so given,
   And hail His coming down to earth,
   Who raises us to heaven.
   Chorus

The Baby in the Cradle

Registration 1
Rhythm: Waltz

By D.G. Corner

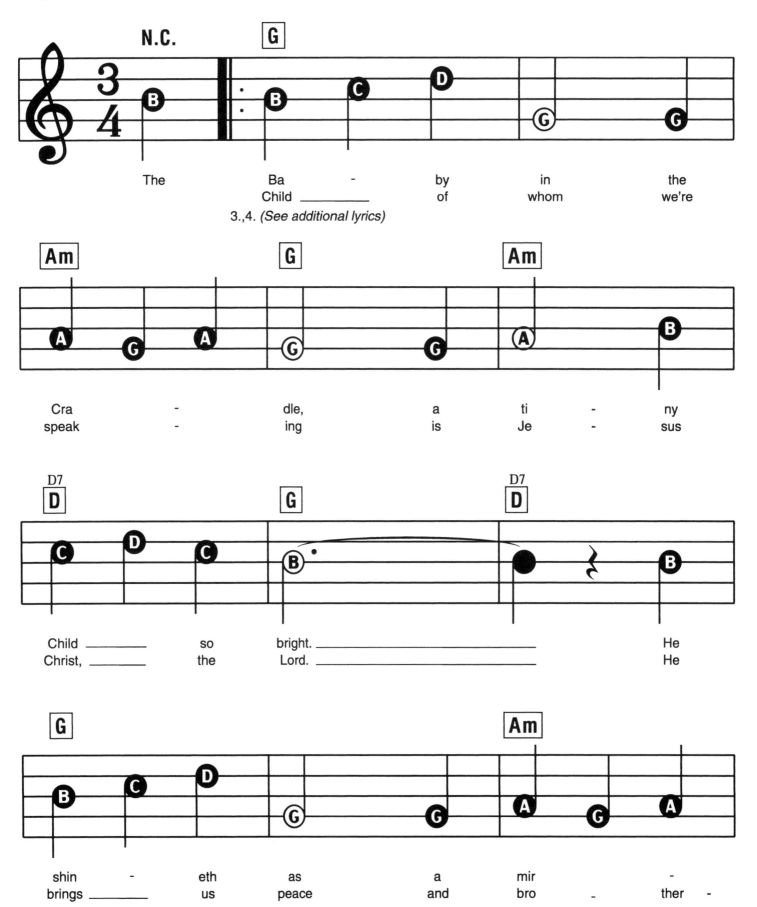

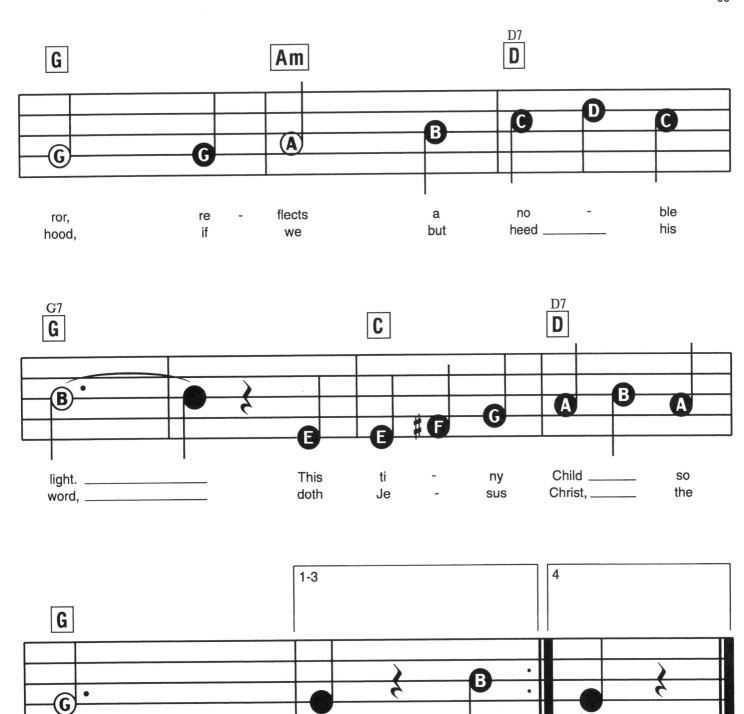

ror,   re - flects   a   no - ble
hood,   if we   but   heed _____ his

light. _____   This   ti - ny   Child _____ so
word, _____   doth   Je - sus   Christ, _____ the

bright. _____
Lord. _____

2. The _____
3. And

Additional Lyrics

3. And he who rocks the cradle
   Of this sweet Child so fine
   Must serve with joy and heartiness,
   Be humble and be kind,
   For Mary's Child so fine.

4. O Jesus, dearest Savior
   Although Thou art so small,
   With Thy great love o'erflowing
   Come flooding through my soul,
   Thou lovely Babe so small.

Beside Thy Cradle Here I Stand

Registration 6
Rhythm: None

Words by Paul Gerhardt
Translated by Rev. J. Troutbeck
Music from the *Geistliche Gesangbuch*
Harmonized by J.S. Bach

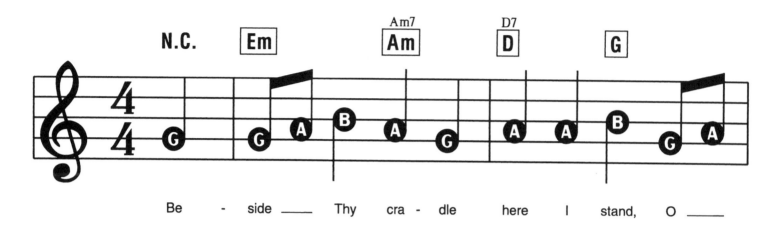

Be - side _____ Thy cra - dle here I stand, O _____

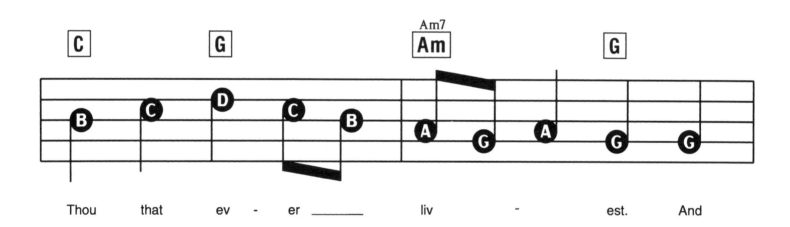

Thou that ev - er _____ liv - est. And

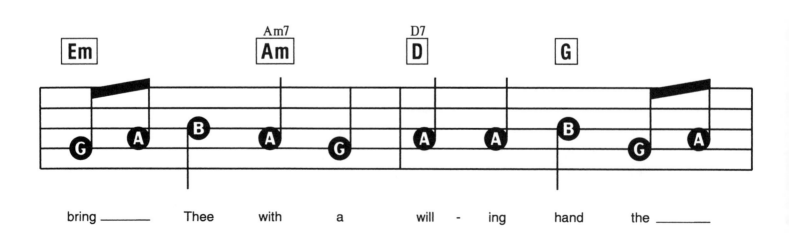

bring _____ Thee with a will - ing hand the _____

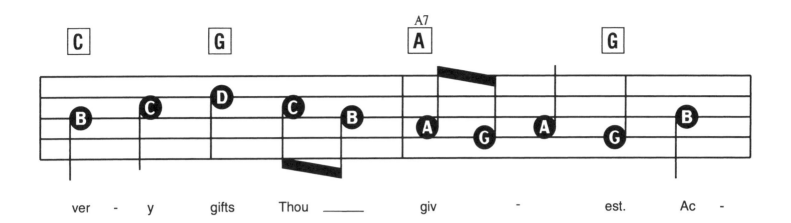

ver - y gifts Thou _____ giv - est. Ac -

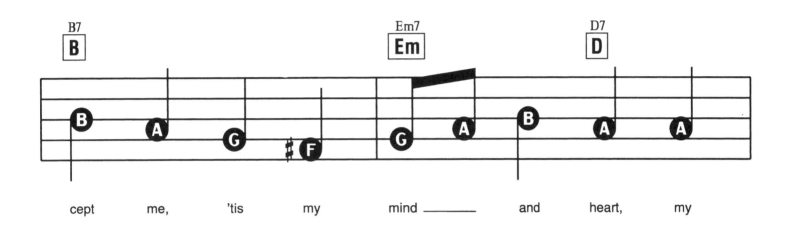

cept me, 'tis my mind _____ and heart, my

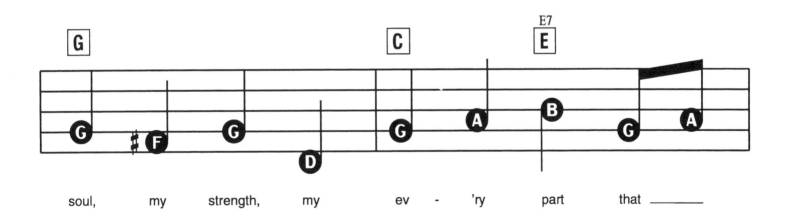

soul, my strength, my ev - 'ry part that _____

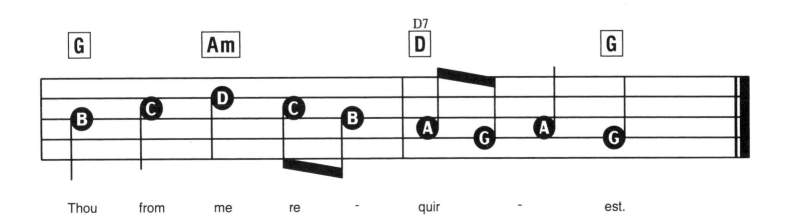

Thou from me re - quir - est.

The Birthday of a King

Registration 5
Rhythm: None

Words and Music by
William H. Neidlinger

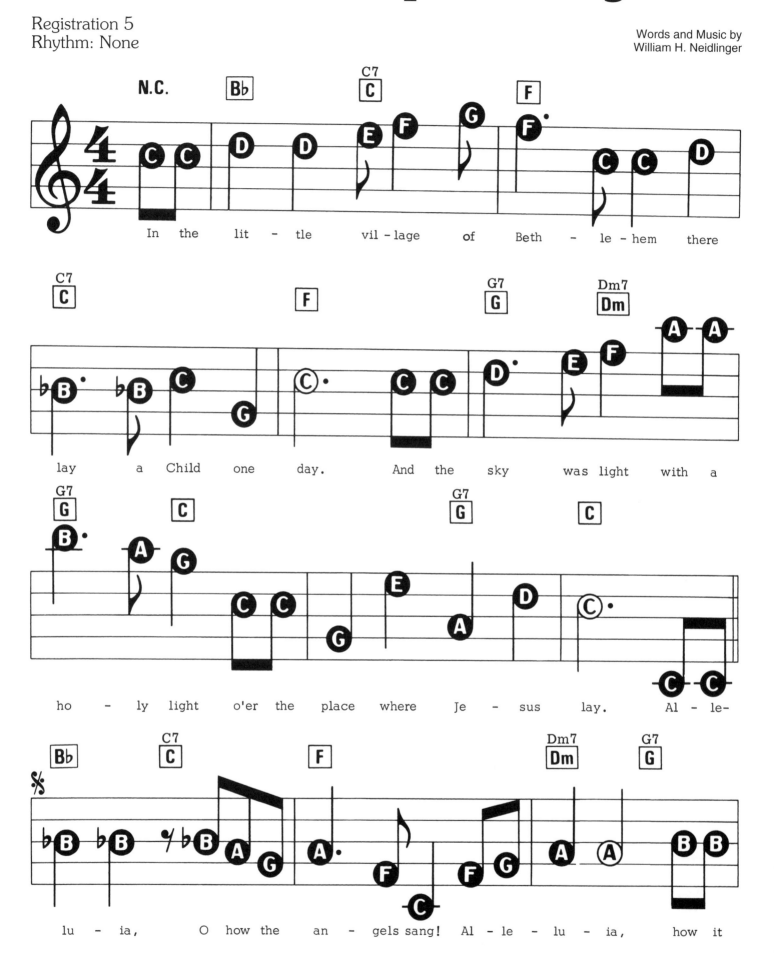

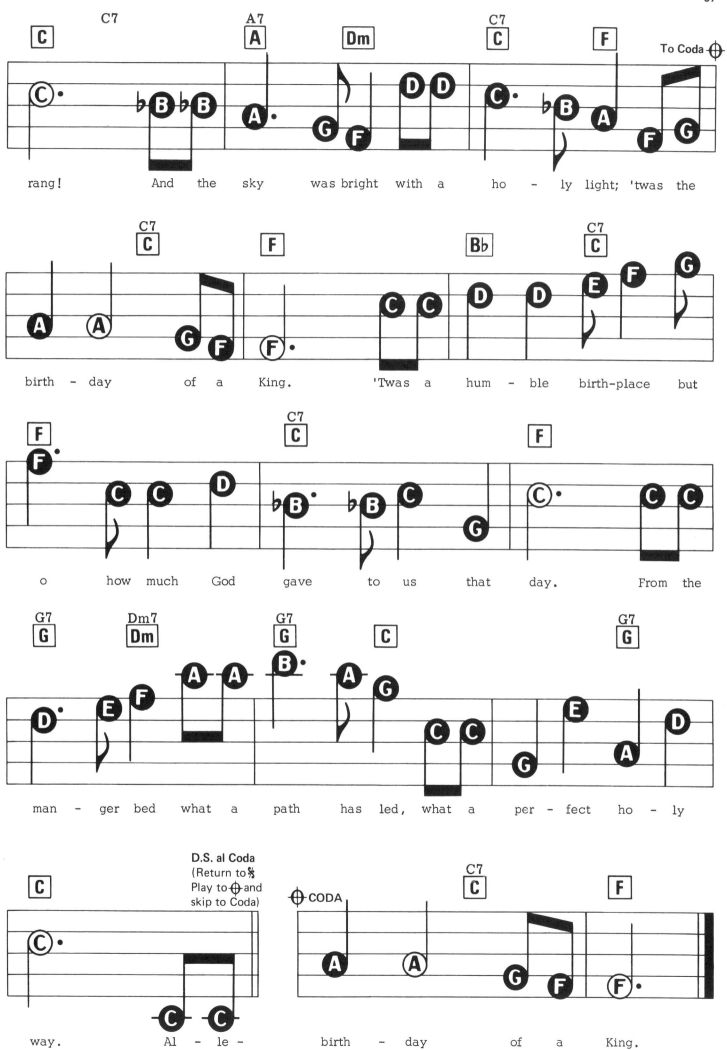

The Boar's Head Carol

Registration 4
Rhythm: None

Traditional English

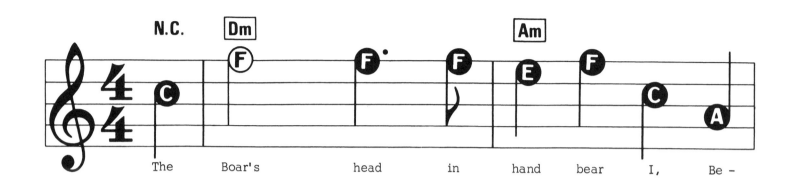

The Boar's head in hand bear I, Be-

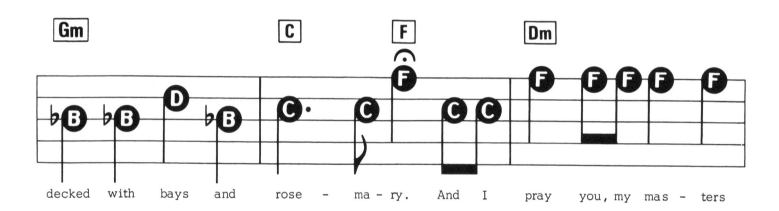

decked with bays and rose — ma - ry. And I pray you, my mas - ters

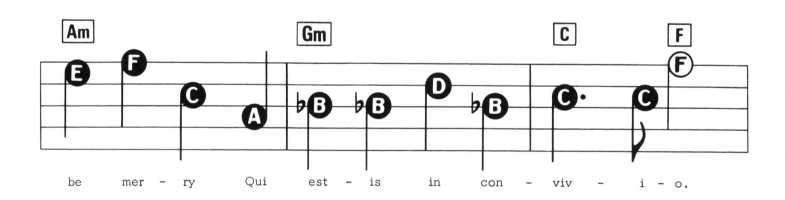

be mer - ry Qui est - is in con - viv - i - o.

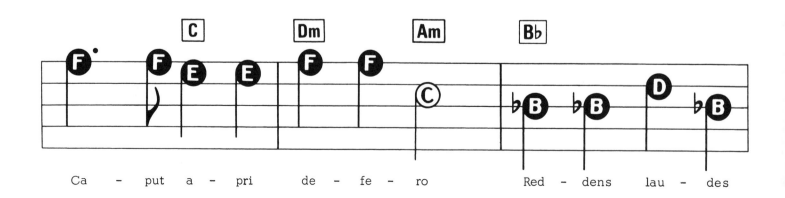

Ca - put a - pri de - fe - ro   Red - dens lau - des

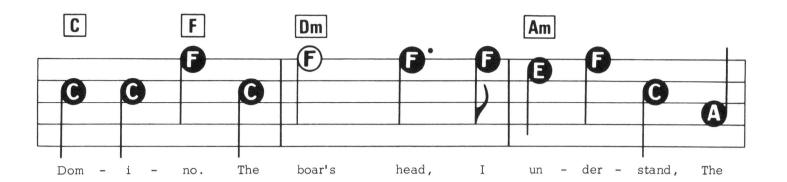

Dom - i - no. The boar's head, I un - der - stand, The

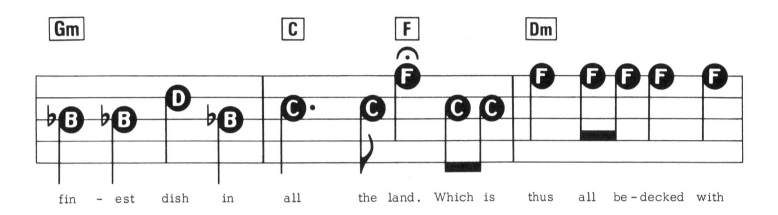

fin - est dish in all the land. Which is thus all be - decked with

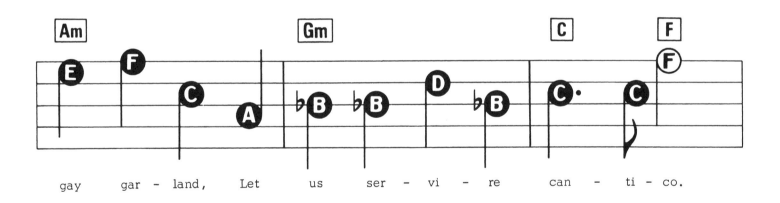

gay gar - land, Let us ser - vi - re can - ti - co.

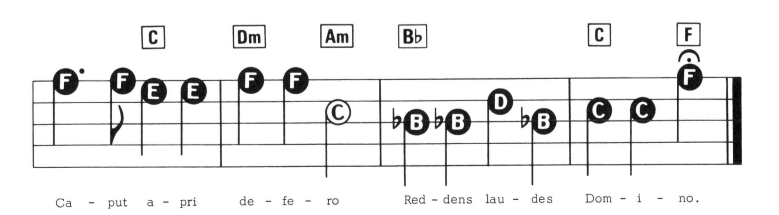

Ca - put a - pri de - fe - ro Red - dens lau - des Dom - i - no.

A Boy Is Born in Bethlehem

Registration 3
Rhythm: Waltz

Traditional

N.C.   **Am**   **Dm**

A   A   A   B   B

1. A   Boy   is   born   in
2. Ga - briel,   Heav'ns   ap -
3.,4. *(See additional lyrics)*

Am   **Em**   **F**

C   B   A   G   C   D

Beth - le - hem, }
point - ed one, }   AL - LE -

G7
G   **Am**

C   B   C   C

LU - JA!   { And
    { The

C   **Dm**

C   C   B   A

joy   is   in   Je -
Vir - gin   bears   a

41

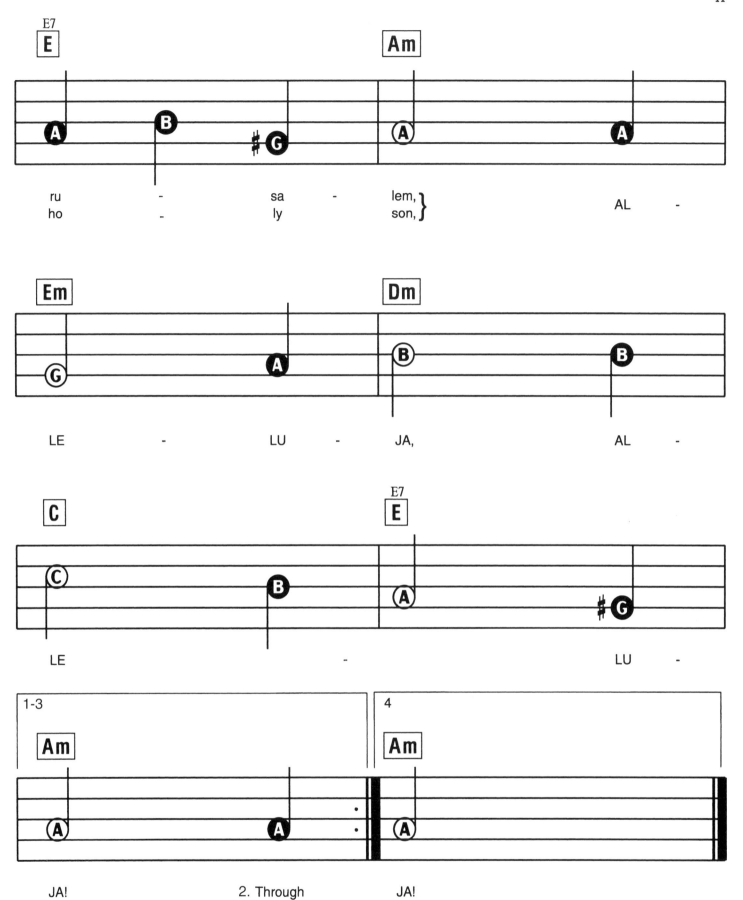

Additional Lyrics

3. The wisest kings of Orient
   Gold, frankincense, and myrrh present.

4. Laud to the Holy Trinity,
   All thanks and praise to God most high.

Break Forth, O Beauteous Heavenly Light

Words by Johann Rist
Translated by Rev. J. Troutbeck
Melody by Johann Schop
Arranged by J.S. Bach

Registration 4
Rhythm: March

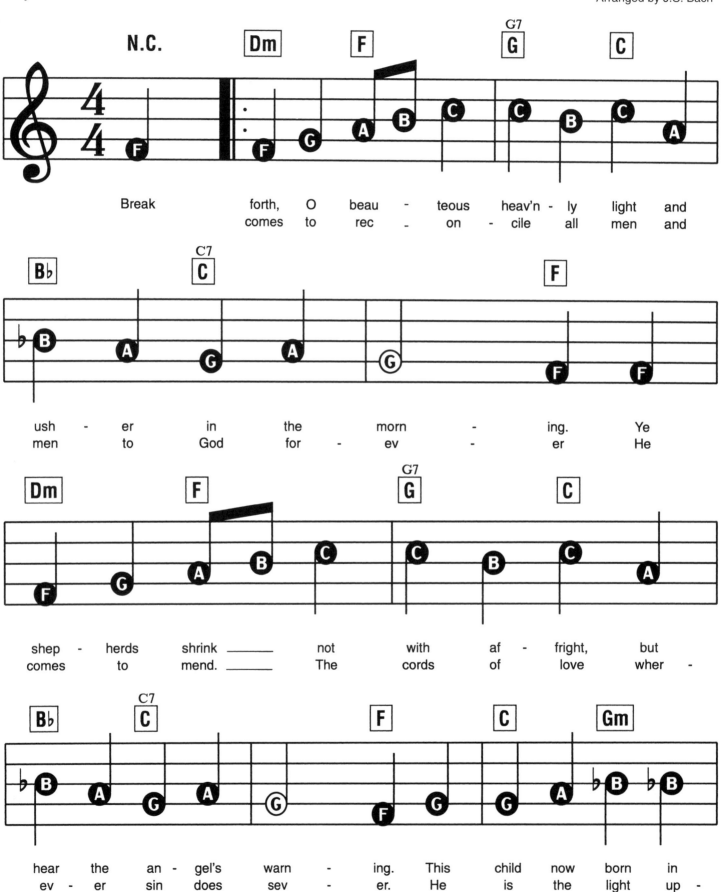

Bring a Torch, Jeannette, Isabella

Registration 3
Rhythm: Waltz

17th Century French Provençal Carol

Bring a torch, _____ Jean - nette, Is - a -
Has - ten now, _____ good folk of the

bel - la, bring a torch, _____ come
vil - lage, has - ten now, _____ the

swift - ly and run. Christ is
Christ Child to see. You will

born, tell the folk of the vil - lage,
find Him a - sleep in a man - ger,

45

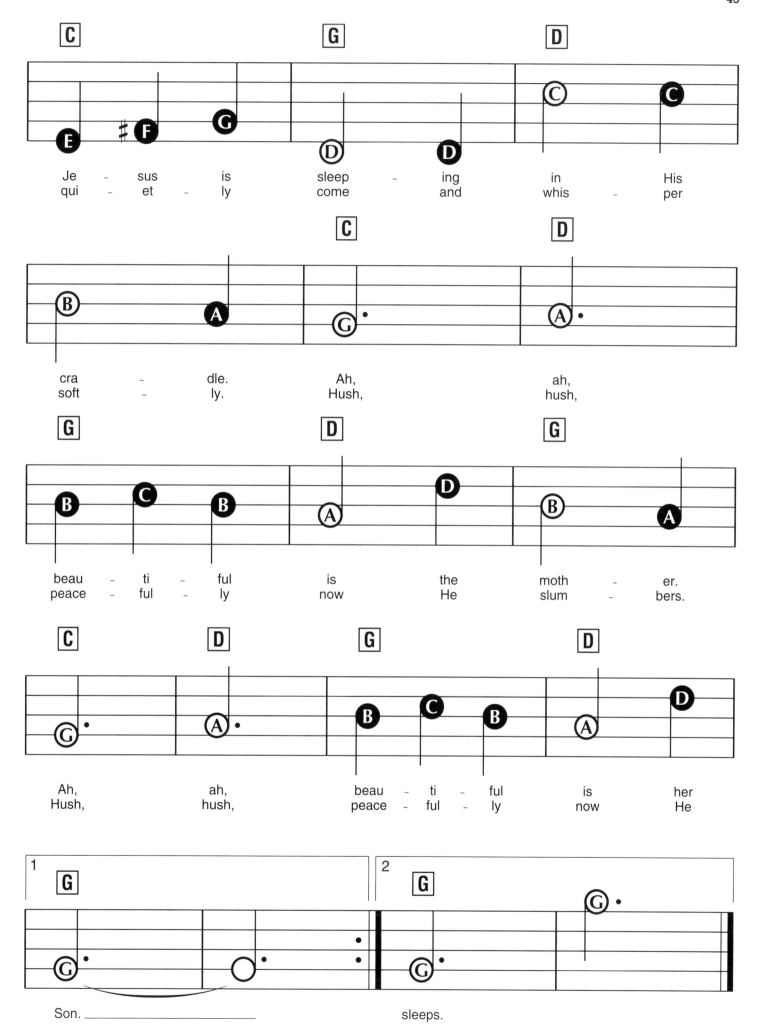

Carol of the Bells

Registration 1
Rhythm: Waltz

Ukrainian Christmas Carol

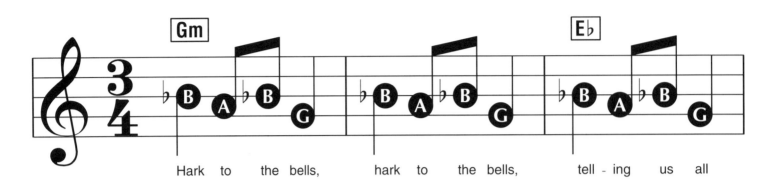

Hark to the bells, hark to the bells, tell - ing us all

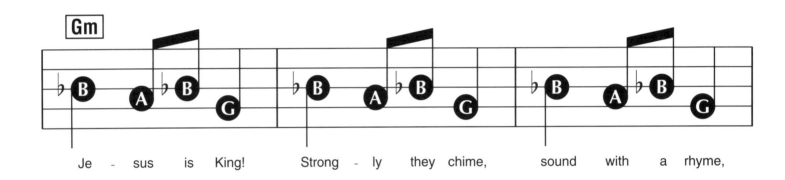

Je - sus is King! Strong - ly they chime, sound with a rhyme,

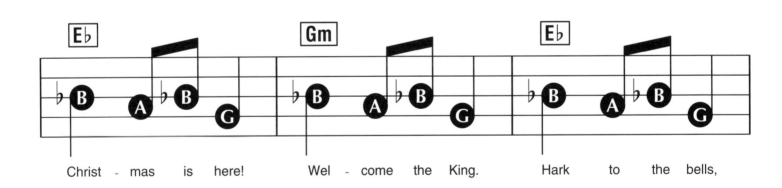

Christ - mas is here! Wel - come the King. Hark to the bells,

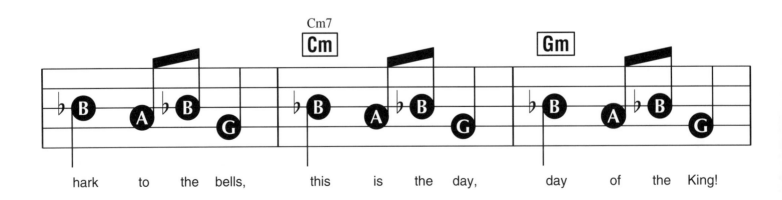

hark to the bells, this is the day, day of the King!

47

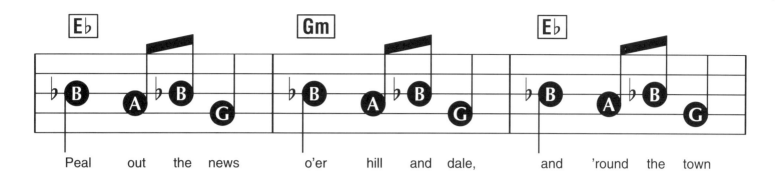

Peal out the news o'er hill and dale, and 'round the town

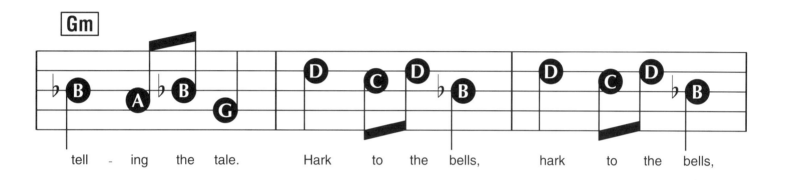

tell - ing the tale. Hark to the bells, hark to the bells,

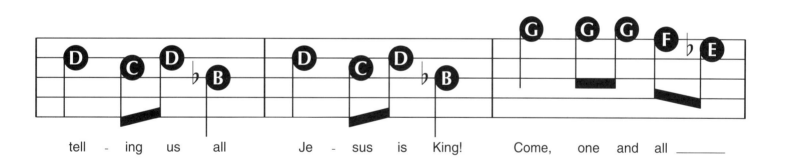

tell - ing us all Je - sus is King! Come, one and all _____

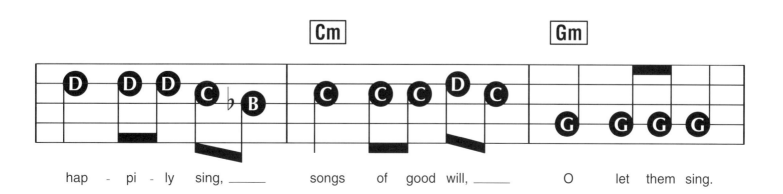

hap - pi - ly sing, _____ songs of good will, _____ O let them sing.

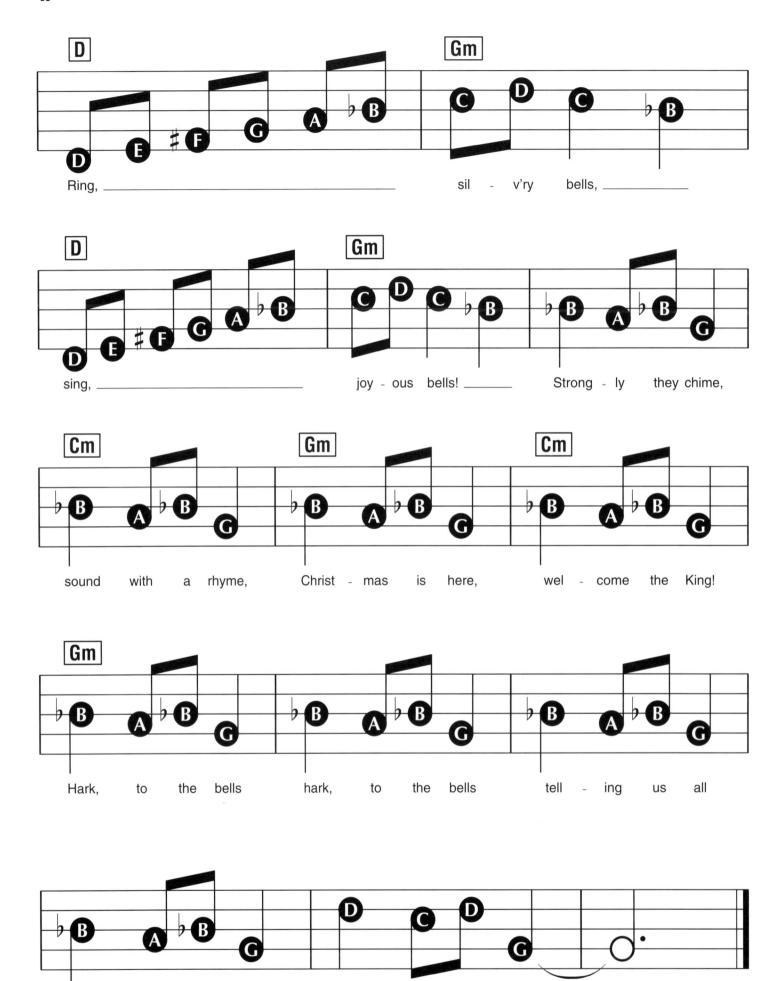

A Child Is Born in Bethlehem

Registration 3
Rhythm: None

14th-Century Latin Text adapted by
Nicolai F.S. Grundtvig
Traditional Danish Melody

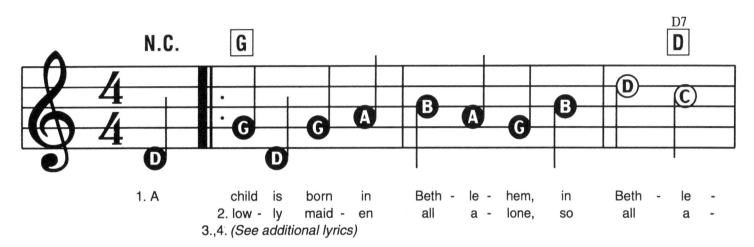

1. A child is born in Beth - le - hem, in Beth - le -
2. low - ly maid - en all a - lone, so all a -
3.,4. *(See additional lyrics)*

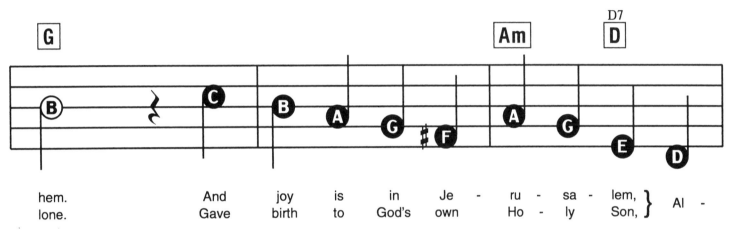

hem. And joy is in Je - ru - sa - lem, } Al -
lone. Gave birth to God's own Ho - ly Son, } Al -

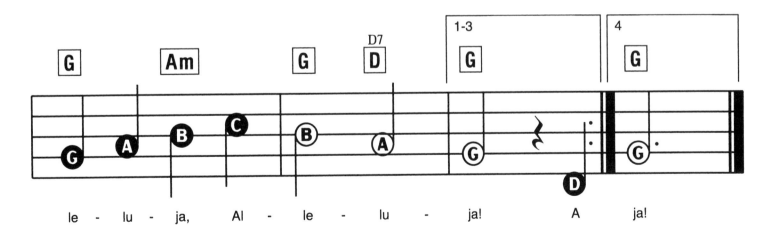

le - lu - ja, Al - le - lu - ja! A ja!

Additional Lyrics

3. She chose a manger for His bed,
   For Jesus' bed.
   God's angels sang for joy o'erhead,
   Alleluja, Alleluja!

4. Give thanks and praise eternally,
   Eternally,
   To God, the Holy Trinity.
   Alleluja, Alleluja!

Carol of the Birds

Registration 1
Rhythm: None

Traditional Catalonian Carol

1. Up - on this ho - ly night,   When
2. The Night - in - gale is first
3.,4. *(See additional lyrics)*

God's great star ap - pears,   And floods the earth with
bring his song of cheer,   And tell us of his

bright - ness   Birds' voi - ces rise in
glad - ness: Je - sus, our Lord, is

song,   And warb - ling all night long,   Ex -
born   To free us from all sin,   And ____

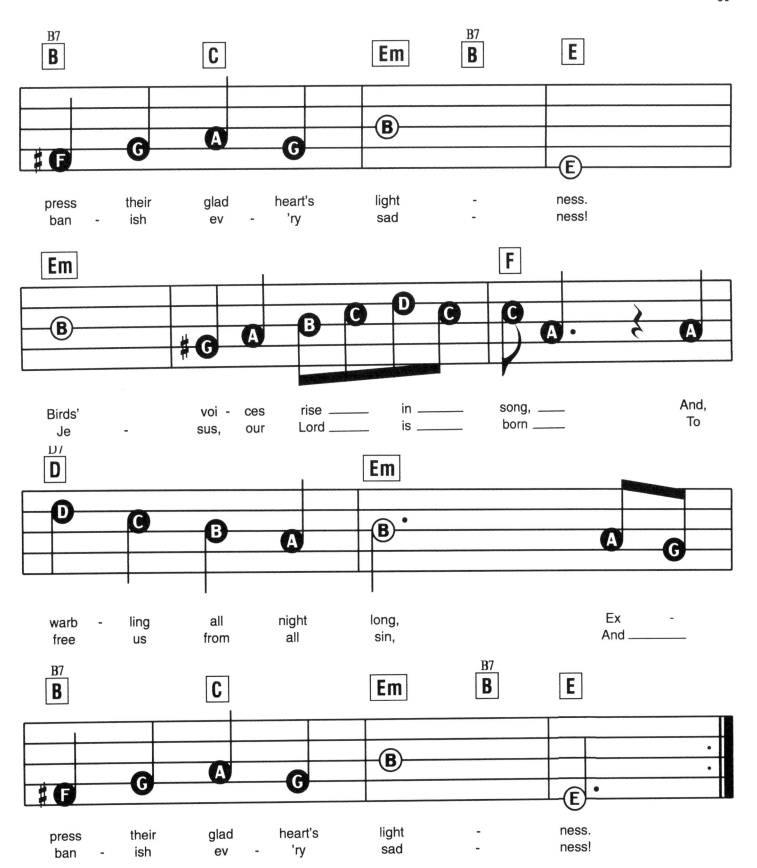

Additional Lyrics

3. The answ'ring Sparrow cries:
"God comes to earth this day
Amid the angels flying."
Trilling in sweetest tones,
The Finch his Lord now owns:
"To Him be all thanksgiving."
Trilling in sweetest tones,
The Finch his Lord now owns:
"To Him be all thanksgiving."

4. The Partridge adds his note:
"To Bethlehem I'll fly,
Where in the stall He's lying.
There, near the manger blest,
I'll build myself a nest,
And sing my love undying.
There, near the manger blest,
I'll build myself a nest,
And sing my love undying.

Child Jesus Came to Earth This Day

Registration 6
Rhythm: None

Traditional Carol

N.C.   **F**

C   D   C   A   B♭

Child   Je - sus   came   to

C   **Gm**   **D7 / D**   **Gm7 / Gm**

A.   G   G   A   C   D   B♭   A

earth   this   day,   to   save   us   sin - ners

C7 / C   **F**

G   F   C   D   C   A   B♭

dy - ing.   And   cra - dle   in   the

C   **Gm**   **G7 / G**   **B7 / B**

A.   G   G   C   E   D   C   B

straw   and   hay,   the   Ho - ly   One   is

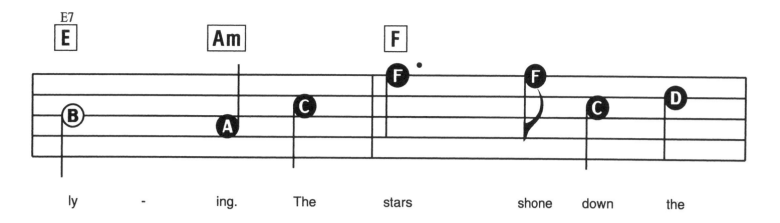

ly - ing. The stars shone down the

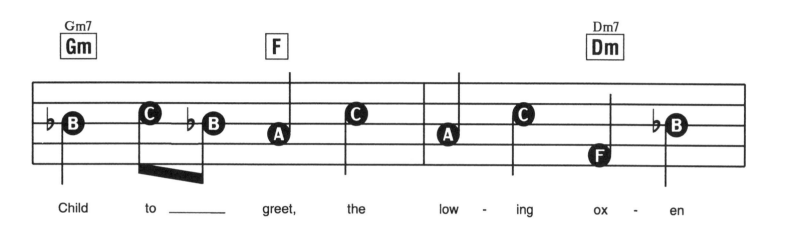

Child to _____ greet, the low - ing ox - en

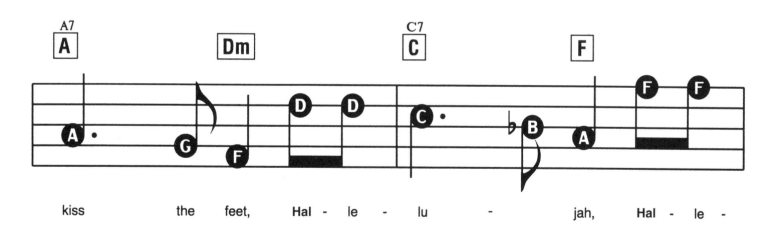

kiss the feet, Hal - le - lu - jah, Hal - le -

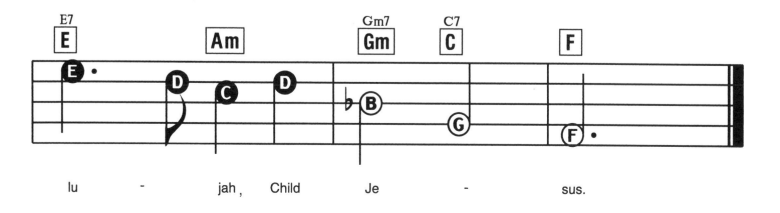

lu - jah, Child Je - sus.

Children Go Where I Send Thee

Registration 9
Rhythm: March

Traditional Spiritual

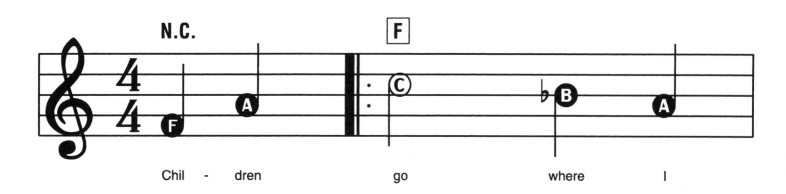

Chil - dren   go   where   I

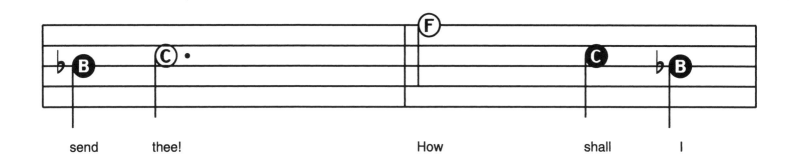

send   thee!   How   shall   I

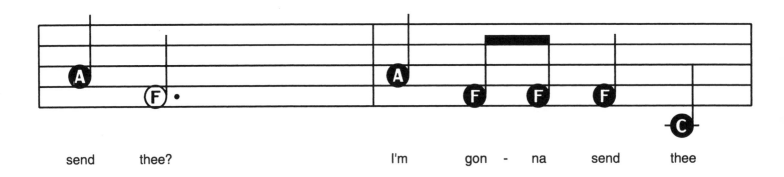

send   thee?   I'm   gon - na   send   thee

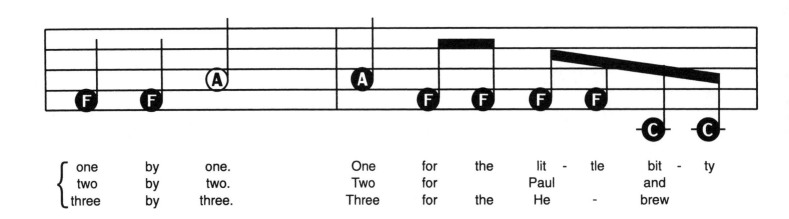

one   by   one.   One   for   the   lit - tle   bit - ty
two   by   two.   Two   for   the   Paul   and
three   by   three.   Three   for   the   He - brew

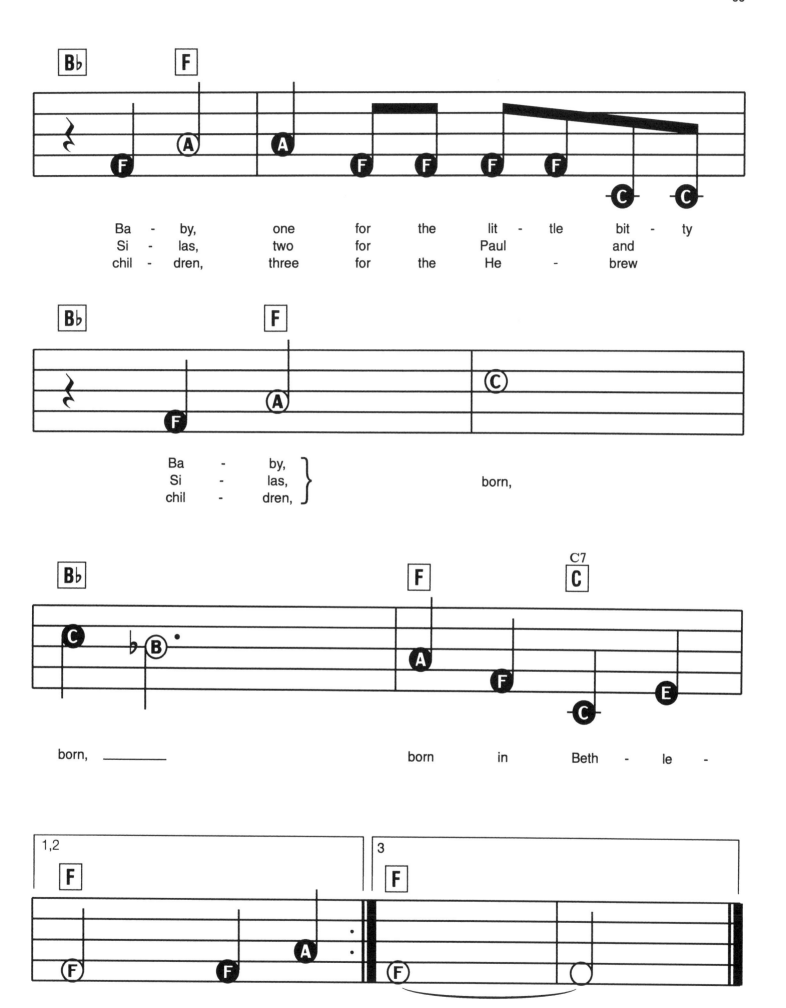

Christ Is Born This Evening

Registration 2
Rhythm: Pops

Traditional

C Am F C

G E C A A G

Christ is born this eve - ning,
Shep - herds, has - ten yon - der,

Am G7 / G Fm C

E E F D D C

let us go re - joic - ing!
where the go Babe most ho - ly,

F C Em

G E C A A G

Though the night is gloom - y,
in this cold De - cem - ber,

Am Dm7 / Dm G7 / G C

E E F D D C

day will soon be dawn - ing!
lies in man - ger low - ly.

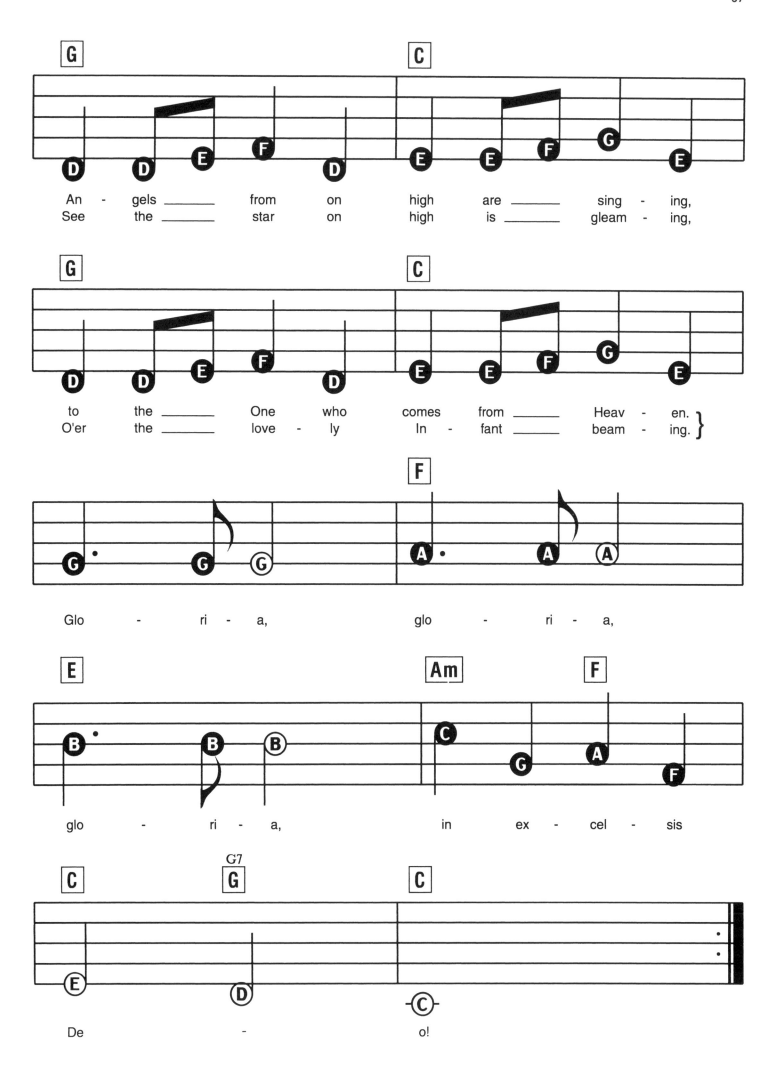

Christ Was Born on Christmas Day

Registration 6
Rhythm: None

Traditional

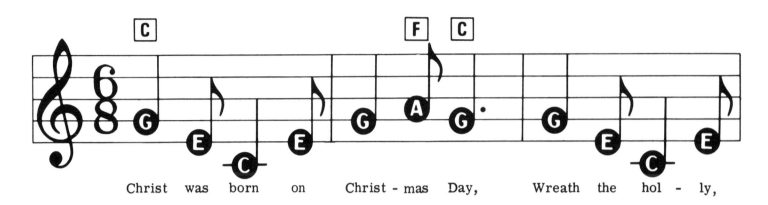

Christ was born on Christ - mas Day, Wreath the hol - ly,

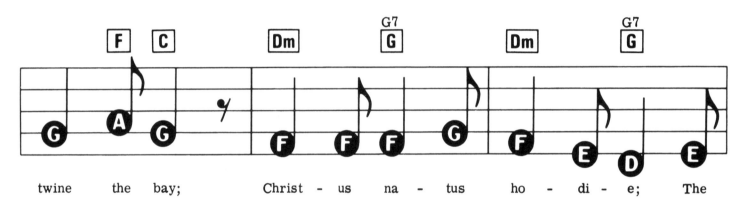

twine the bay; Christ - us na - tus ho - di - e; The

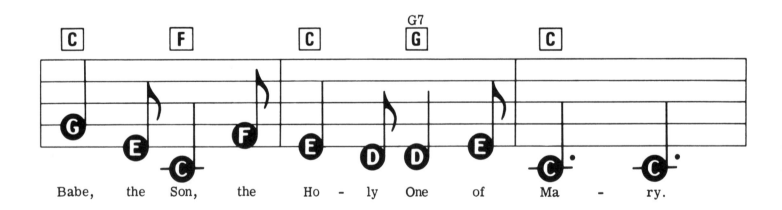

Babe, the Son, the Ho - ly One of Ma - ry.

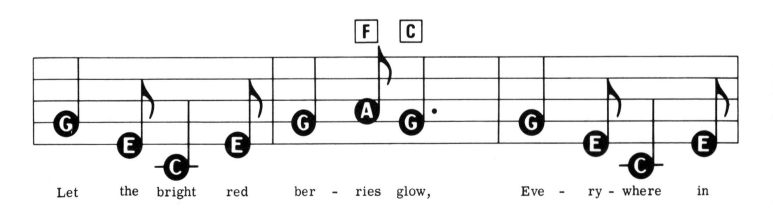

Let the bright red ber - ries glow, Eve - ry - where in

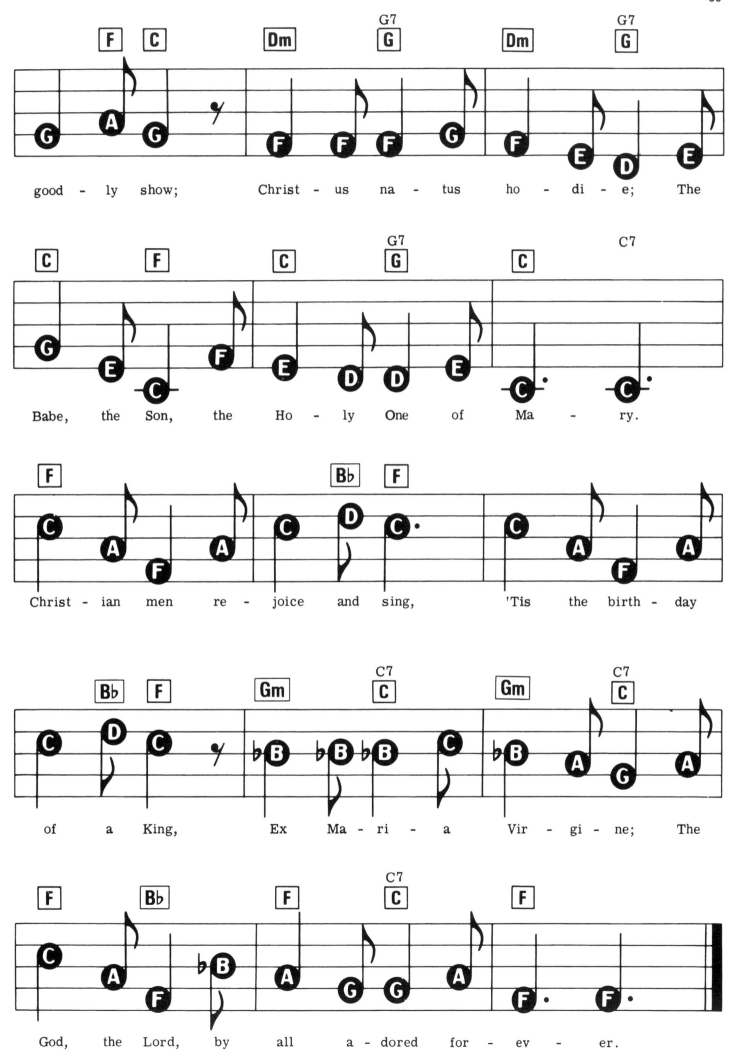

Christians, Awake! Salute the Happy Morn

Registration 4
Rhythm: None

Traditional

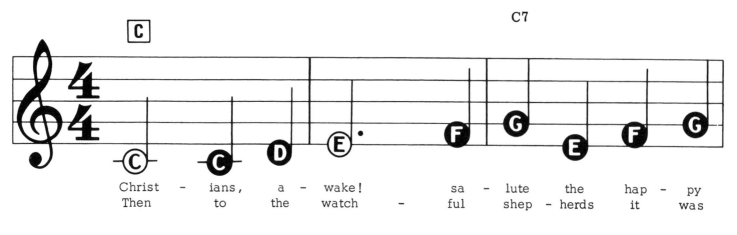

Christ - ians, a - wake! sa - lute the hap - py
Then to the watch - ful shep - herds it was

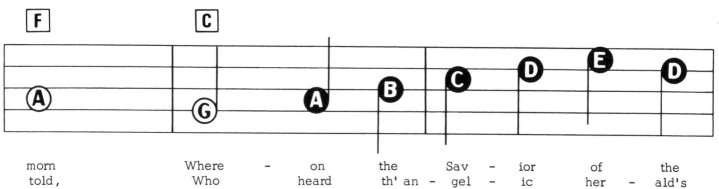

morn Where - on the Sav - ior of the
told, Who heard th' an - gel - ic her - ald's

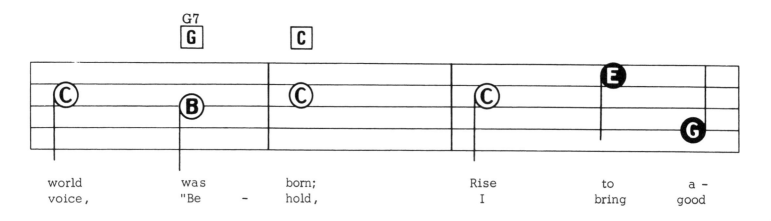

world was born; Rise to a -
voice, "Be - hold, I bring good

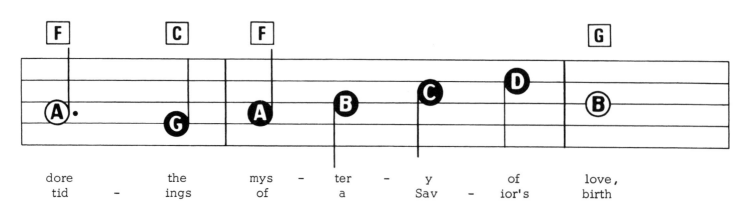

dore the mys - ter - y of love,
tid - ings of a Sav - ior's birth

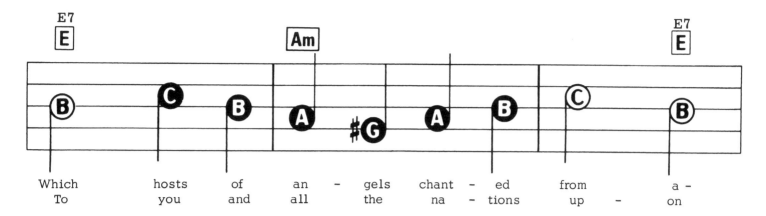

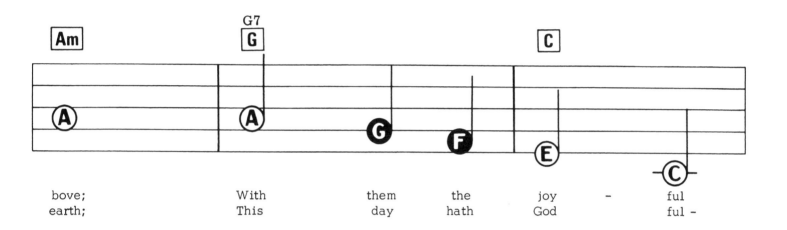

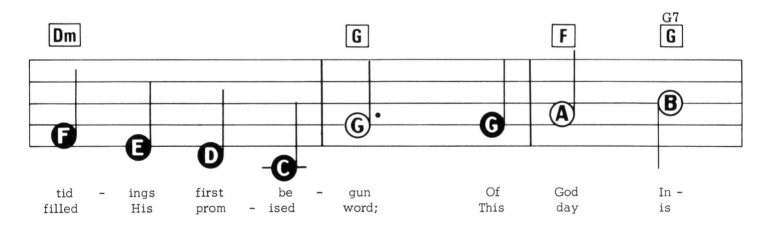

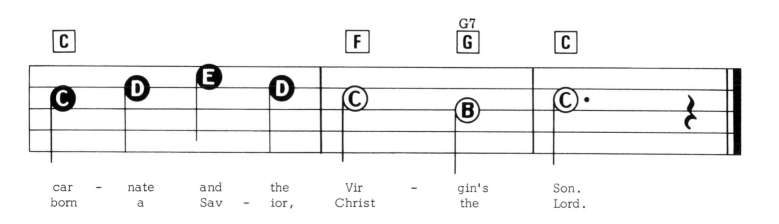

Christmas Comes Anew

Registration 2
Rhythm: 8 Beat

Traditional French

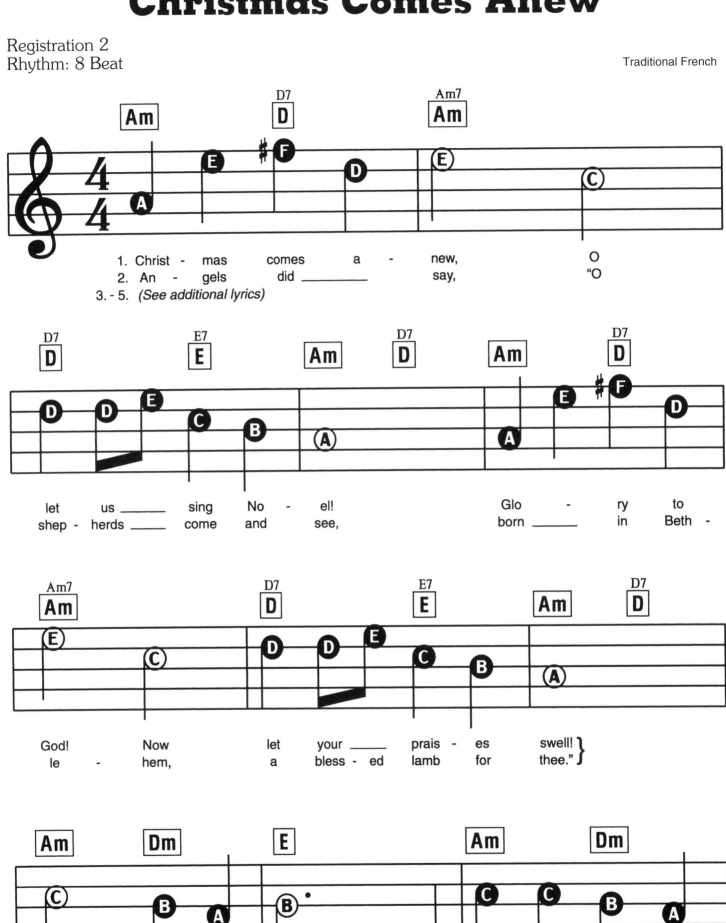

1. Christ - mas comes a - new, O
2. An - gels did _____ say, "O
3. - 5. *(See additional lyrics)*

let us _____ sing No - el! Glo - ry to
shep - herds _____ come and see, born _____ in Beth -

God! Now let your _____ prais - es swell! }
le - hem, a bless - ed lamb for thee." }

Sing we No - el for Christ, the new - born

63

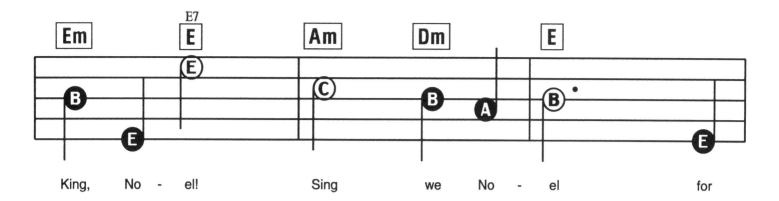

King, No - el! Sing we No - el for

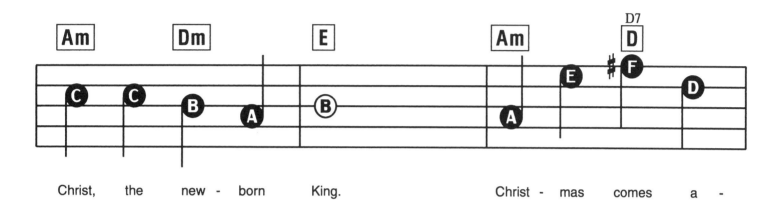

Christ, the new - born King. Christ - mas comes a -

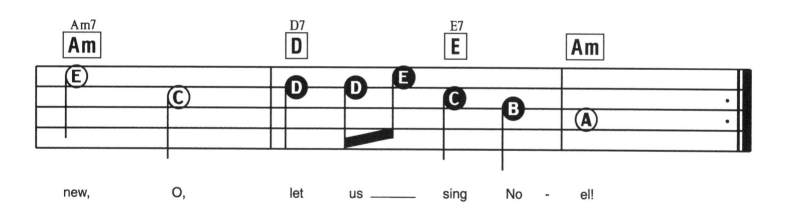

new, O, let us _____ sing No - el!

Additional Lyrics

3. In the manger bed,
   The shepherds found the child;
   Joseph was there,
   And the Mother Mary mild.
   Refrain

4. Soon came the kings
   From following the star,
   Bearing costly gifts
   From Eastern lands afar.
   Refrain

5. Brought to Him gold
   And incense of great price;
   Then the stable bare
   Resembled Paradise.
   Refrain

Christmas Greeting

Registration 7
Rhythm: 8 Beat or Pops

Traditional

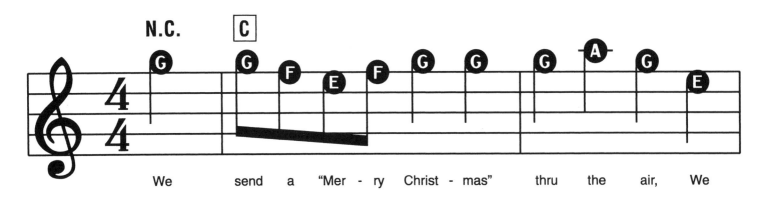

We send a "Mer - ry Christ - mas" thru the air, We

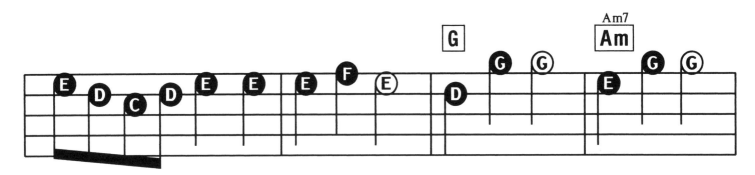

send a "Mer - ry Christ - mas" ev - 'ry - where. Christ - mas bells, Christ - mas bells,

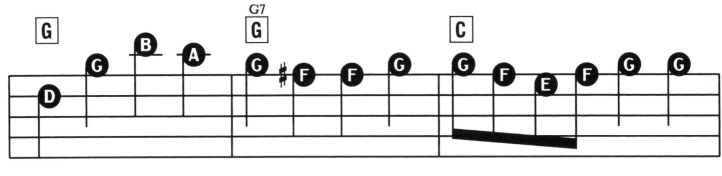

Christ - mas voic - es on the breeze. We wish you "Mer - ry Christ - mas"

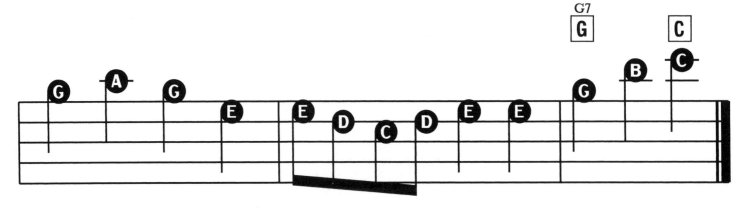

dear Ma - ma, We wish you "Mer - ry Christ - mas" dear Pa - pa.

The Christmas Tree
with Its Candles Gleaming

Registration 1
Rhythm: Waltz

Traditional Czech Text
Traditional Bohemian-Czech Tune

Come, Hear the Wonderful Tidings

Registration 4
Rhythm: None

Traditional Czech Text
Traditional Bohemian-Czech Tune

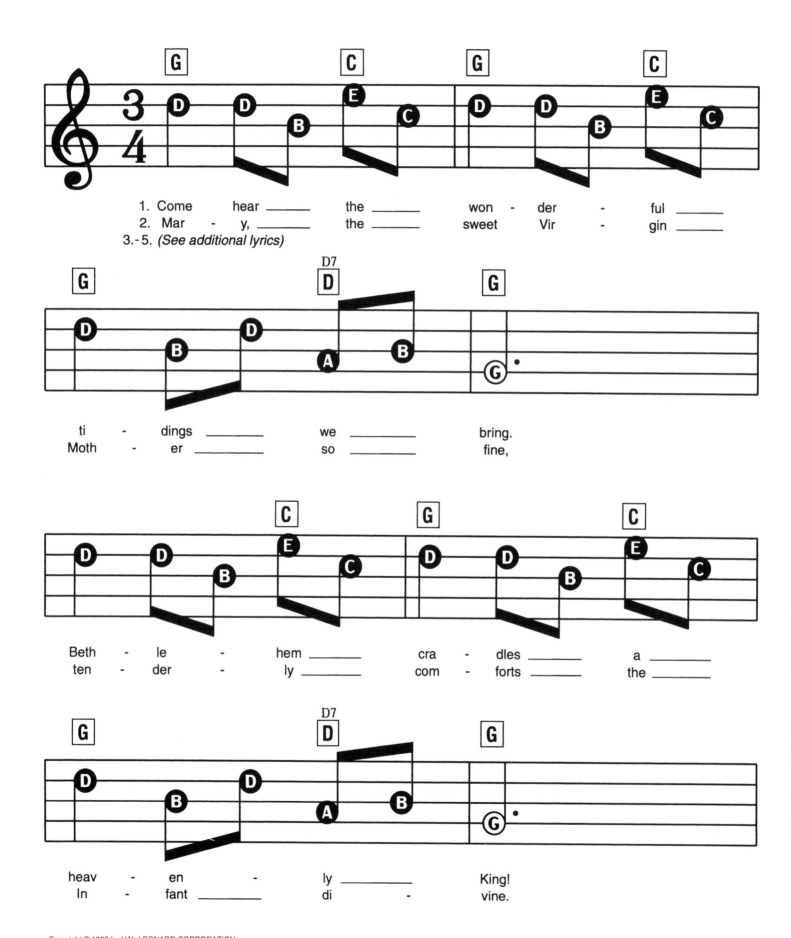

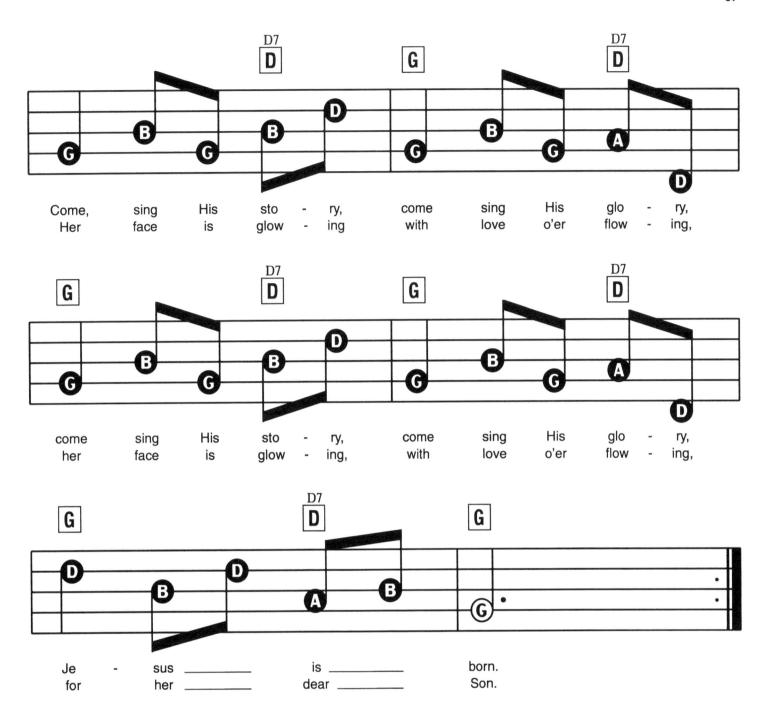

Come, sing His sto - ry, come sing His glo - ry,
Her face is glow - ing with love o'er flow - ing,

come sing His sto - ry, come sing His glo - ry,
her face is glow - ing, with love o'er flow - ing,

Je - sus _____ is _____ born.
for her _____ dear _____ Son.

Additional Lyrics

3. Angels from Heaven are singing His praise
   Shepherds in wonder and joy on Him gaze;
   Bringing Him honor, presents they offer,
   Bringing Him honor, presents they offer,
   Jesus their Lord.

4. Over the desert shines God's radiant star
   Guiding the kings who come journeying far
   Here to discover, in lowly manger,
   Here to discover, in lowly manger,
   Wisdom divine.

5. Prophecy now is fulfilled in this hour;
   Darkness is scattered by Heaven's great pow'r
   God's glory beaming, o'er Jesus streaming,
   God's glory beaming, o'er Jesus streaming,
   Shines through the night.

Come, Thou Long-Expected Jesus

Registration 1
Rhythm: Waltz

Words by Charles Wesley
Music by Rowland Hugh Prichard

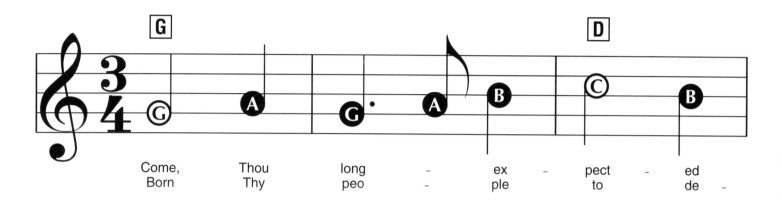

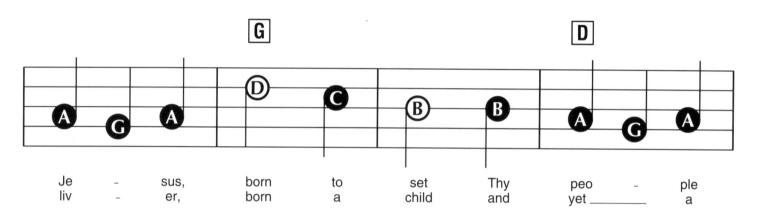

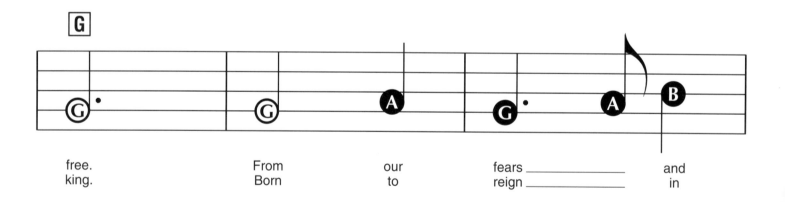

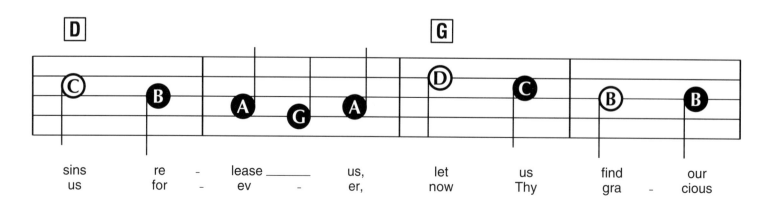

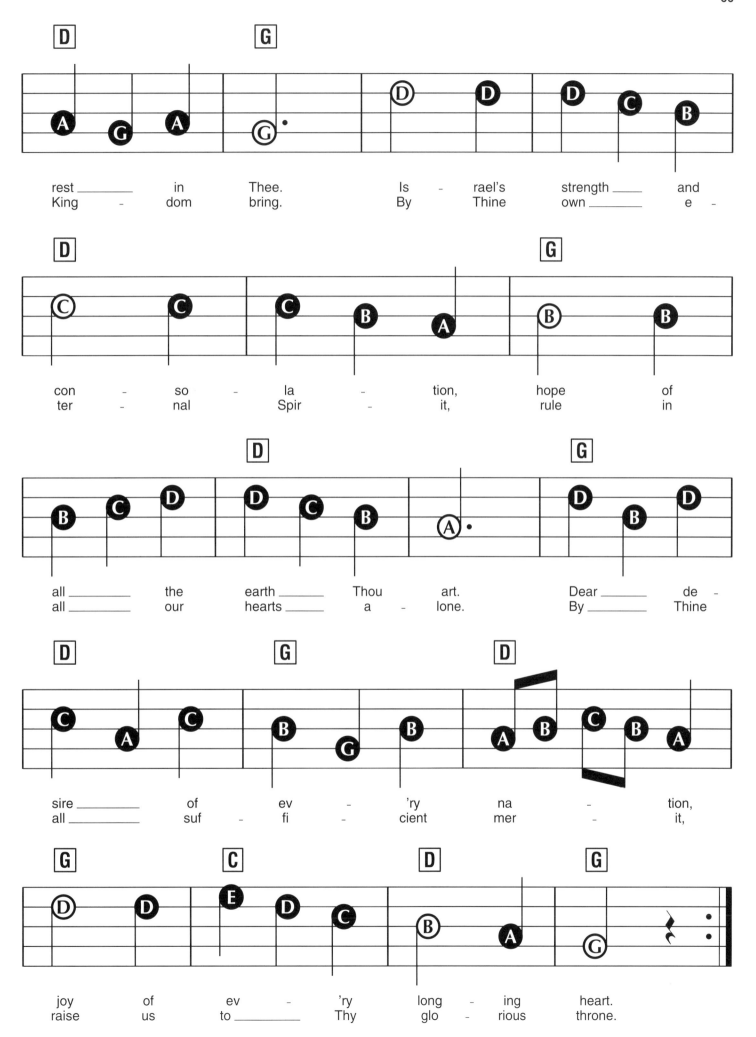

The Coventry Carol

Registration 1
Rhythm: None

Words by Robert Croo
Traditional English Melody

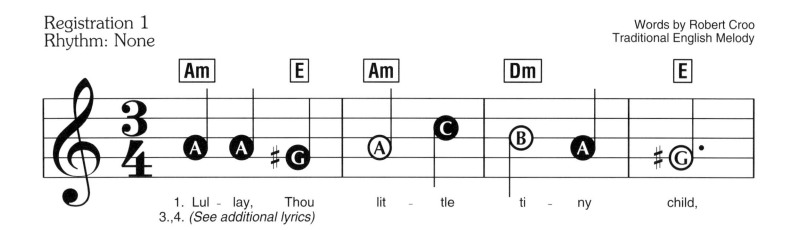

1. Lul - lay, Thou lit - tle ti - ny child,
3.,4. *(See additional lyrics)*

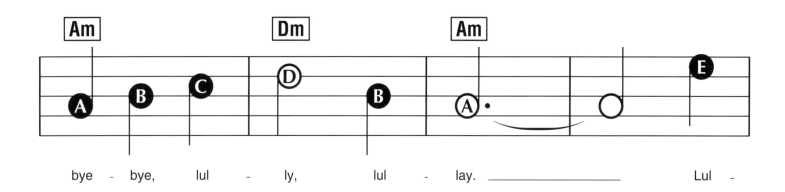

bye - bye, lul - ly, lul - lay. _____ Lul -

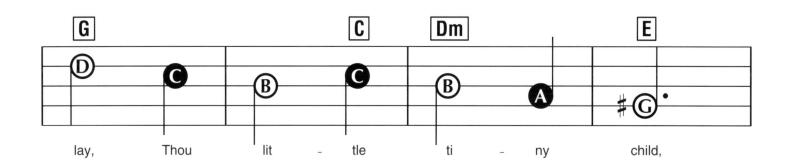

lay, Thou lit - tle ti - ny child,

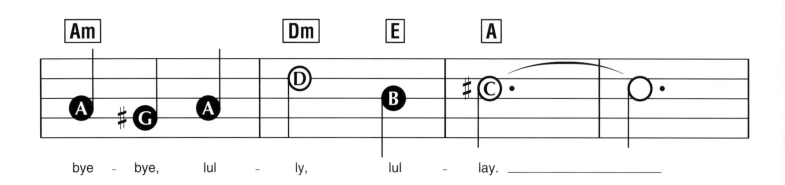

bye - bye, lul - ly, lul - lay. _____

71

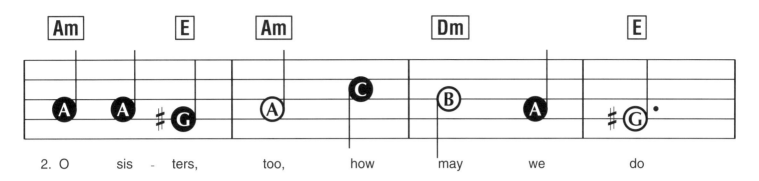

2. O sis - ters, too, how may we do

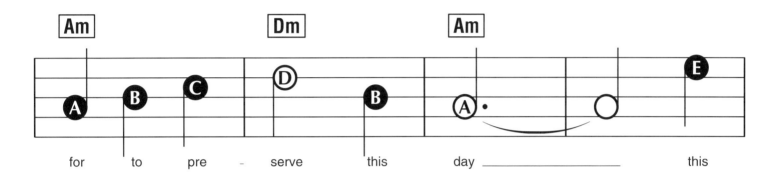

for to pre - serve this day _____ this

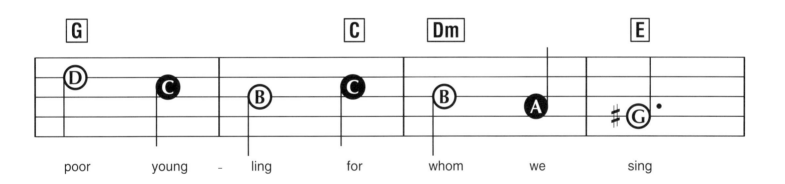

poor young - ling for whom we sing

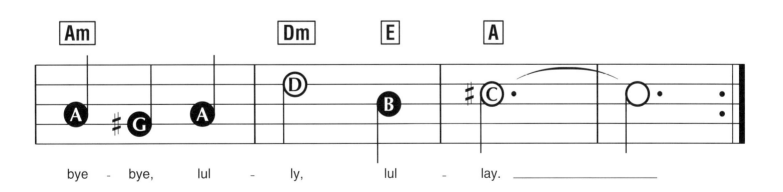

bye - bye, lul - ly, lul - lay. _____

Additional Lyrics

3. Herod the king, in his raging,
   Charged he hath this day
   His men of might, in his own sight,
   All young children to slay.

4. That woe is me, poor child for thee!
   And ever morn and day,
   For they parting neither say nor sing
   bye-bye, lully, lullay!

Dance of the Sugar Plum Fairy
from THE NUTCRACKER

Registration 7
Rhythm: March

By Pyotr Il'yich Tchaikovsky

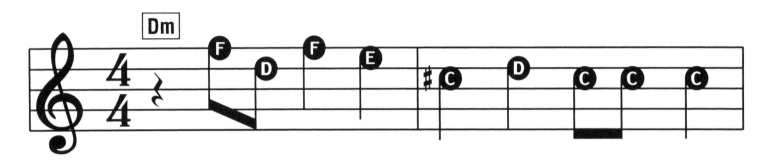

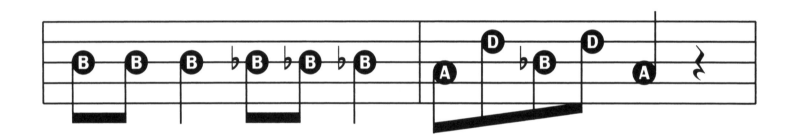

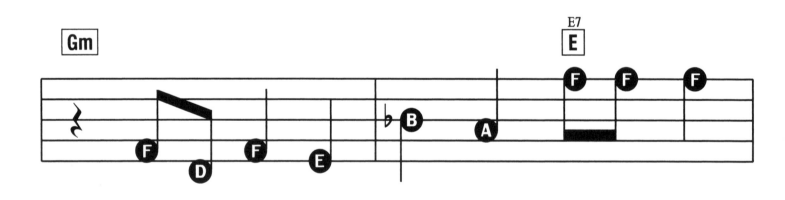

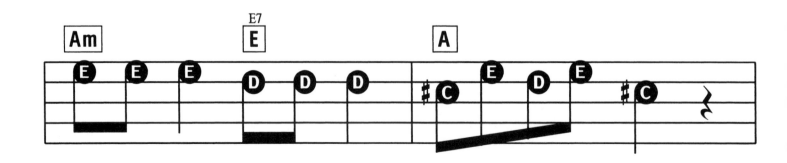

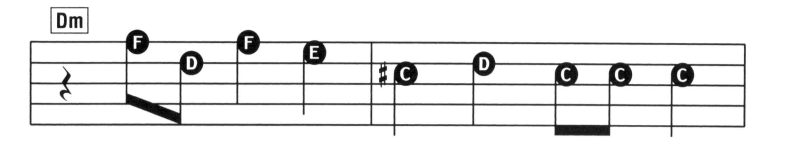

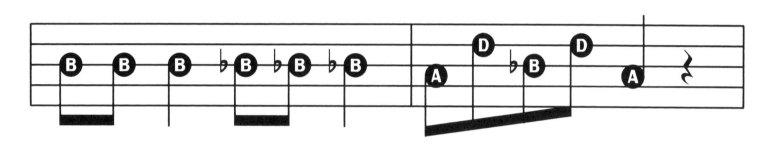

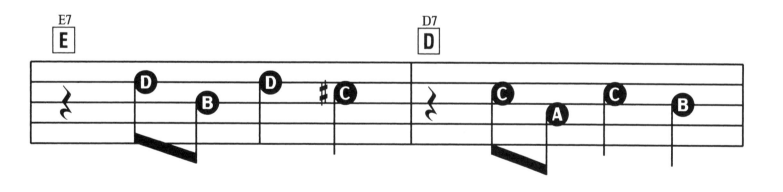

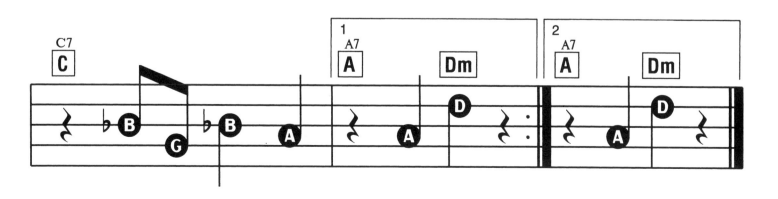

A Day, Bright Day of Glory

Registration 4
Rhythm: Waltz

Traditional

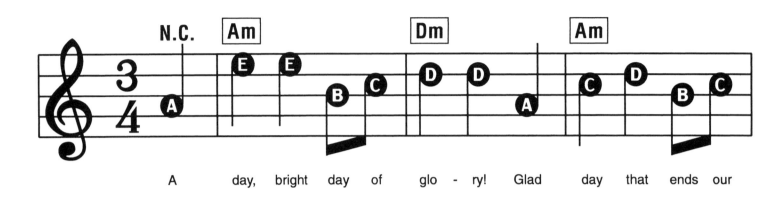

A   day,   bright   day   of   glo - ry!   Glad   day   that   ends   our

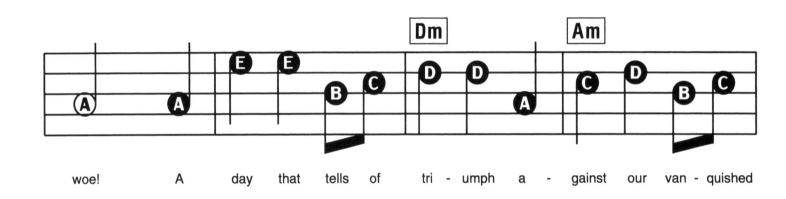

woe!   A   day   that   tells   of   tri - umph   a - gainst   our   van - quished

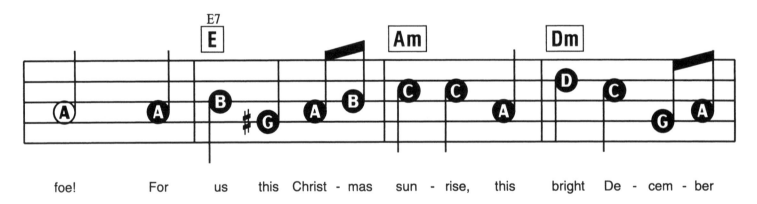

foe!   For   us   this   Christ - mas   sun - rise,   this   bright   De - cem - ber

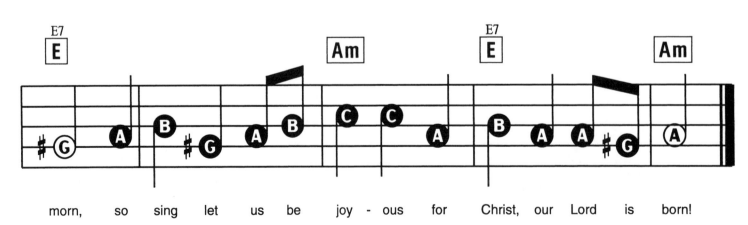

morn,   so   sing   let   us   be   joy - ous   for   Christ,   our   Lord   is   born!

Deck the Hall

Registration 5
Rhythm: Fox Trot

Traditional Welsh Carol

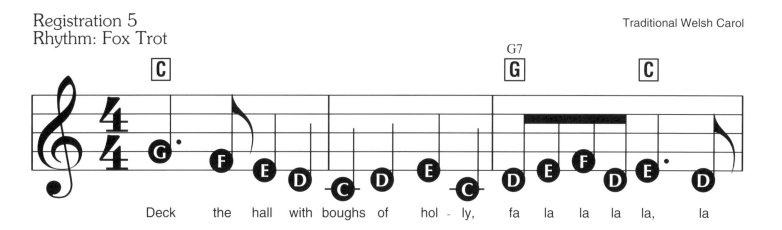

Deck the hall with boughs of hol - ly, fa la la la la, la

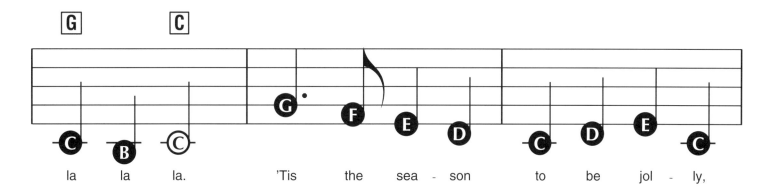

la la la. 'Tis the sea - son to be jol - ly,

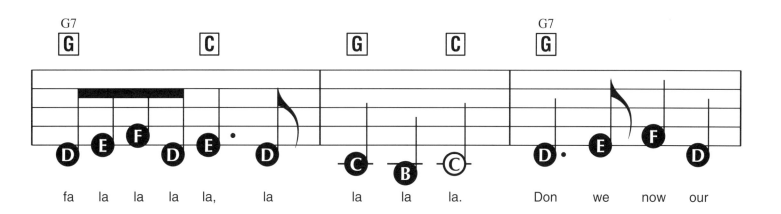

fa la la la la, la la la la. Don we now our

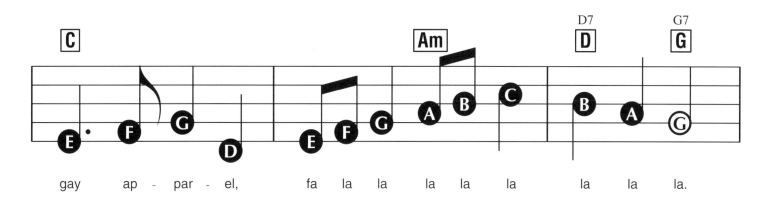

gay ap - par - el, fa la la la la la la la la.

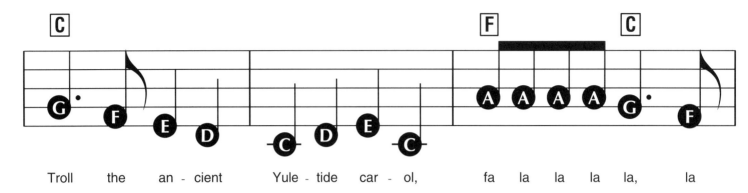

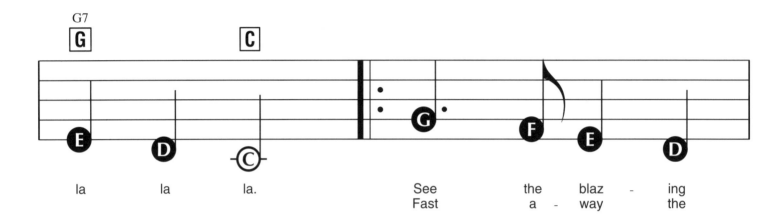

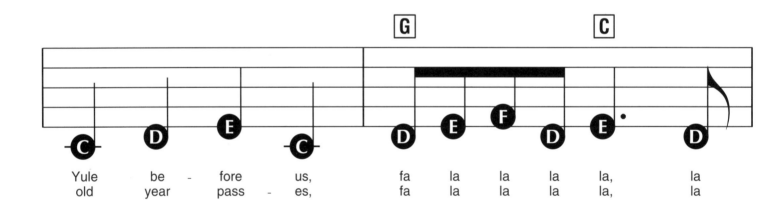

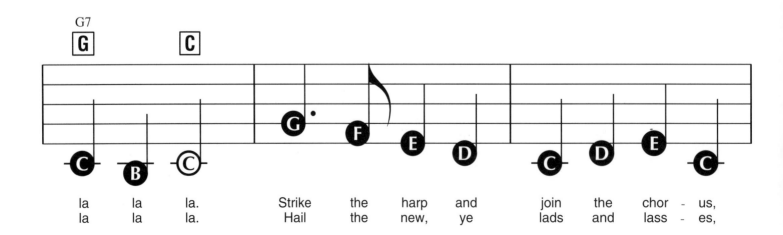

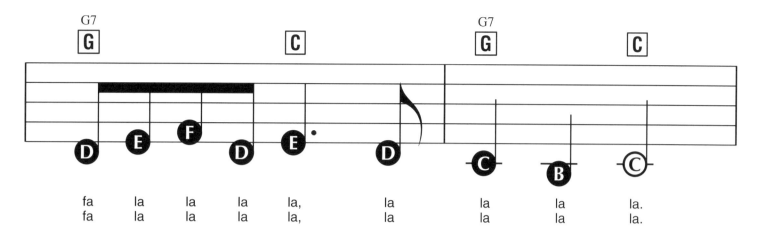

fa la la la la, la la la la.
fa la la la la, la la la la.

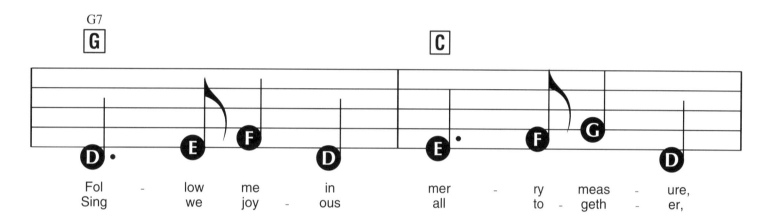

Fol - low me in mer - ry meas - ure,
Sing we joy - ous all to - geth - er,

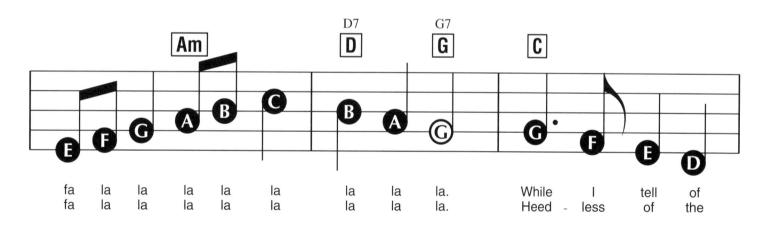

fa la la la la la la la la. While I tell of
fa la la la la la la la la. Heed - less of the

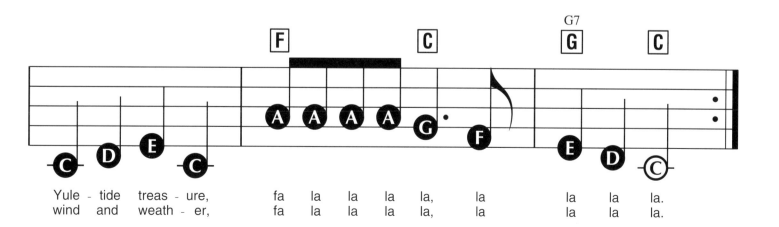

Yule - tide treas - ure, fa la la la la, la la la la.
wind and weath - er, fa la la la la, la la la la.

Ding Dong! Merrily on High!

Registration 5
Rhythm: March

French Carol

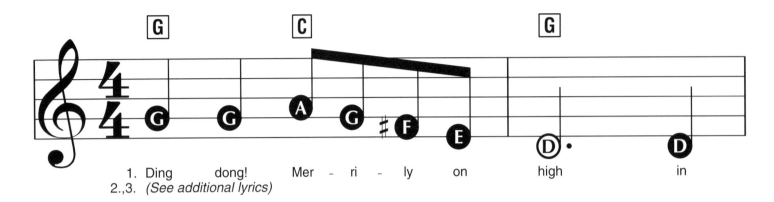

1. Ding   dong!   Mer – ri – ly   on   high   in
2.,3. *(See additional lyrics)*

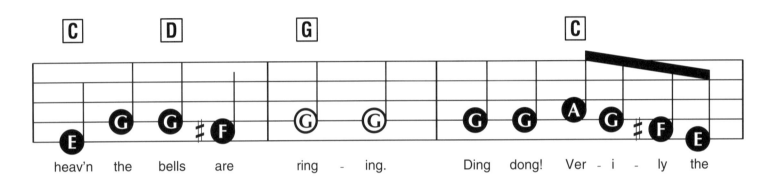

heav'n   the   bells   are   ring – ing.   Ding   dong!   Ver – i – ly   the

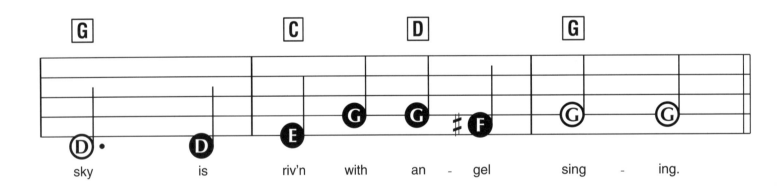

sky   is   riv'n   with   an – gel   sing – ing.

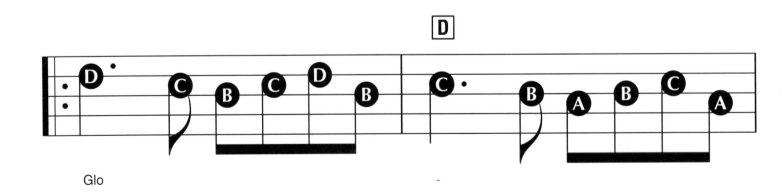

Glo   –

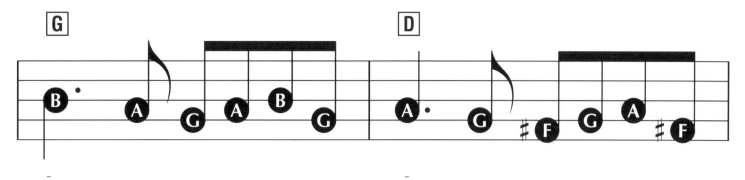

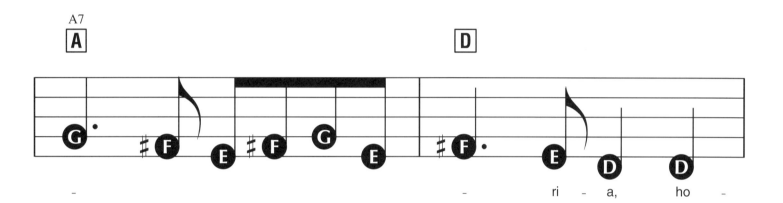

ri - a, ho -

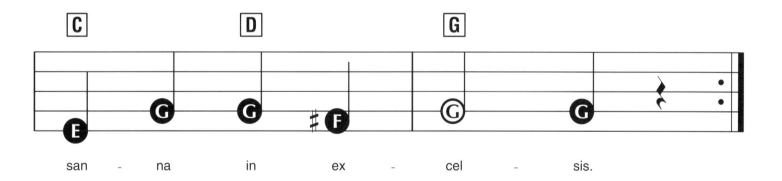

san - na in ex - cel - sis.

Additional Lyrics

2. E'en so here below, below,
   Let steeple bells be swungen,
   And io, io, io,
   By priest and people sungen.

   Gloria, hosanna in excelsis!
   Gloria, hosanna in excelsis!

3. Pray you, dutifully prime
   Your matin chime, ye ringers.
   May you beautifully rime
   Your evetime song, ye singers.

   Gloria, hosanna in excelsis!
   Gloria, hosanna in excelsis!

Everywhere, Everywhere, Christmas Tonight

Registration 10
Rhythm: Waltz

By Lewis H. Redner
and Phillip Brooks

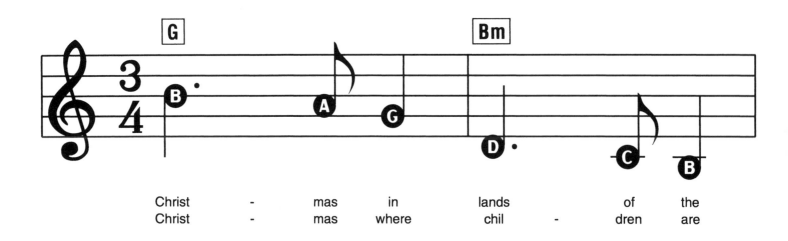

Christ - mas in lands of the
Christ - mas in where chil - dren are

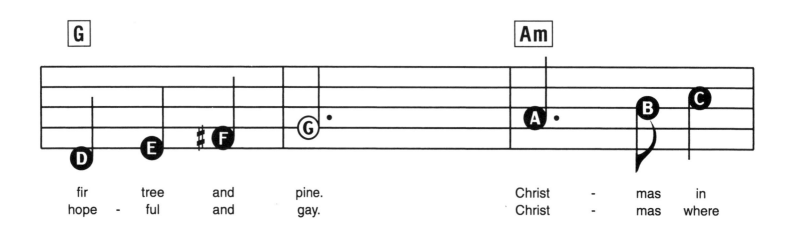

fir tree and pine.
hope - ful and gay.

Christ - mas in
Christ - mas where

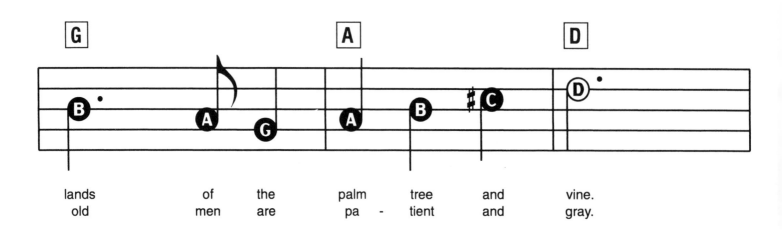

lands of the palm tree and vine.
old men are pa - tient and gray.

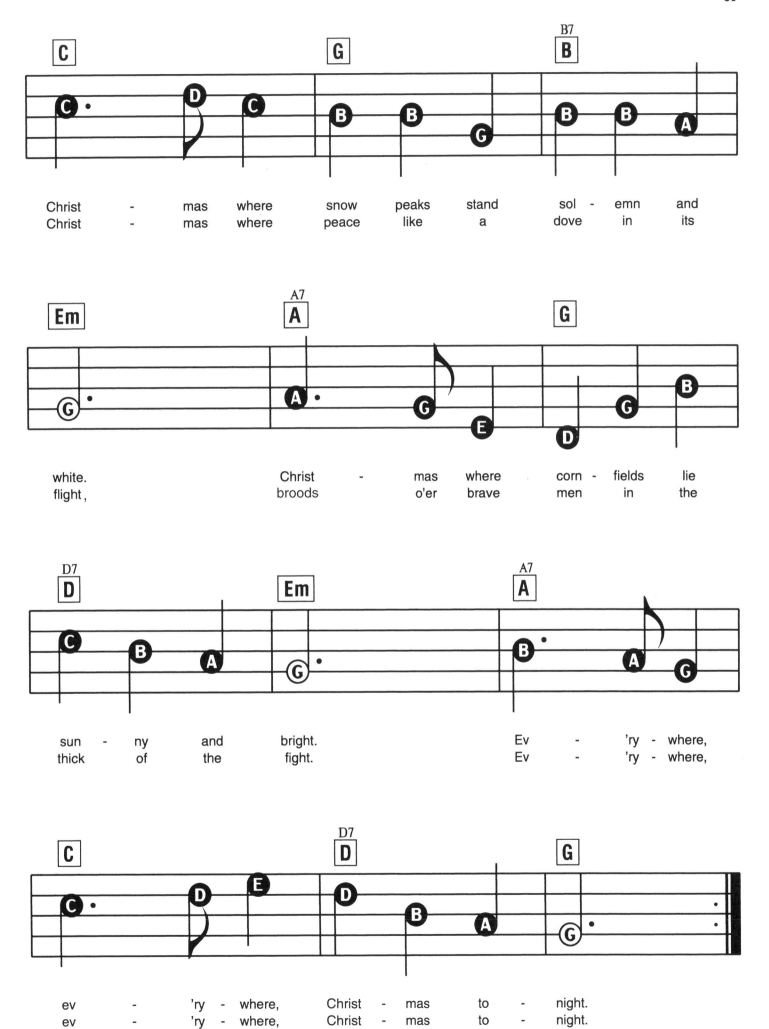

The First Noël

Registration 10
Rhythm: None

17th Century English Carol
Music from W. Sandys' *Christmas Carols*

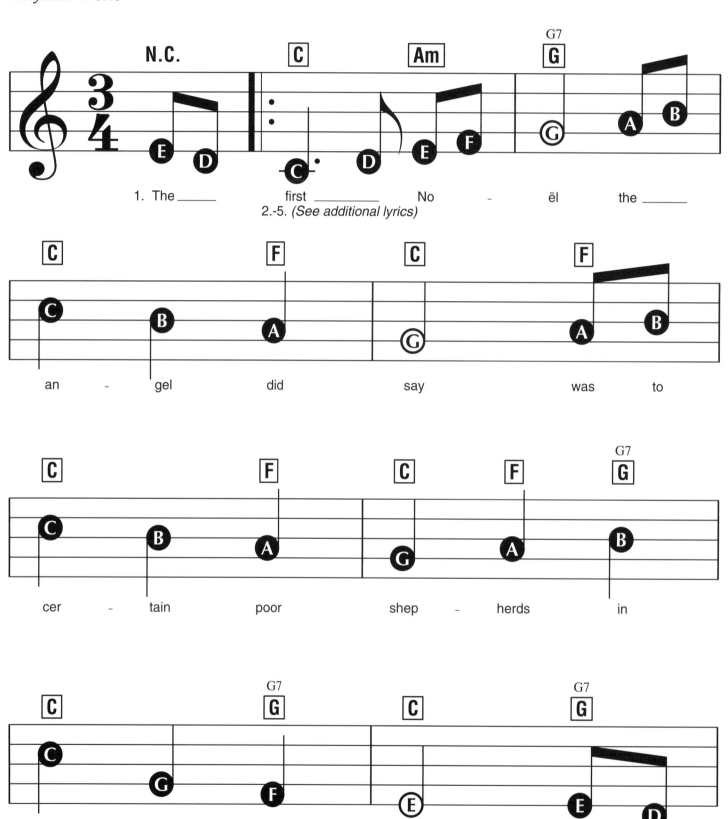

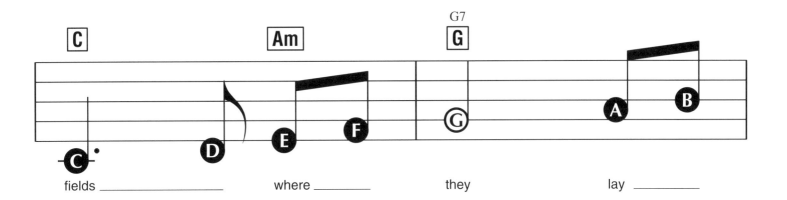

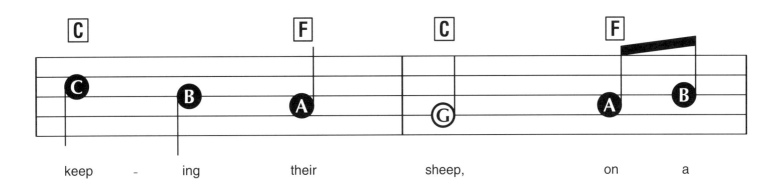

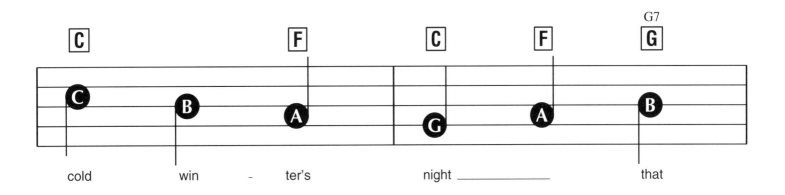

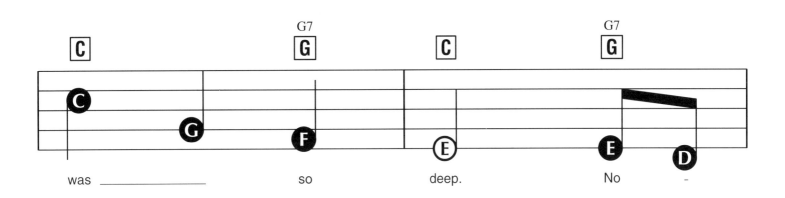

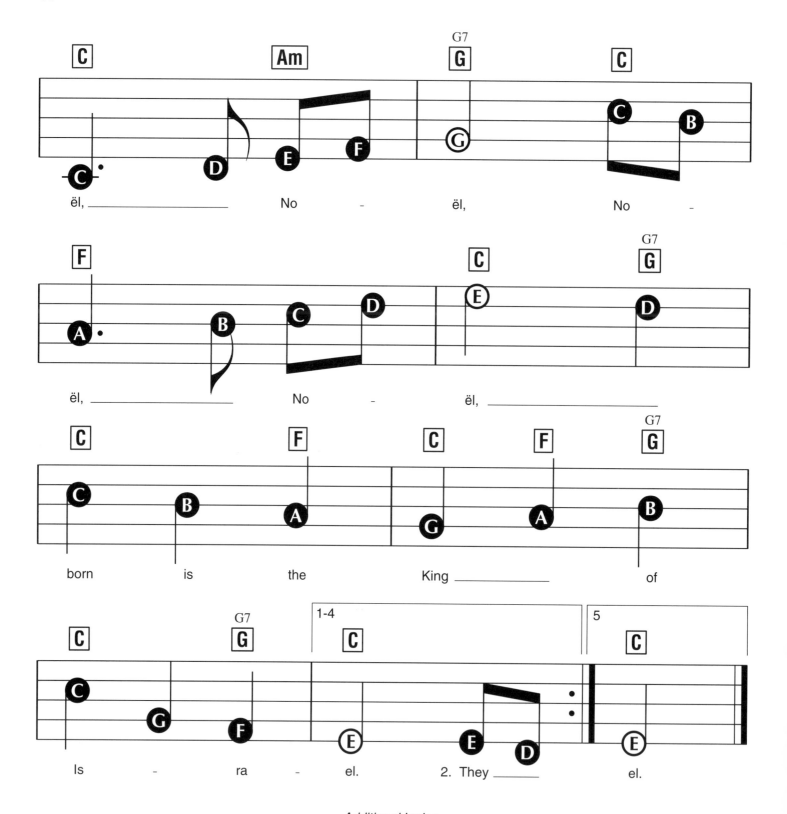

Additional Lyrics

2. They looked up and saw a star
   Shining in the east beyond them far.
   And to the earth it gave great light,
   And so it continued both day and night.
   Noël, noël, noël, noël,
   Born is the King of Israel.

3. And by the light of that same star
   Three wise men came from country far.
   To seek for a King was their intent,
   And to follow the star wherever it went.
   Noël, Noël, Noël, Noël,
   Born is the King of Israel.

4. This star drew nigh to the northwest,
   O'er Bethlehem it took its rest.
   And there it did both stop and stay
   Right over the place where Jesus lay.
   Noël, Noël, Noël, Noël,
   Born is the King of Israel.

5. Then entered in those wise men three
   Full reverently upon their knee,
   And offered there, in His presence,
   Their gold, and myrrh, and frankincense.
   Noël, Noël, Noël, Noël,
   Born is the King of Israel.

From the Eastern Mountains

Registration 9
Rhythm: None

Traditional

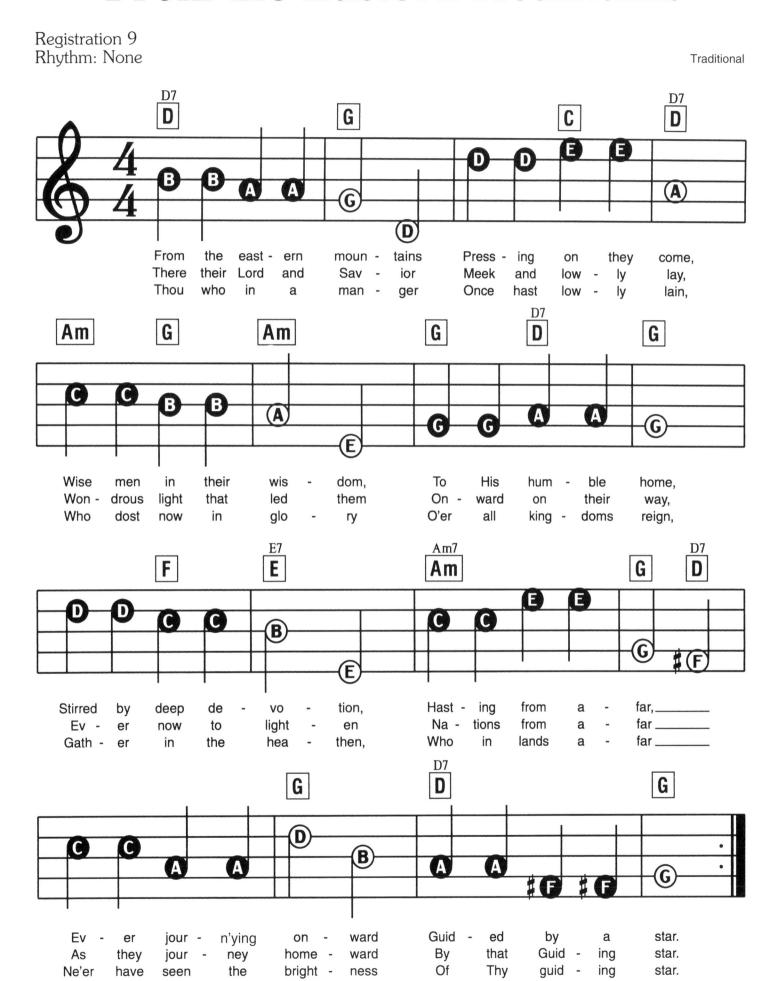

From the east - ern moun - tains Press - ing on they come,
There their Lord and Sav - ior Meek and low - ly lay,
Thou who in a man - ger Once hast low - ly lain,

Wise men in their wis - dom, To His hum - ble home,
Won - drous light that led them On - ward on their way,
Who dost now in glo - ry O'er all king - doms reign,

Stirred by deep de - vo - tion, Hast - ing from a - far,_____
Ev - er now to light - en Na - tions from a - far_____
Gath - er in the hea - then, Who in lands a - far_____

Ev - er jour - n'ying on - ward Guid - ed by a star.
As they jour - ney home - ward By that Guid - ing star.
Ne'er have seen the bright - ness Of Thy guid - ing star.

The Friendly Beasts

Registration 2
Rhythm: Waltz

Traditional English Carol

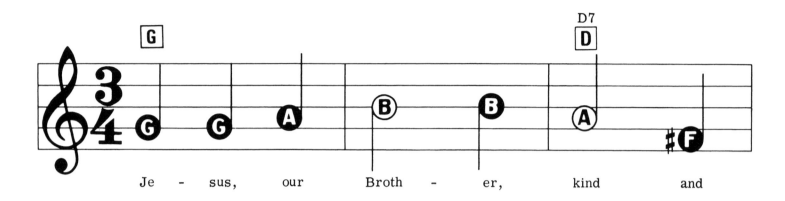

Je - sus, our Broth - er, kind and

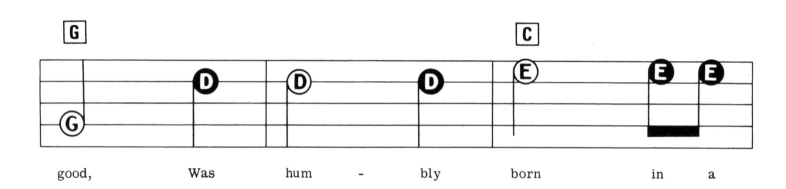

good, Was hum - bly born in a

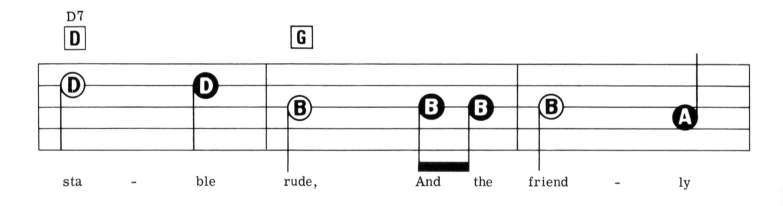

sta - ble rude, And the friend - ly

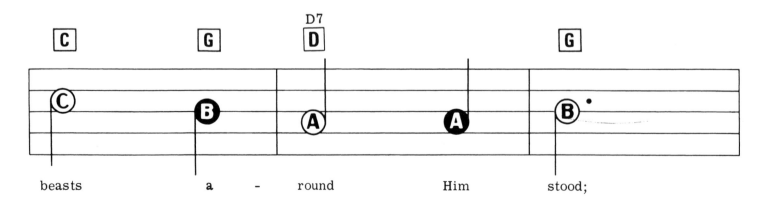

beasts a - round Him stood;

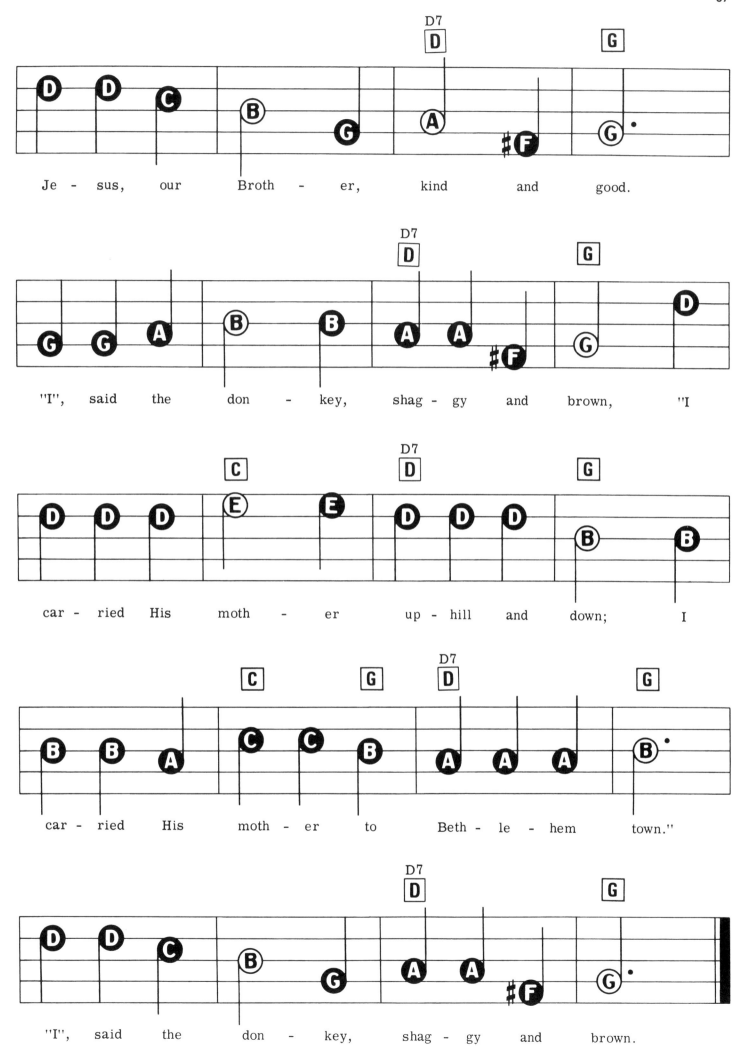

From Heaven Above to Earth I Come

Registration 10
Rhythm: None

Words and Music by
Martin Luther

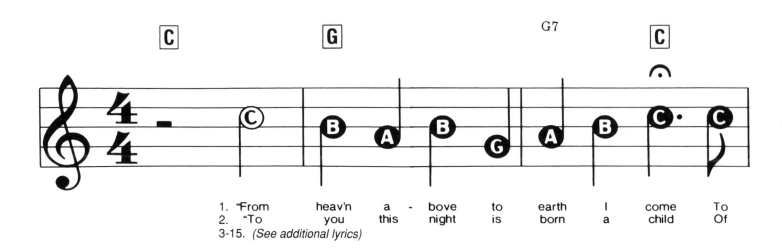

1. "From heav'n a - bove to earth I come To
2. "To you this night is born a child Of
3-15. *(See additional lyrics)*

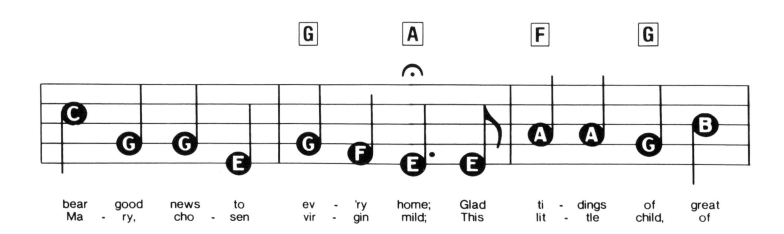

bear good news to ev - 'ry home; Glad ti - dings of great
Ma - ry, cho - sen vir - gin mild; This lit - tle child, of

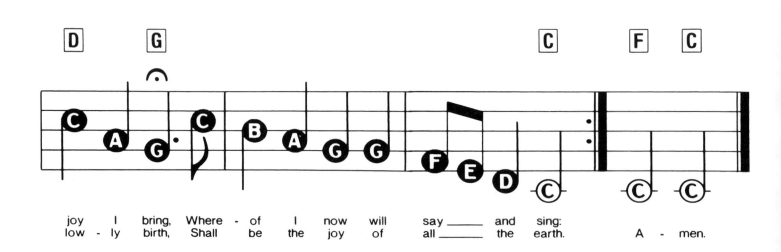

joy I bring, Where - of I now will say _____ and sing:
low - ly birth, Shall be the joy of all _____ the earth. A - men.

Additional Lyrics

3. "This is the Christ, our God and Lord,
   Who in all need shall aid afford;
   He will Himself your Savior be
   From all your sins to set you free.

4. "He will on you the gifts bestow
   Prepared by God for all below,
   That in His kingdom, bright and fair,
   You may with us His glory share.

5. "These are the tokens ye shall mark:
   The swaddling - clothes and manger dark;
   There ye shall find the Infant laid
   By whom the heavens and earth were made."

6. Now let us all with gladsome cheer
   Go with the shepherds and draw near
   To see the precious **Gift** of God,
   Who hath His own dear Son bestowed.

7. Give heed, my heart, lift up thine eyes!
   What is it in yon manger lies?
   Who is this child, so young and fair?
   The blessed Christ-child lieth there.

8. Welcome to earth, Thou noble Guest,
   Through whom the sinful world is blest!
   Thou com'st to share my misery;
   What thanks shall I return to Thee?

9. Ah, Lord, who hast created all,
   How weak art Thou, how poor and small,
   That Thou dost choose Thine infant bed
   Where humble cattle lately fed!

10. Were earth a thousand **times** as fair.
    Beset with gold and jewels rare,
    It yet were far too poor to be
    A narrow cradle, Lord, for Thee.

11. For velvets soft and silken stuff
    Thou hast but hay and straw so rough,
    Whereon Thou, King, so rich and great,
    As 'twere Thy heaven, art throned in state.

12. And thus, dear Lord, it pleaseth Thee
    To make this truth quite plain to me,
    That all the world's wealth, honor, might,
    Are naught and worthless in Thy sight.

13. Ah, dearest Jesus, holy Child,
    Make Thee a bed, soft, undefiled,
    Within my heart, that it may be
    A quiet chamber kept for Thee.

14. My heart for very joy doth leap,
    My lips no more can silence keep;
    I, too, must sing with joyful tongue
    That sweetest ancient cradle-song:

15. Glory to God in highest heaven,
    Who unto us His Son hath given!
    While angels sing with pious mirth
    A glad new year to all the earth.

Gather Around the Christmas Tree

Registration 3
Rhythm: None

By John H. Hopkins

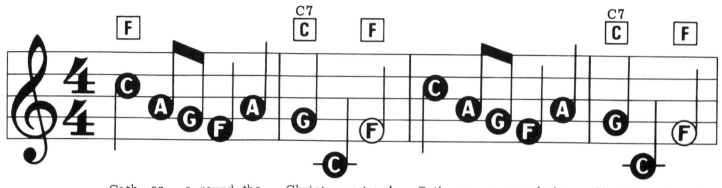

Gath - er a-round the Christ-mas tree! Gath- er a-round the Christ-mas tree!

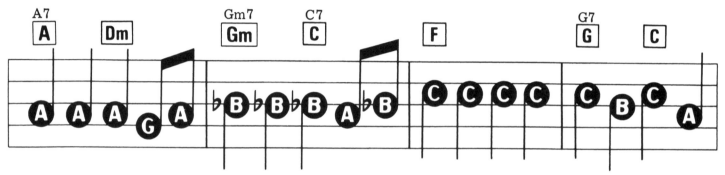

Ev - er green have it's branch - es been, It is king of all the wood-land scene; For

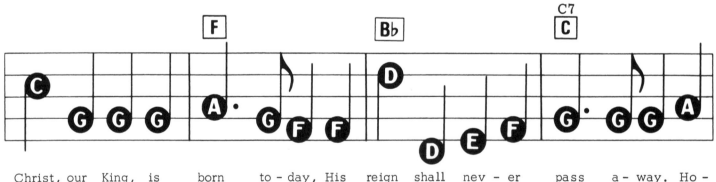

Christ, our King, is born to - day, His reign shall nev - er pass a - way. Ho -

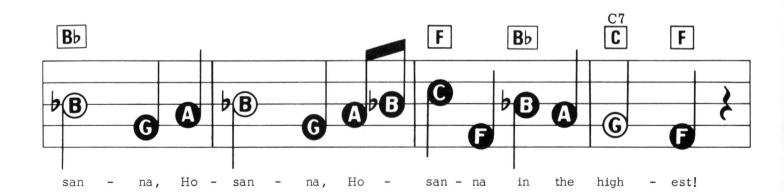

san - na, Ho - san - na, Ho - san - na in the high - est!

91

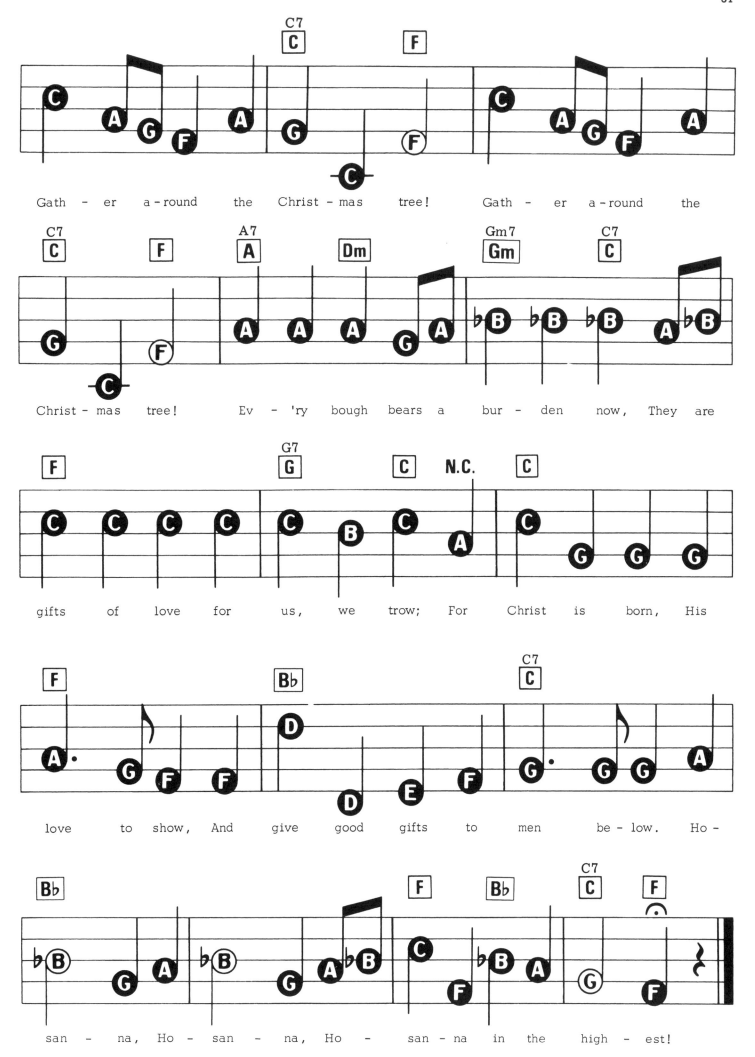

Glad Christmas Bells

Registration 8
Rhythm: Waltz

Traditional American Carol

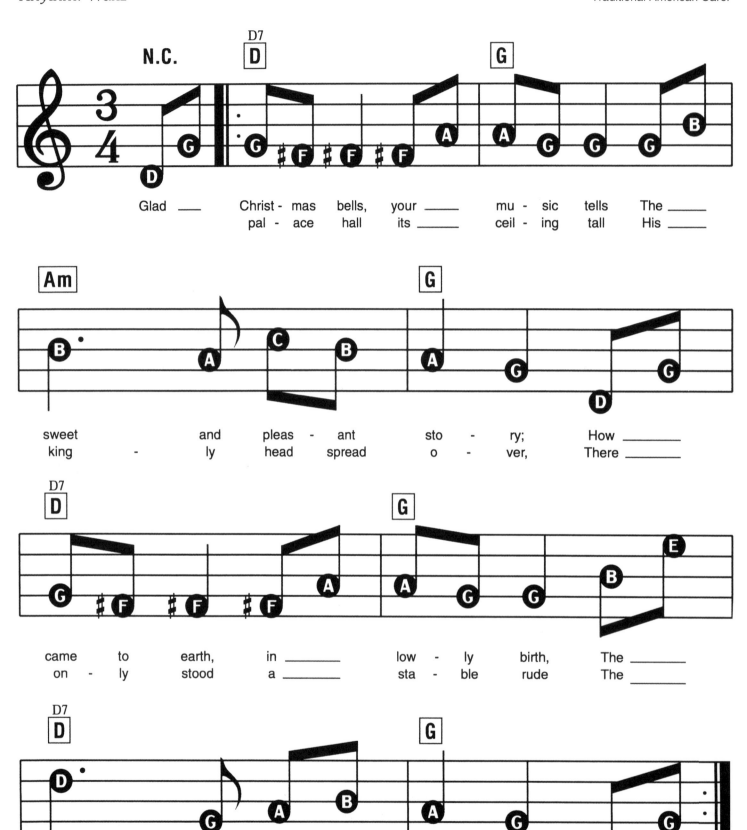

93

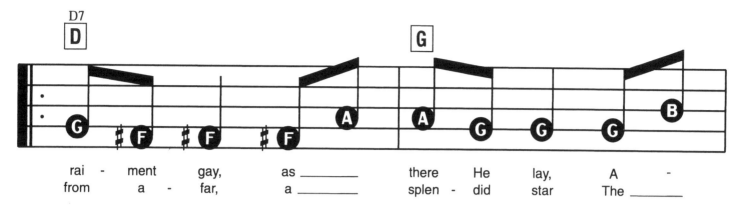

rai - ment gay, as _____ there He lay, A -
from a - far, a _____ splen - did star The _____

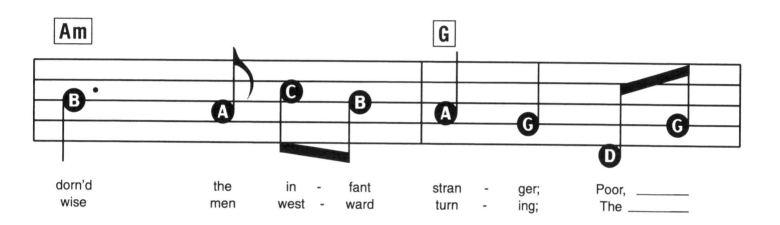

dorn'd the in - fant stran - ger; Poor, _____
wise men west - ward turn - ing; The _____

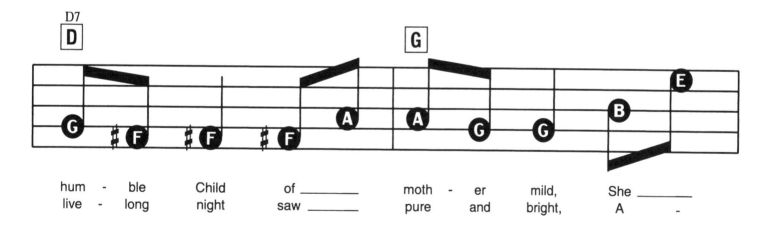

hum - ble Child of _____ moth - er mild, She _____
live - long night saw _____ pure and bright, A -

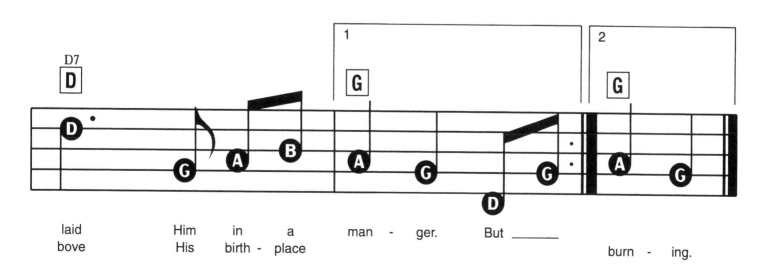

laid Him in a man - ger. But _____
bove His birth - place burn - ing.

Fum, Fum, Fum

Registration 9
Rhythm: March

Traditional Catalonian Carol

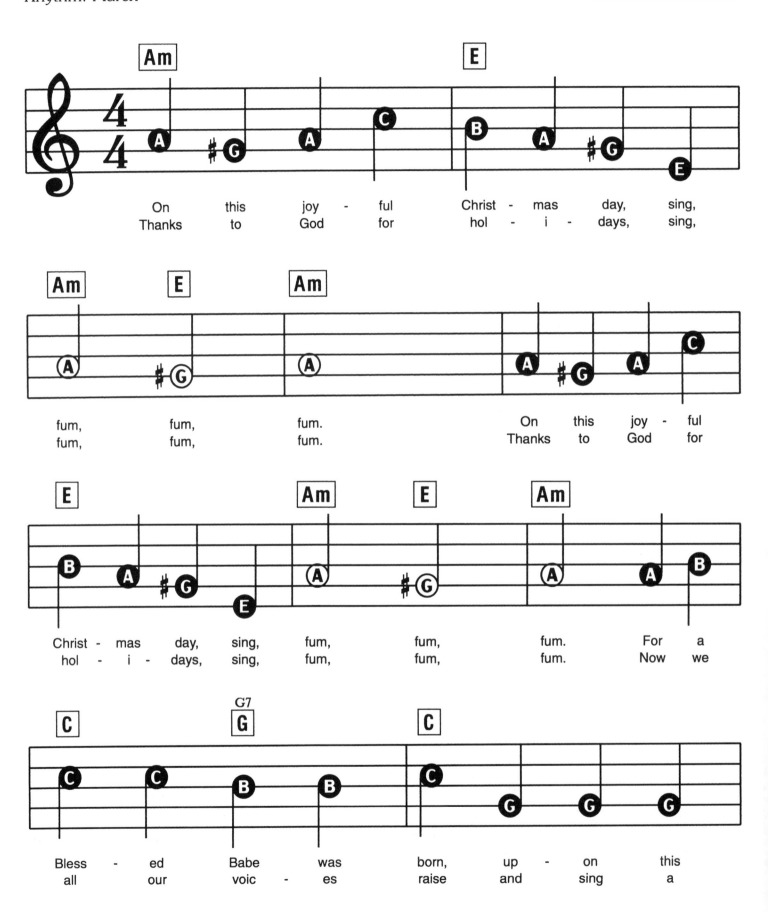

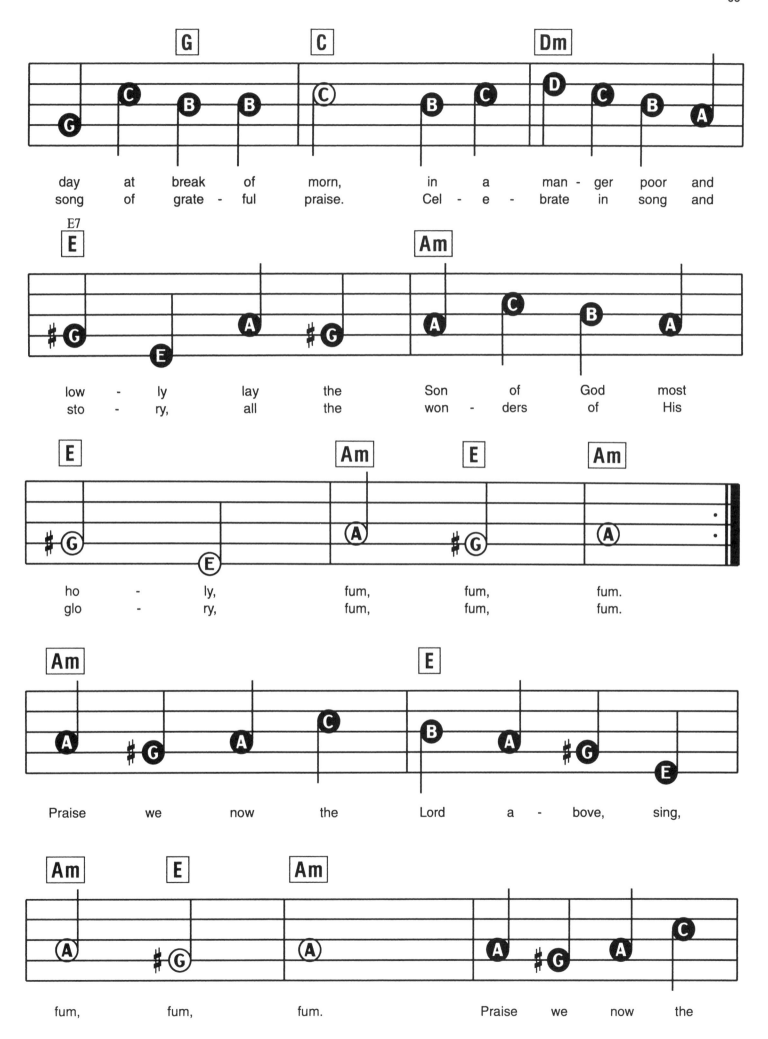

96

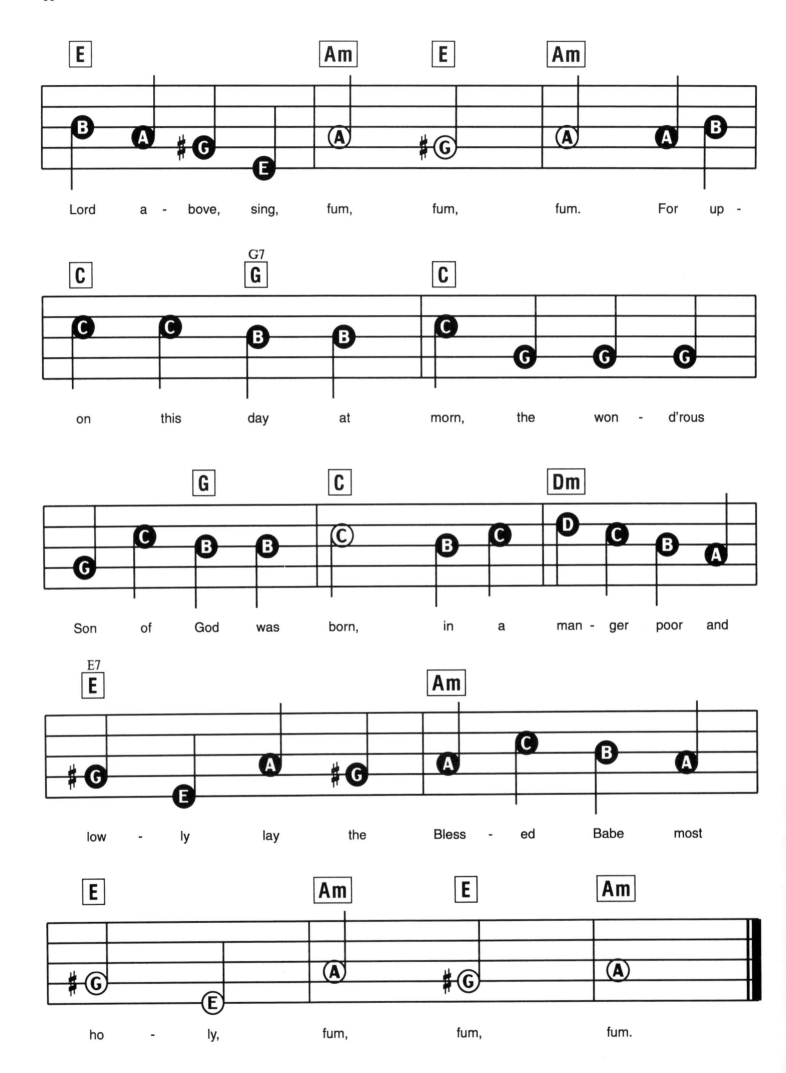

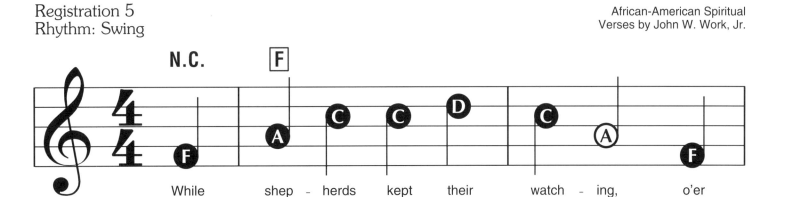
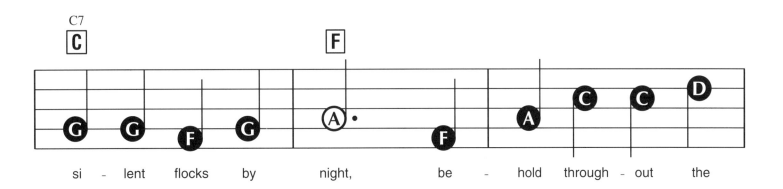
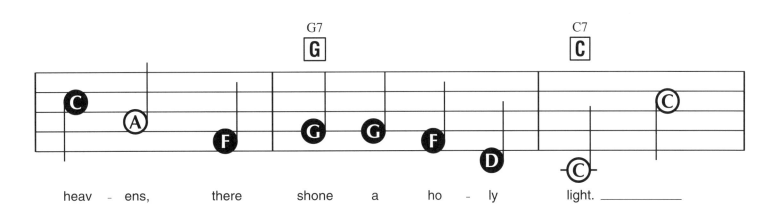
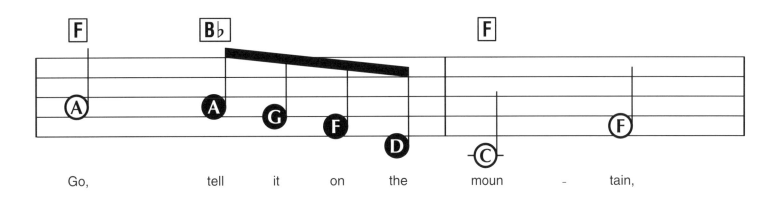

Go, Tell It on the Mountain

Registration 5
Rhythm: Swing

African-American Spiritual
Verses by John W. Work, Jr.

98

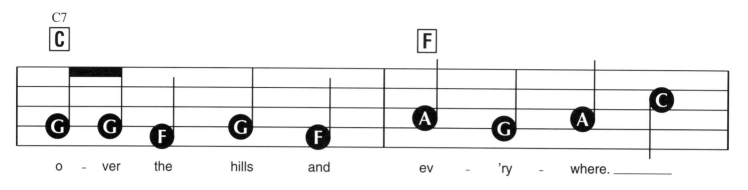

o - ver the hills and ev - 'ry - where. _____

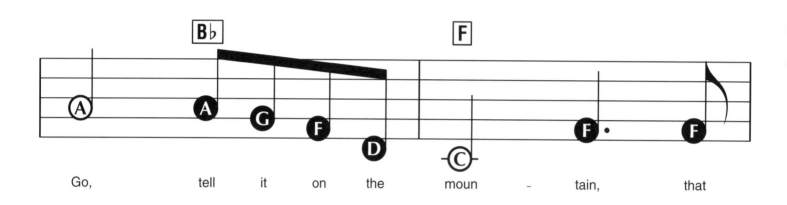

Go, tell it on the moun - tain, that

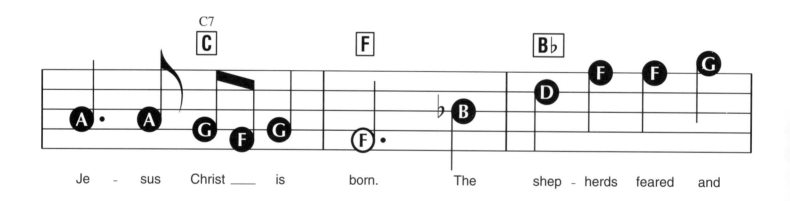

Je - sus Christ ___ is born. The shep - herds feared and

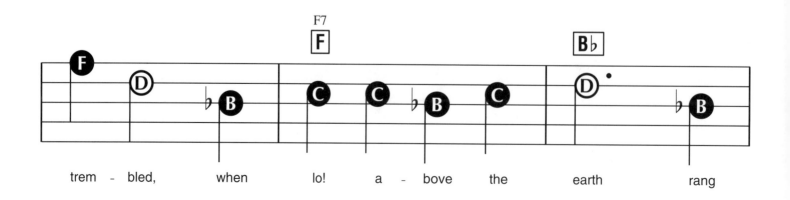

trem - bled, when lo! a - bove the earth rang

99

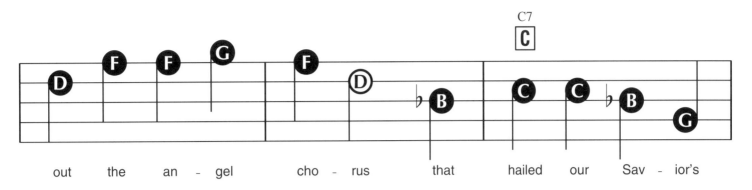

out the an - gel cho - rus that hailed our Sav - ior's

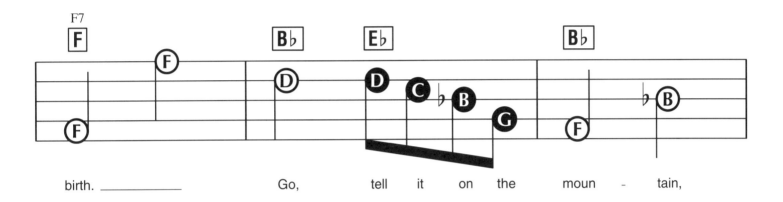

birth. _____ Go, tell it on the moun - tain,

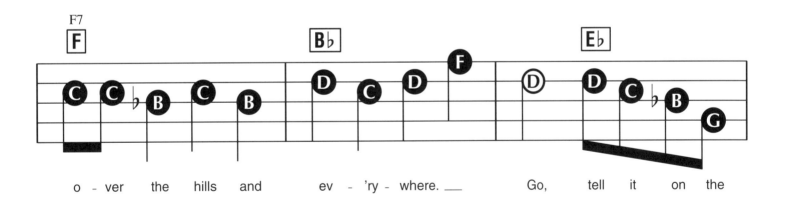

o - ver the hills and ev - 'ry - where. __ Go, tell it on the

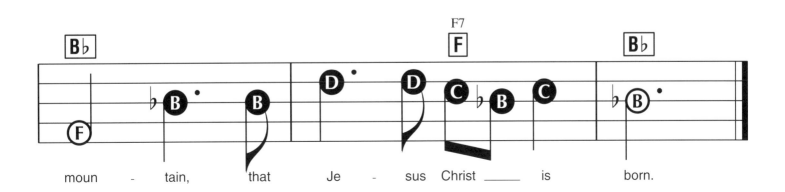

moun - tain, that Je - sus Christ _____ is born.

God Rest Ye Merry, Gentlemen

Registration 6
Rhythm: None

19th Century English Carol

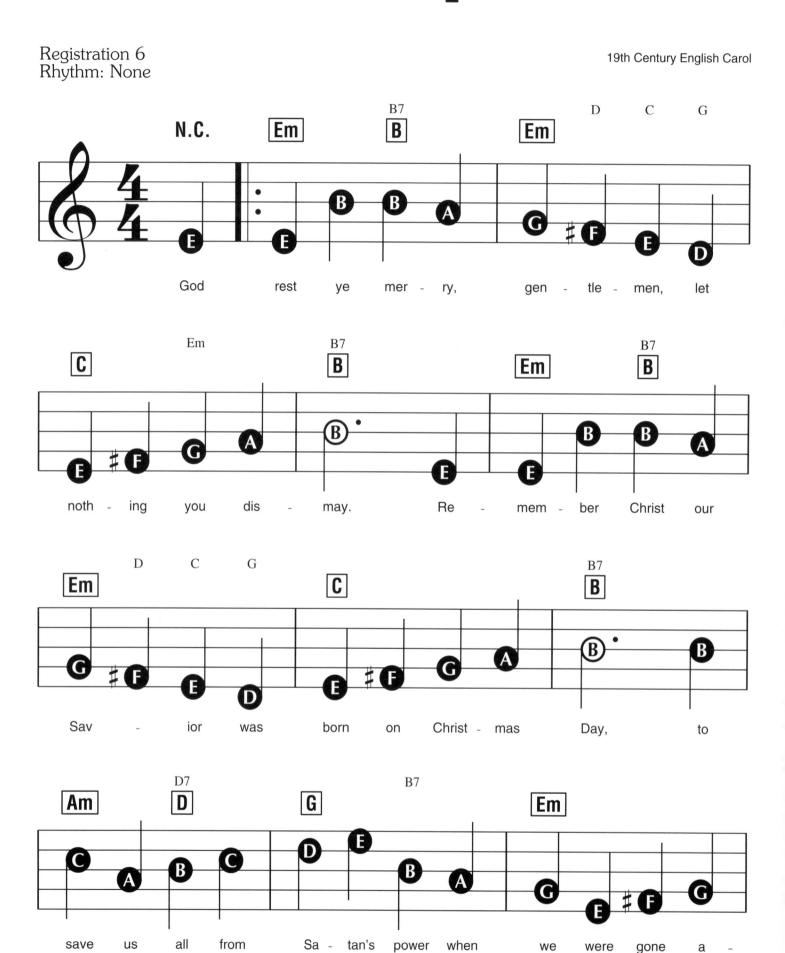

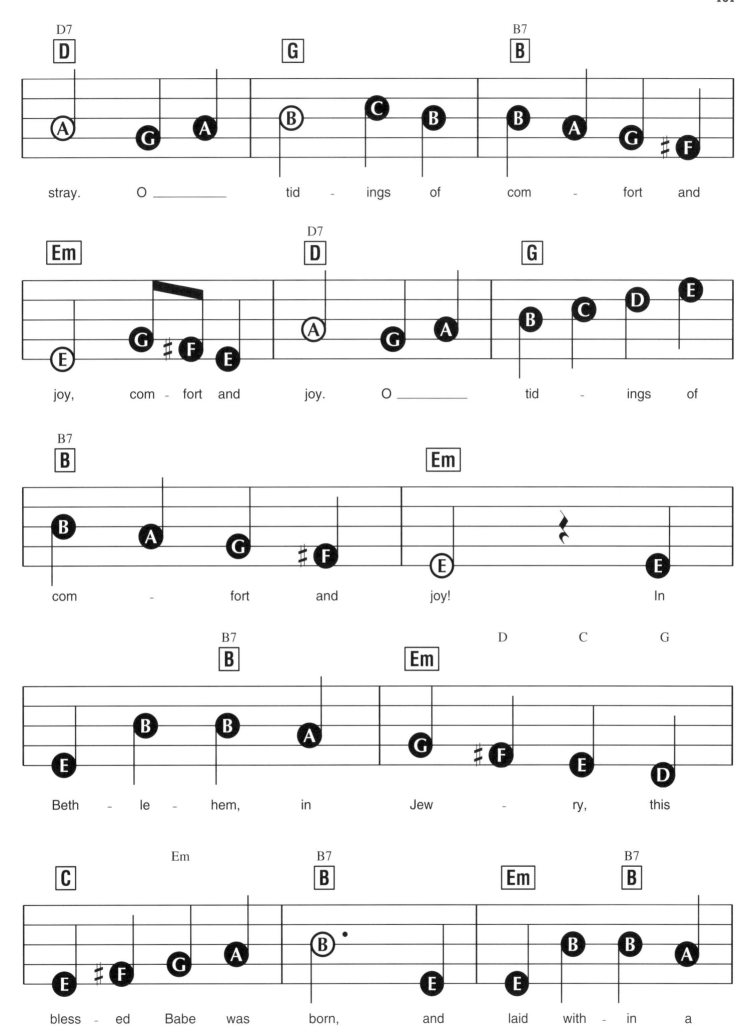

102

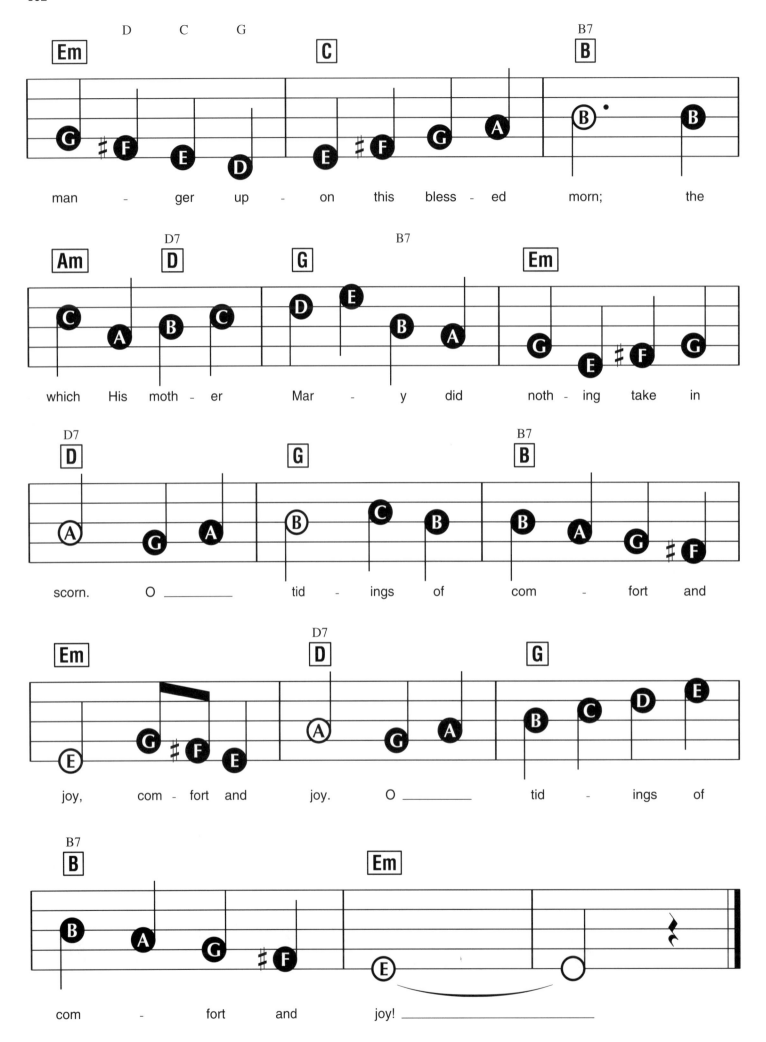

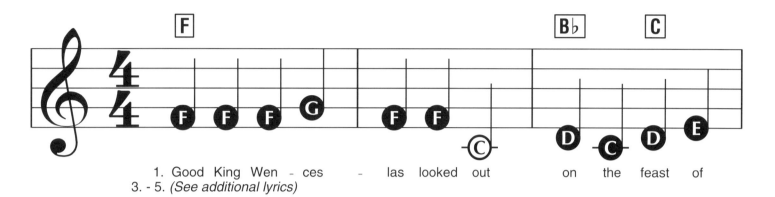

Good King Wenceslas

Registration 4
Rhythm: March

Words by John M. Neale
Music from *Piae Cantiones*

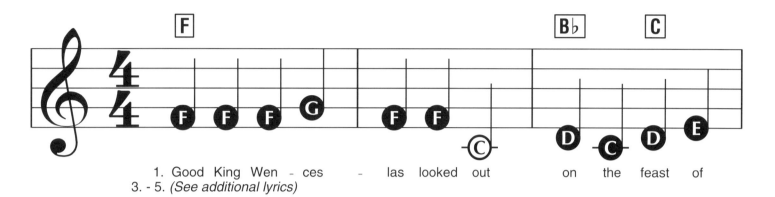

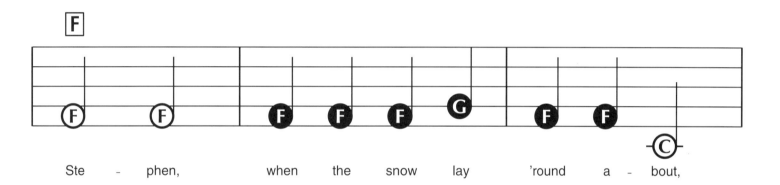

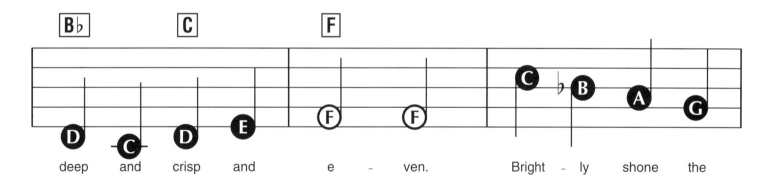

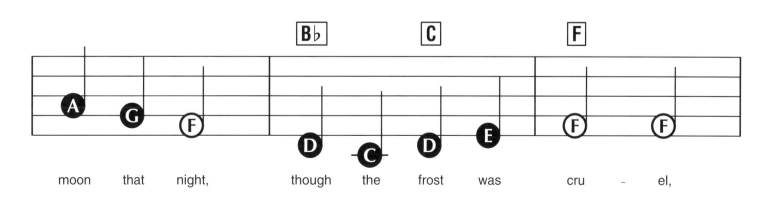

104

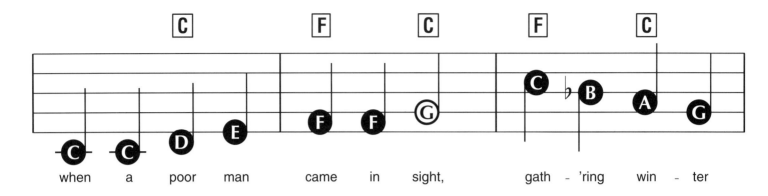

when a poor man came in sight, gath - 'ring win - ter

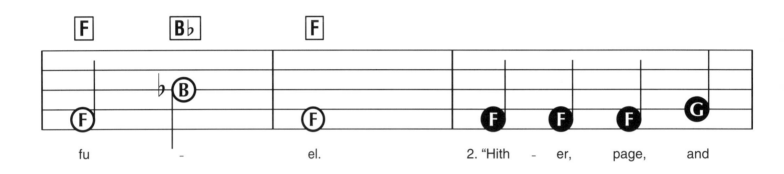

fu - el. 2. "Hith - er, page, and

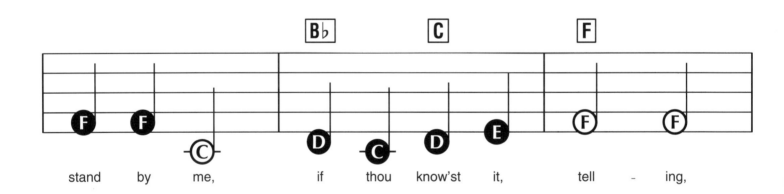

stand by me, if thou know'st it, tell - ing,

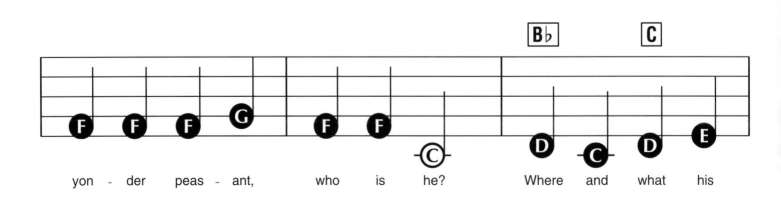

yon - der peas - ant, who is he? Where and what his

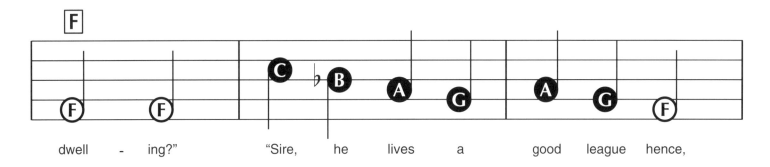

dwell - ing?" "Sire, he lives a good league hence,

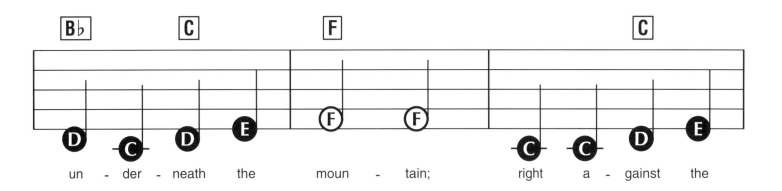

un - der - neath the moun - tain; right a - gainst the

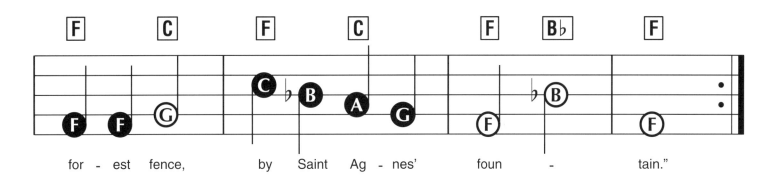

for - est fence, by Saint Ag - nes' foun - tain."

Additional Lyrics

3. "Bring me flesh, and bring me wine,
   Bring me pine logs hither.
   Thou and I will see him dine,
   When we bear them thither."
   Page and monarch forth they went,
   Forth they went together,
   Through the rude wind's wild lament,
   And the bitter weather.

4. "Sire, the night is darker now,
   And the wind blows stronger.
   Fails my heart, I know not how,
   I can go no longer."
   "Mark my footsteps, my good page,
   Tread thou in them boldly.
   Thou shalt find the winter's rage
   Freeze thy blood less coldly."

5. In his master's steps he trod,
   Where the snow lay dinted;
   Heat was in the very sod,
   Which the saint had printed.
   Therefore, Christian men, be sure,
   Wealth or rank possessing,
   Ye who now will bless the poor
   Shall yourselves find blessing.

Good Christian Men, Rejoice

Registration 6
Rhythm: None

14th Century Latin Text
Translated by John Mason Neale
14th Century German Melody

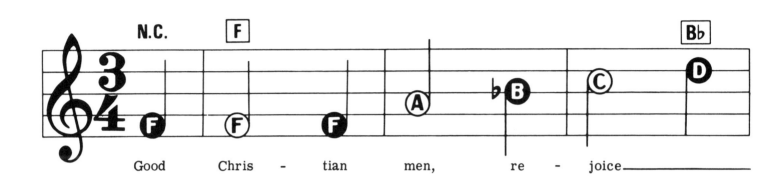

Good Chris - tian men, re - joice

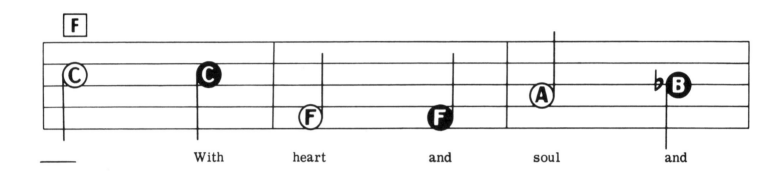

With heart and soul and

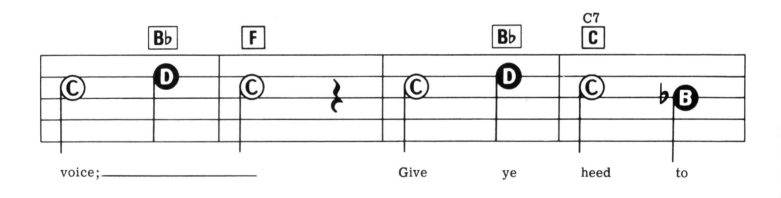

voice; Give ye heed to

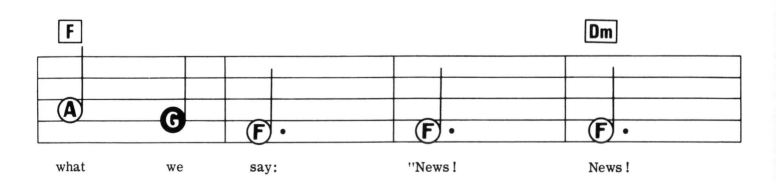

what we say: "News! News!

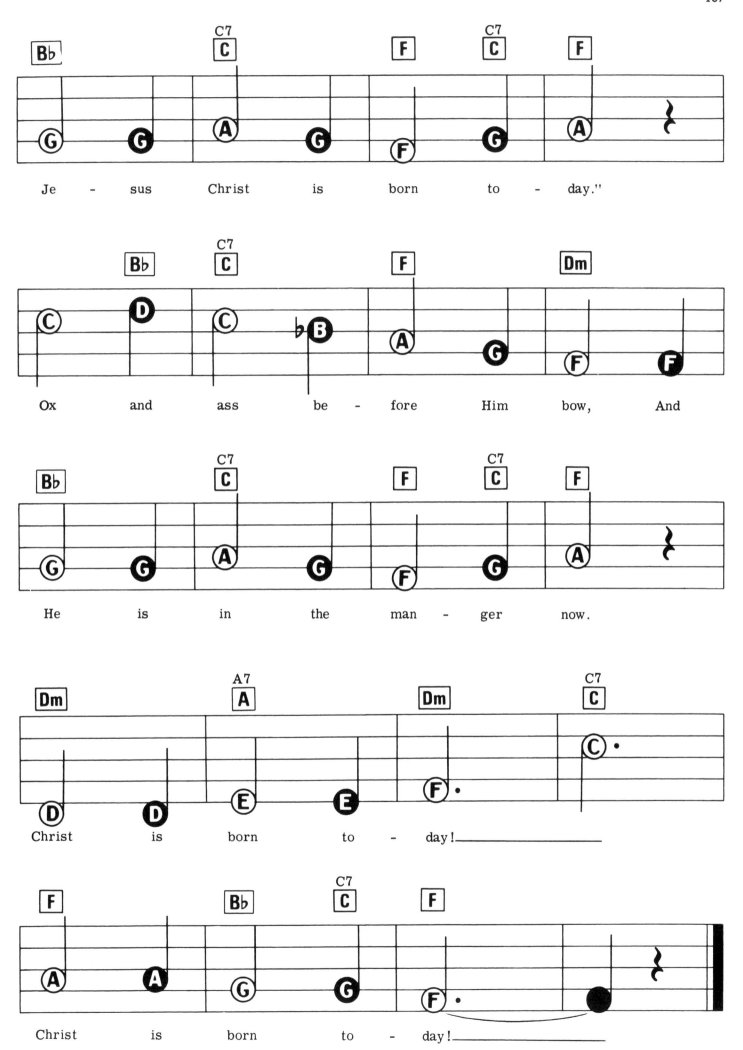

Hallelujah Chorus
from MESSIAH

Registration 4
Rhythm: None

By George Frideric Handel

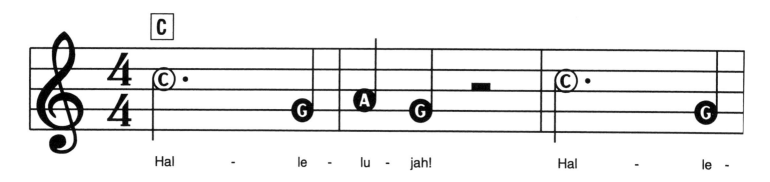

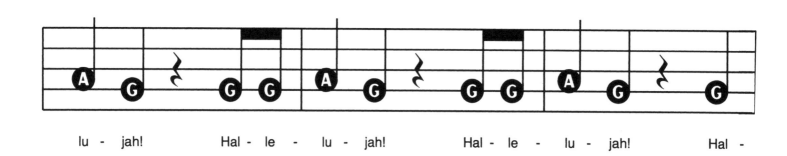

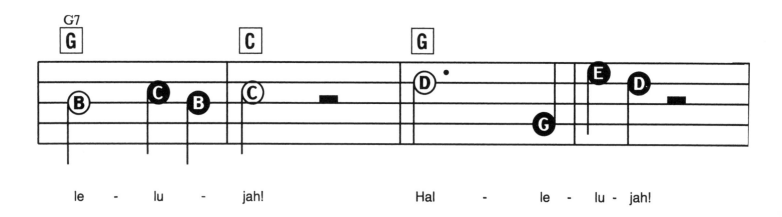

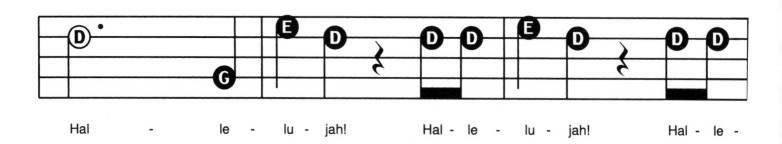

109

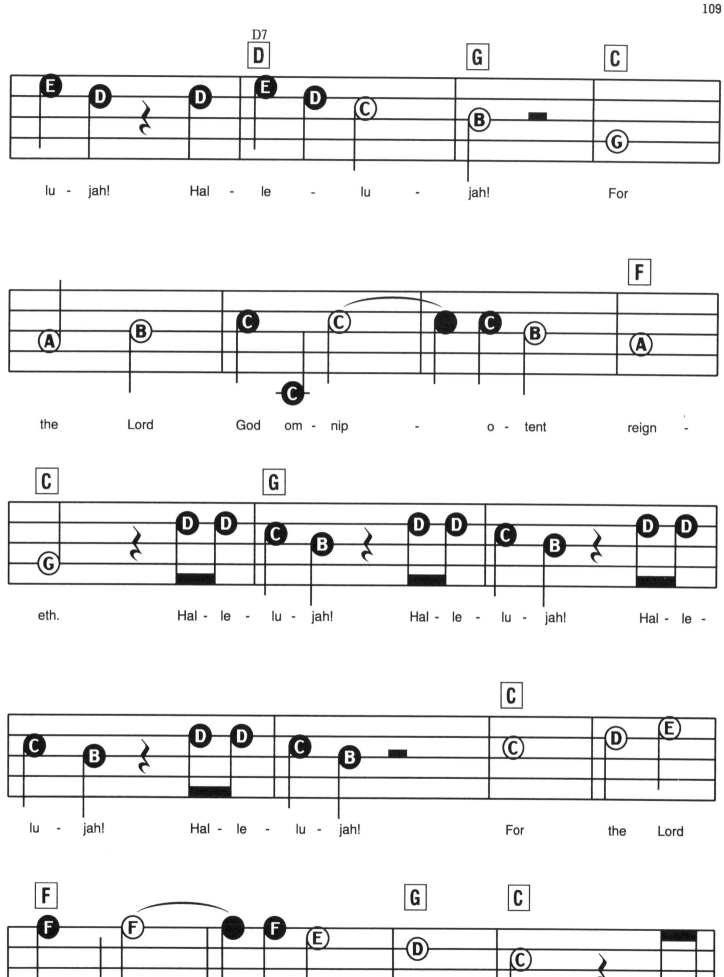

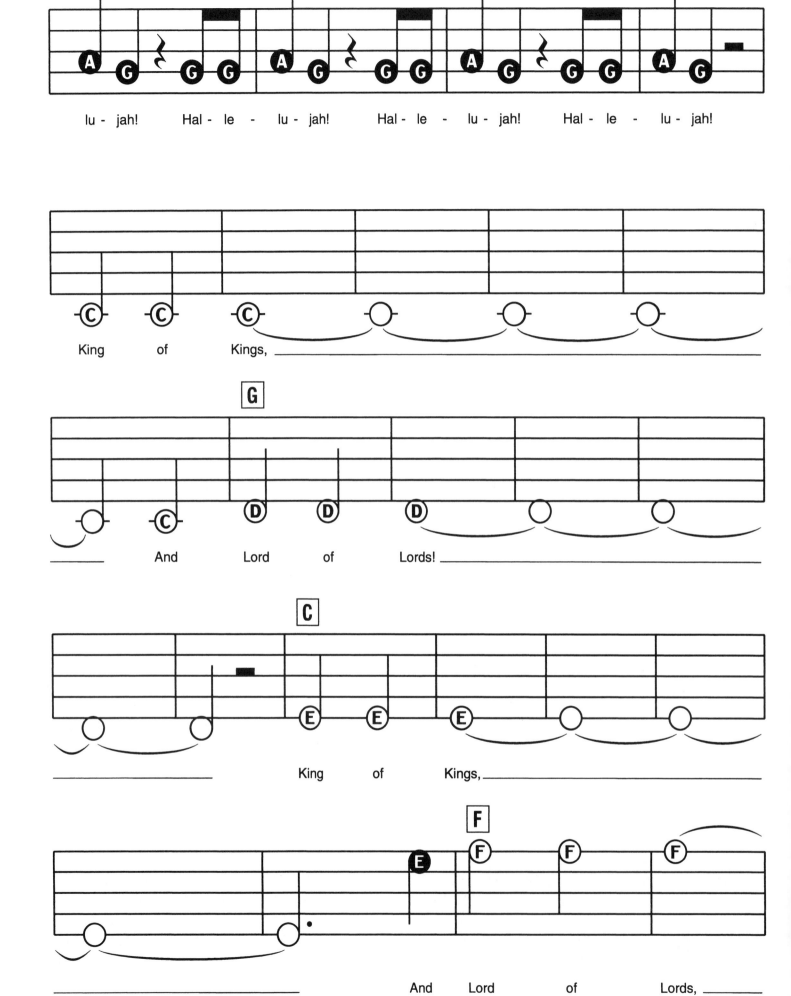

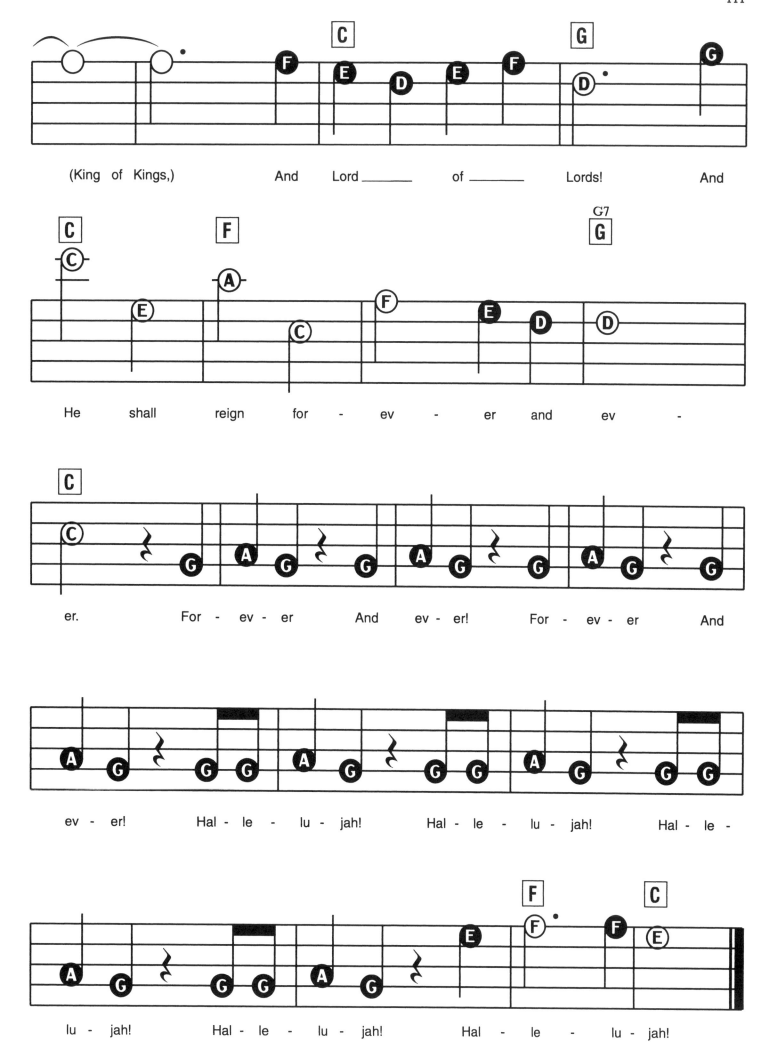

The Happy Christmas Comes Once More

Registration 1
Rhythm: Waltz

Words by Nicolai F.S. Grundtvig
Music by C. Balle

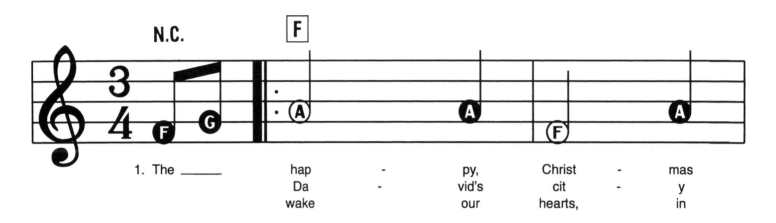

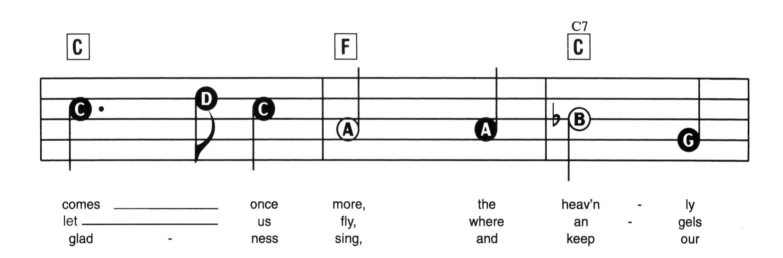

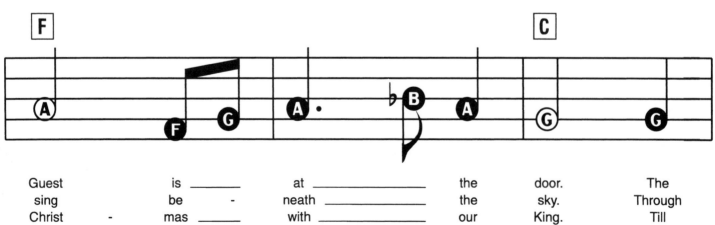

113

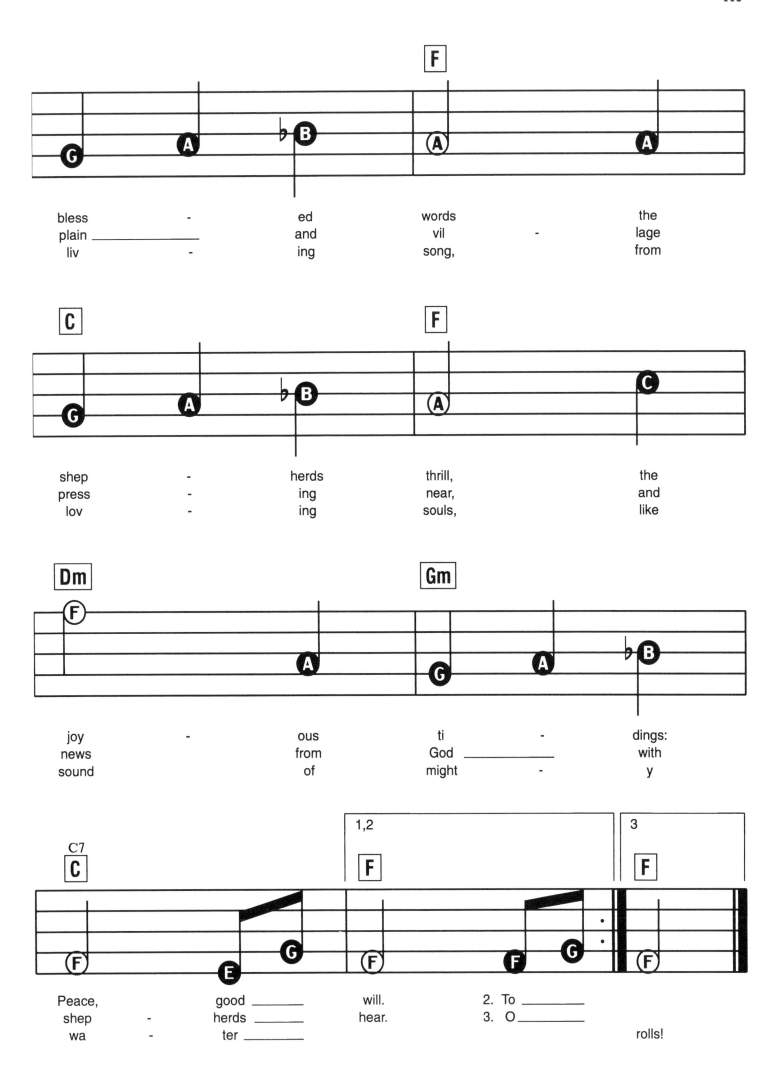

Hark! The Herald Angels Sing

Registration 5
Rhythm: None

Words by Charles Wesley
Altered by George Whitefield
Music by Felix Mendelssohn-Bartholdy
Arranged by William H. Cummings

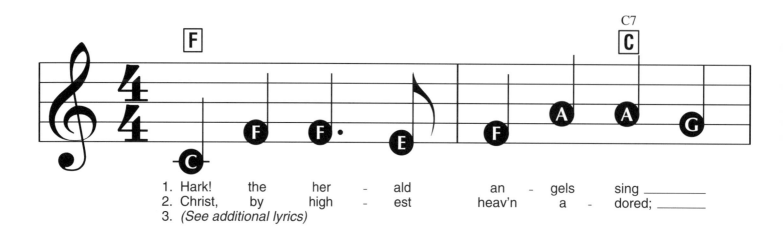

1. Hark! the her - ald an - gels sing _____
2. Christ, by high - est heav'n a - dored; _____
3. *(See additional lyrics)*

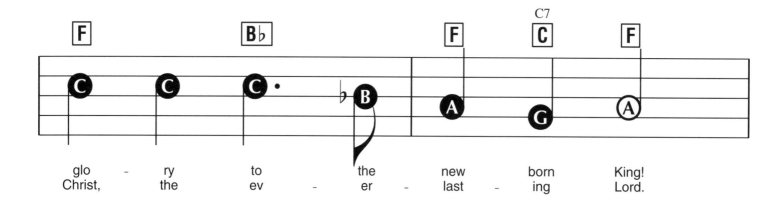

glo - ry to the new born King!
Christ, the ev - er - last - ing Lord.

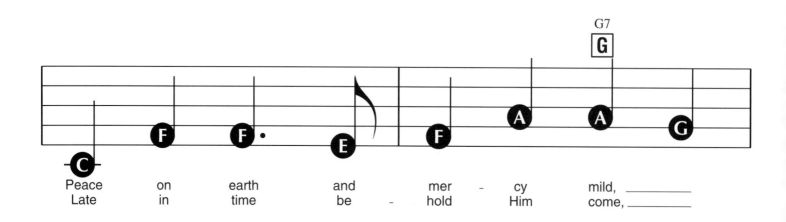

Peace on earth and mer - cy mild, _____
Late in time be - hold Him come, _____

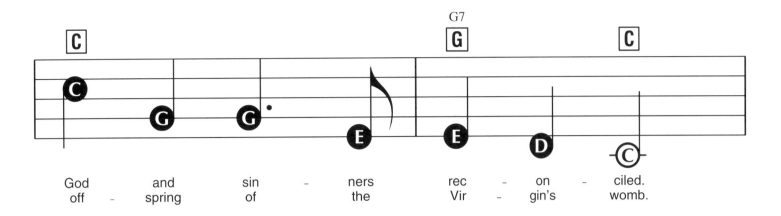

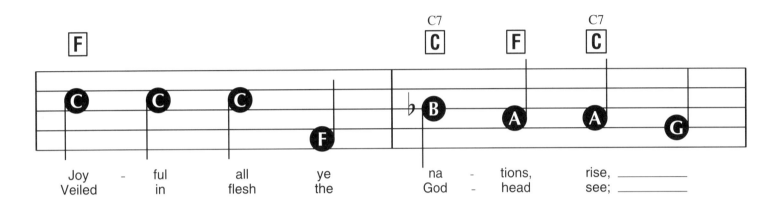

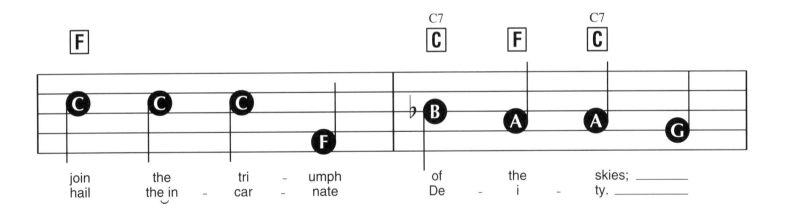

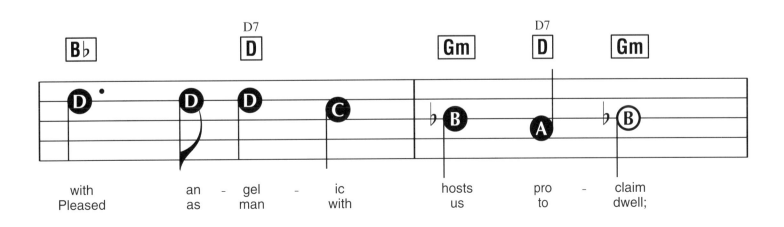

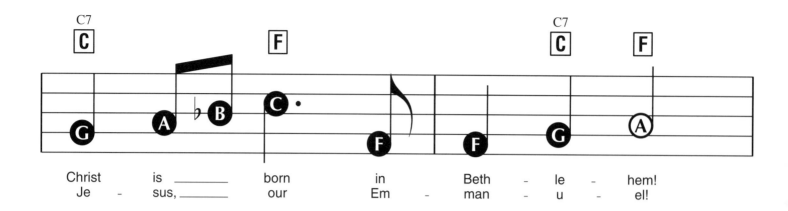

Christ is _____ born in Beth - le - hem!
Je - sus, _____ our Em - man - u - el!

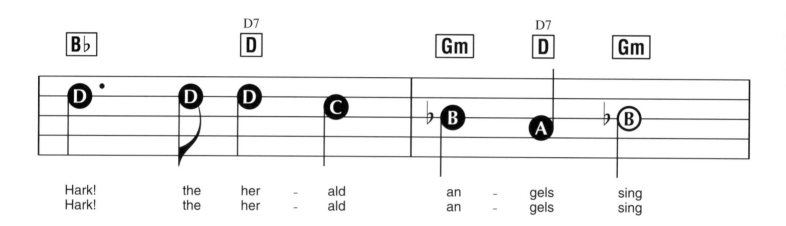

Hark! the her - ald an - gels sing
Hark! the her - ald an - gels sing

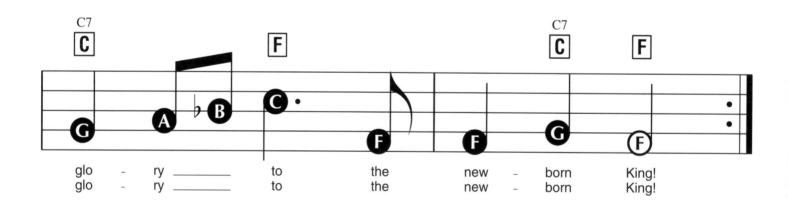

glo - ry _____ to the new - born King!
glo - ry _____ to the new new - born King!

Additional Lyrics

3. Hail, the heaven-born Prince of Peace!
   Hail, the Sun of Righteousness!
   Light and life to all he brings,
   Risen with healing in His wings.
   Mild He lays His glory by,
   Born that man no more may die.
   Born to raise the sons of earth,
   Born to give them second birth.

   Hark! the hearald angels sing
   Glory to the newborn King!

In the Silence of the Night

Registration 9
Rhythm: None

Traditional Carol

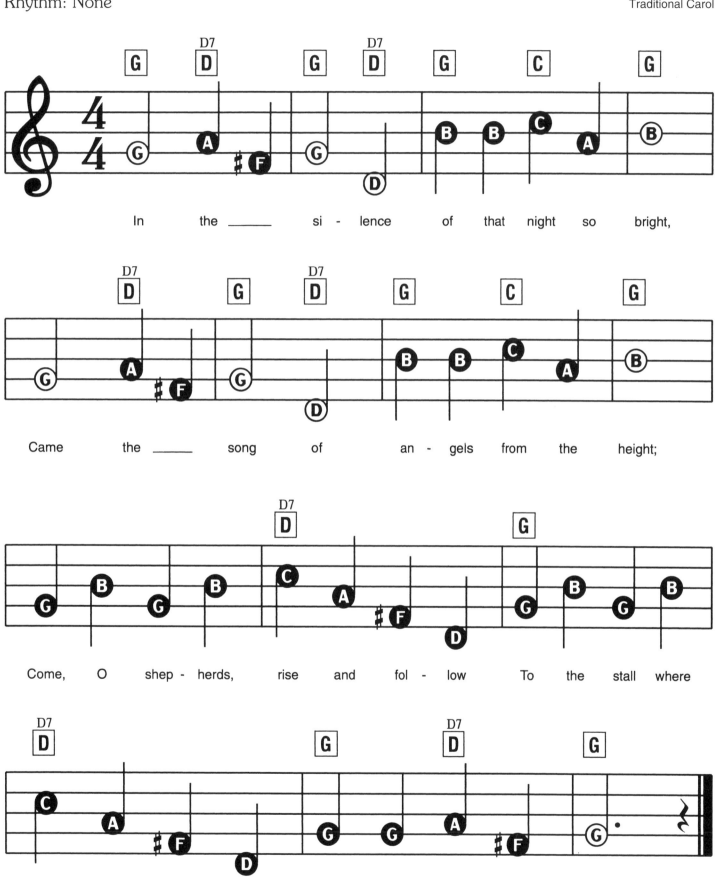

He Is Born

Registration 3
Rhythm: Pops

Traditional French Carol

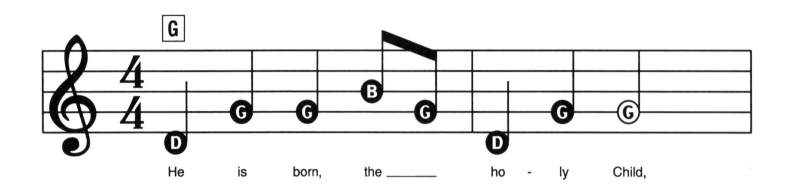

He   is   born,   the _____   ho - ly   Child,

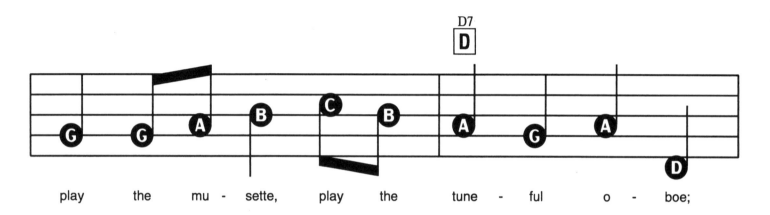

play   the   mu - sette,   play   the   tune - ful   o - boe;

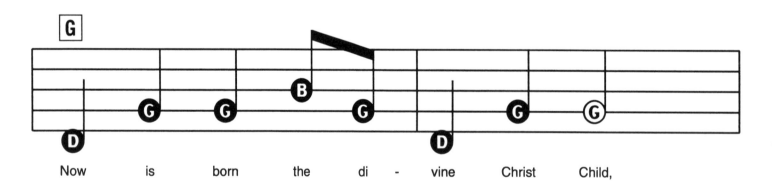

Now   is   born   the   di - vine   Christ   Child,

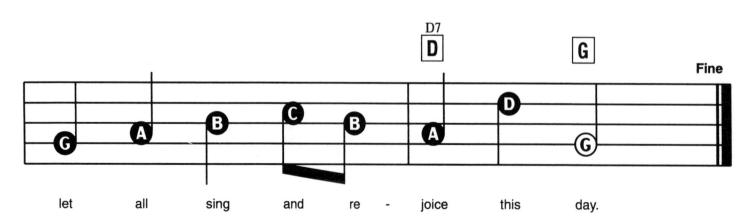

let   all   sing   and   re - joice   this   day.

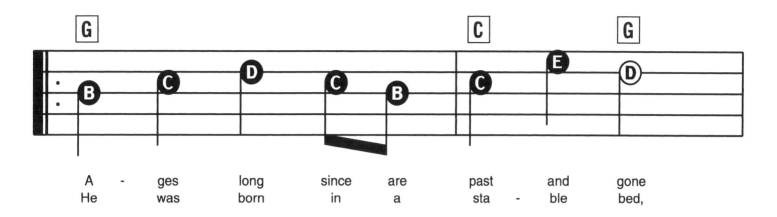

A - ges long since are past and gone
He was long born in a sta - ble bed,

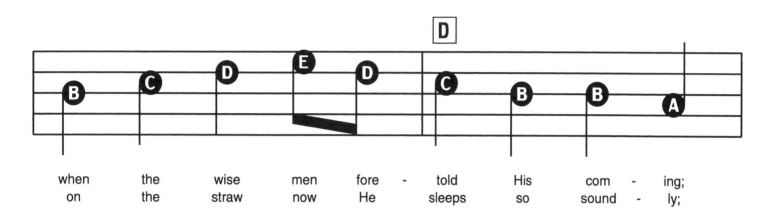

when the wise men fore - told His com - ing;
on the straw men now He sleeps so sound - ly;

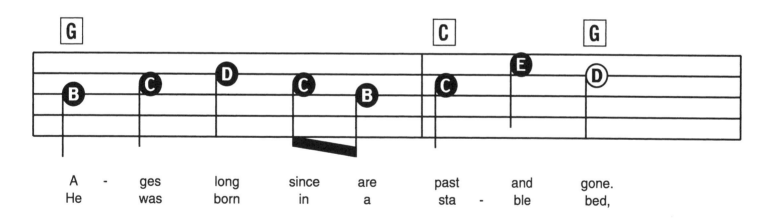

A - ges long since are past and gone.
He was long born in a sta - ble bed,

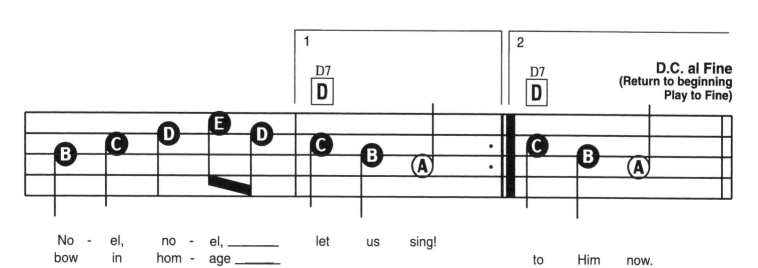

No - el, no - el, _____ let us sing!
bow in hom - age _____ to Him now.

Hear Them Bells

Registration 7
Rhythm: 8 Beat

Words and Music by
D.S. McCosh

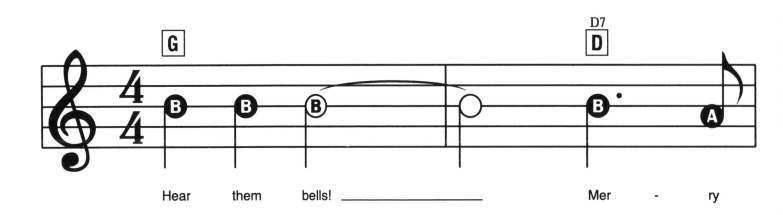

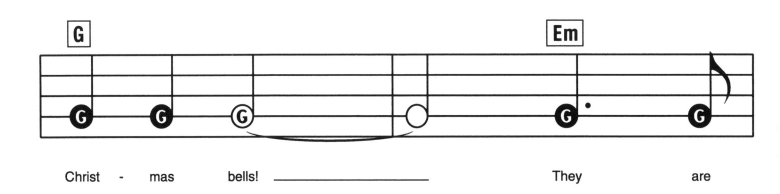

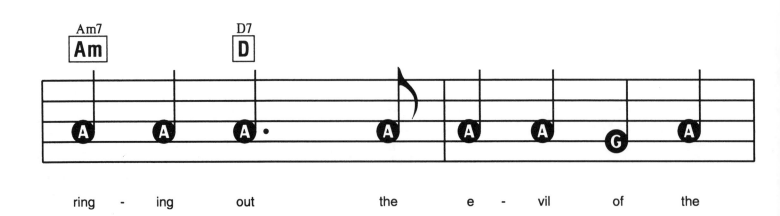

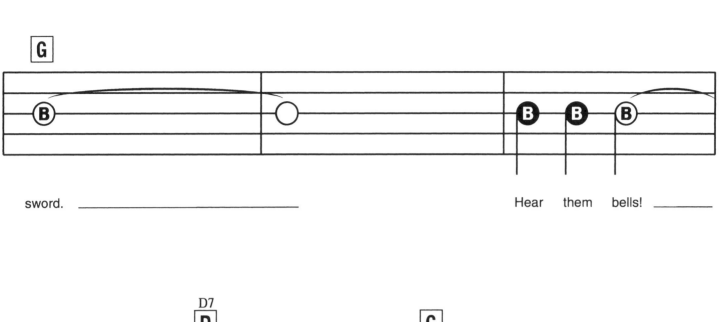

sword. _____ Hear them bells! _____

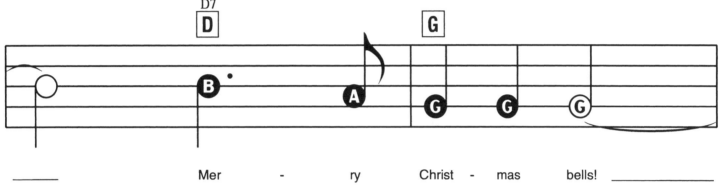

_____ Mer - ry Christ - mas bells! _____

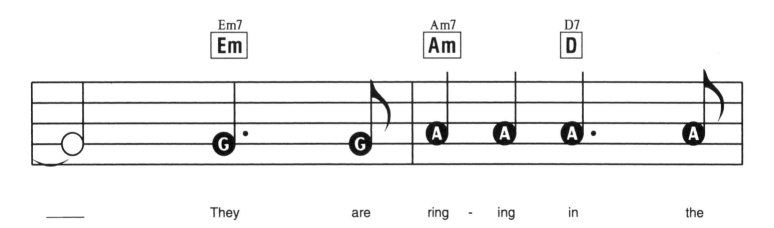

_____ They are ring - ing in the

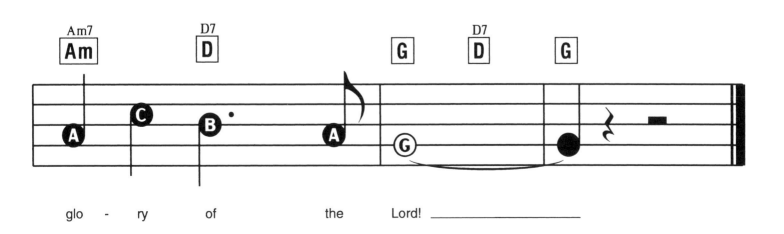

glo - ry of the Lord! _____

Here We Come A-Wassailing

Registration 3
Rhythm: 6/8 March

Traditional

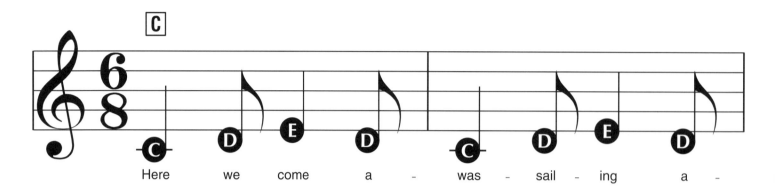

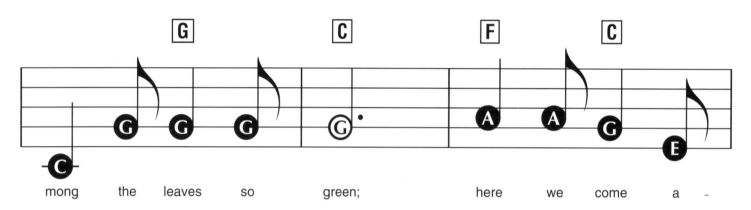

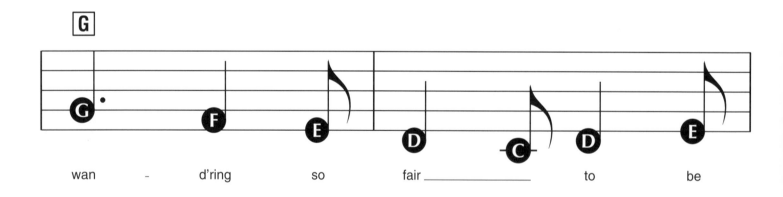

Rhythm: Fox Trot

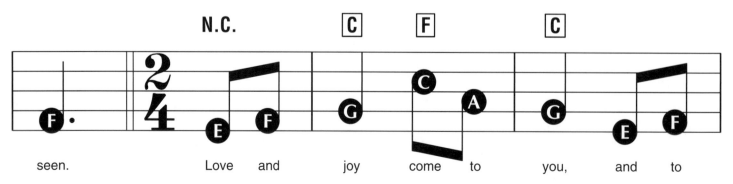

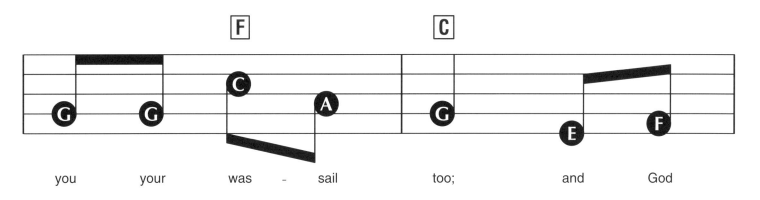

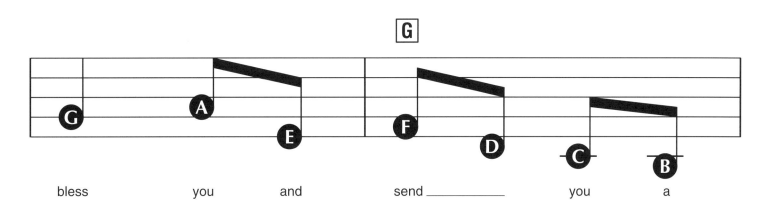

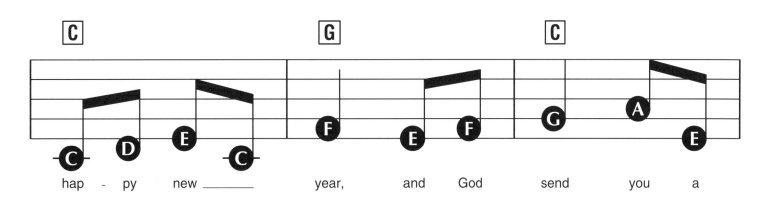

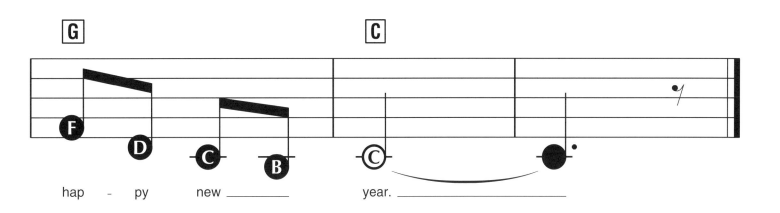

The Holly and the Ivy

Registration 1
Rhythm: None

18th Century English Carol

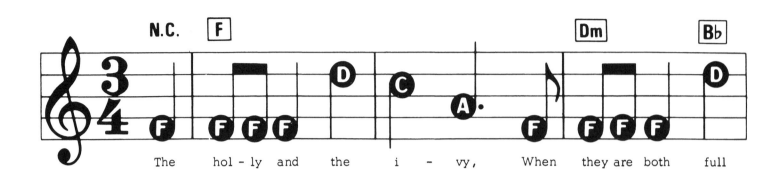

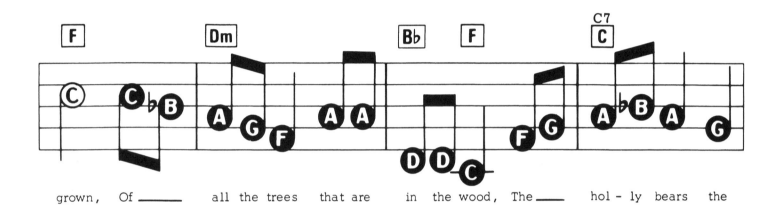

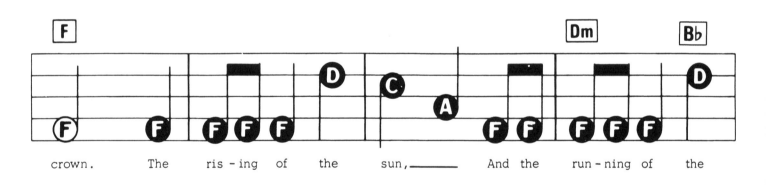

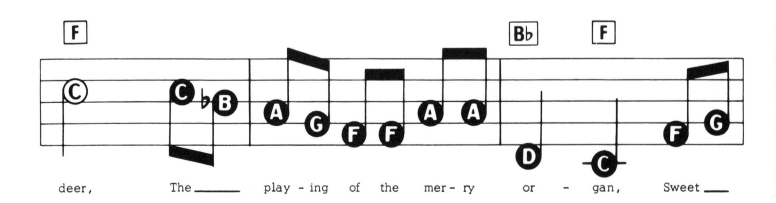

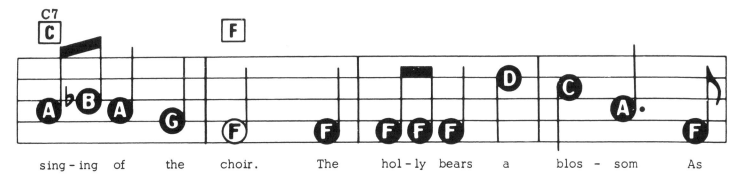

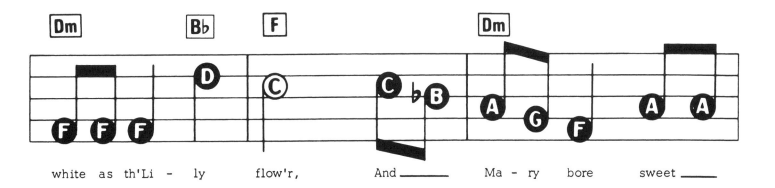

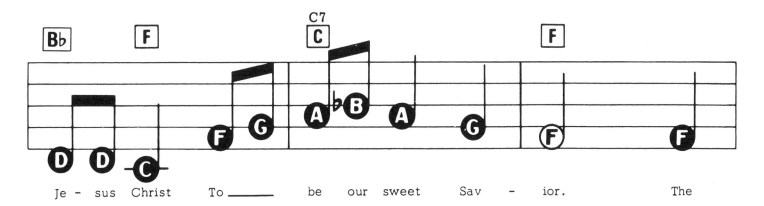

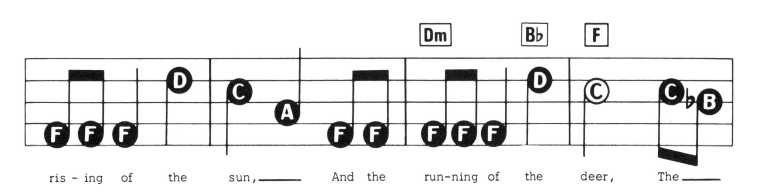

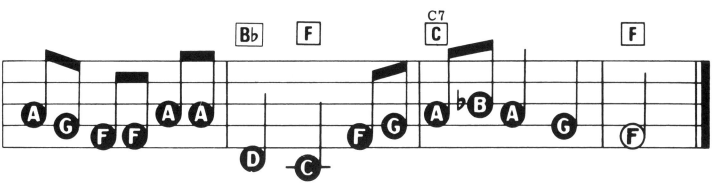

I Am So Glad on Christmas Eve

Registration 9
Rhythm: Waltz

Words by Marie Wexelsen
Music by Peder Knudsen

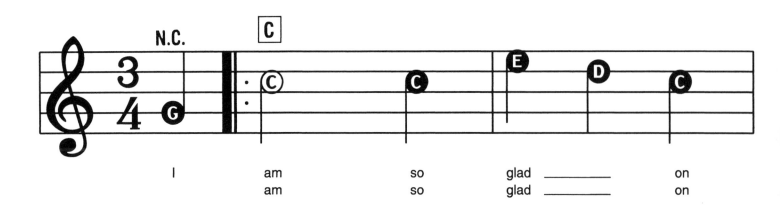

I am so glad on
am so glad on

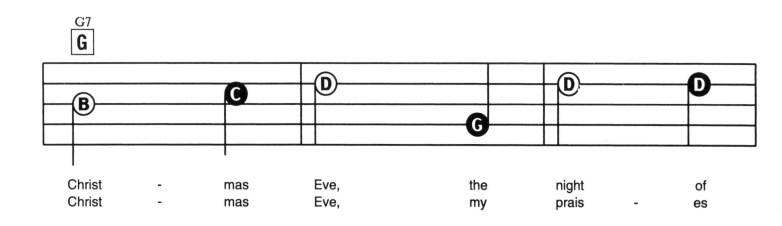

Christ - mas Eve, the night of
Christ - mas Eve, my prais - es

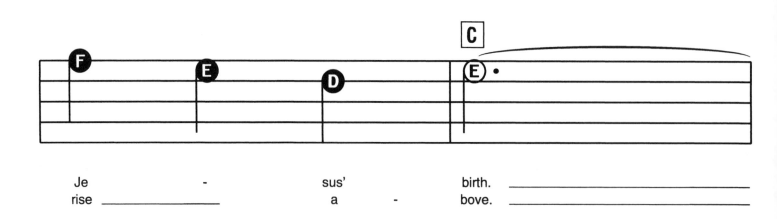

Je - sus' birth. _____
rise _____ a - bove. _____

127

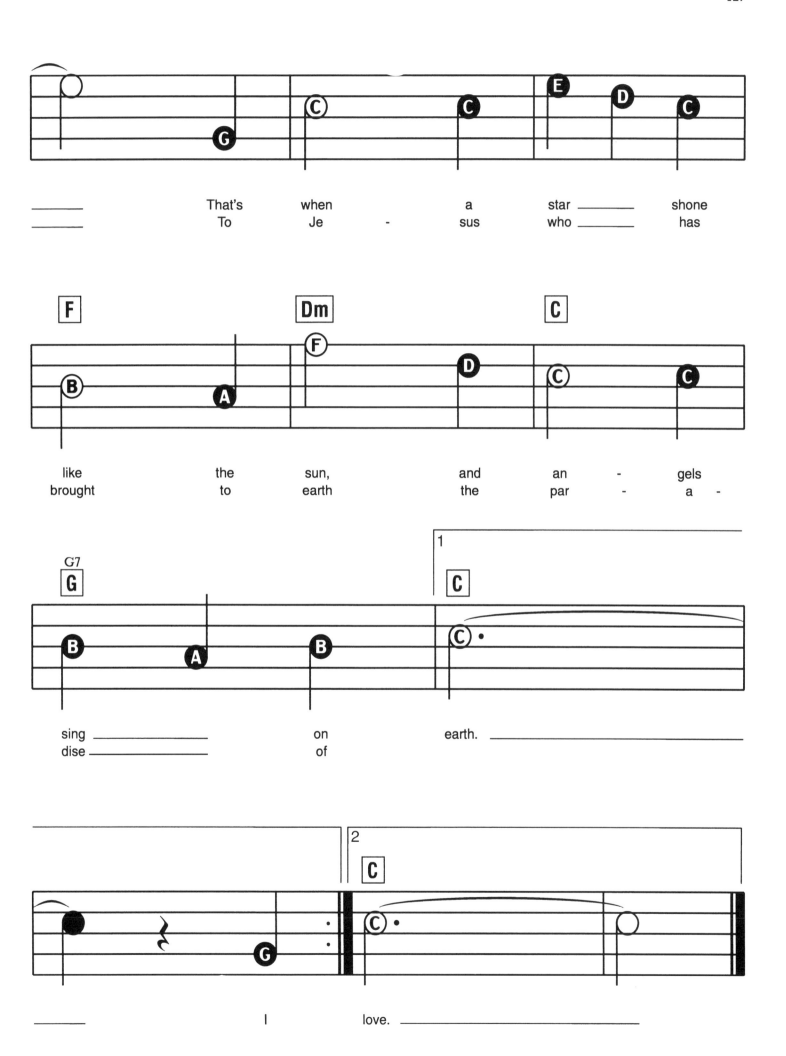

I Heard the Bells on Christmas Day

Registration 7
Rhythm: Ballad or Fox Trot

Words by Henry Wadsworth Longfellow
Music by John Baptiste Calkin

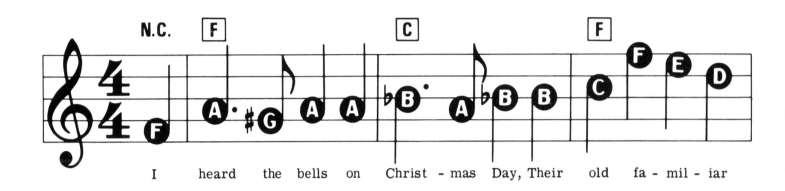

I heard the bells on Christ - mas Day, Their old fa - mil - iar

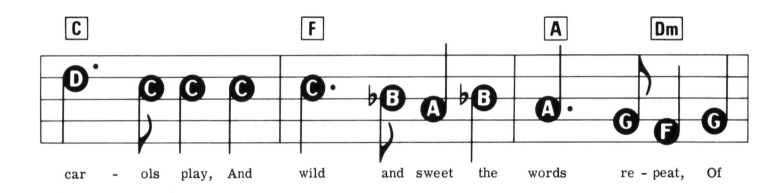

car - ols play, And wild and sweet the words re - peat, Of

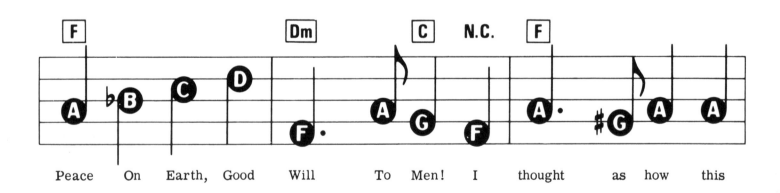

Peace On Earth, Good Will To Men! I thought as how this

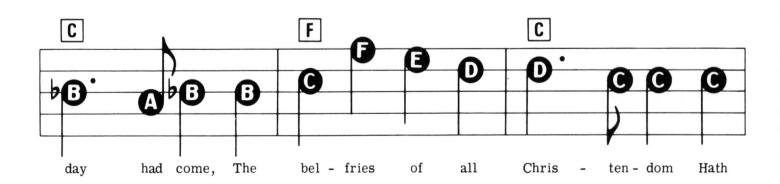

day had come, The bel - fries of all Chris - ten - dom Hath

129

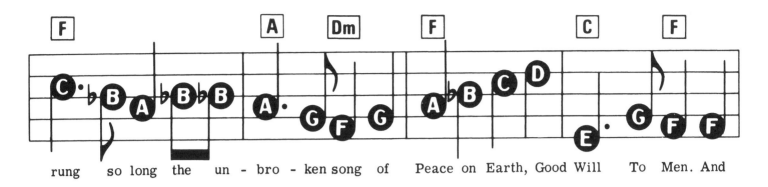

rung so long the un - bro - ken song of Peace on Earth, Good Will To Men. And

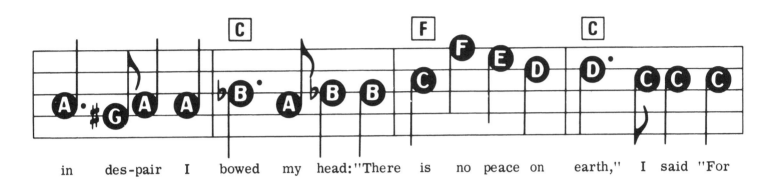

in des-pair I bowed my head:"There is no peace on earth," I said "For

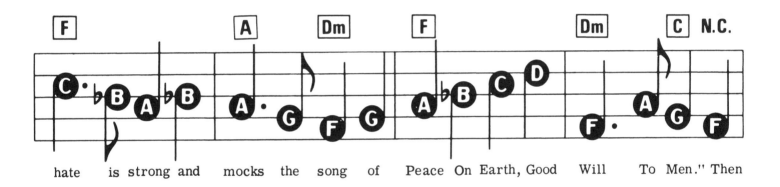

hate is strong and mocks the song of Peace On Earth, Good Will To Men." Then

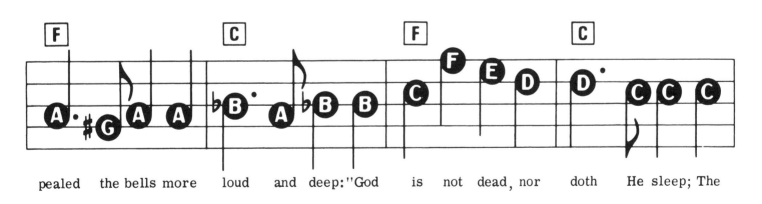

pealed the bells more loud and deep:"God is not dead, nor doth He sleep; The

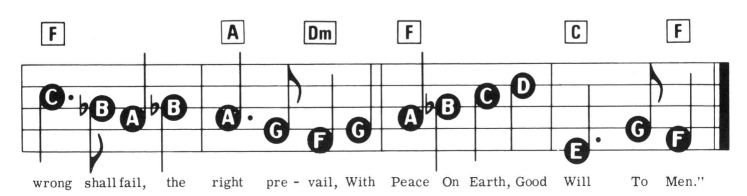

wrong shall fail, the right pre - vail, With Peace On Earth, Good Will To Men."

I Saw Three Ships

Registration 2
Rhythm: 6/8 March

Traditional English Carol

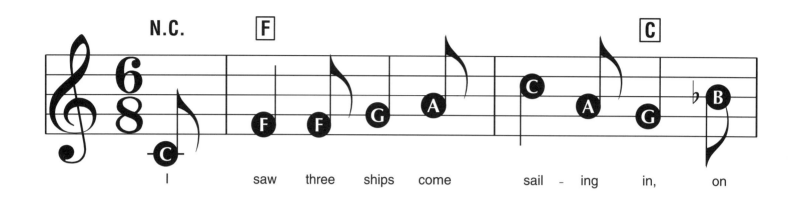

I saw three ships come sail - ing in, on

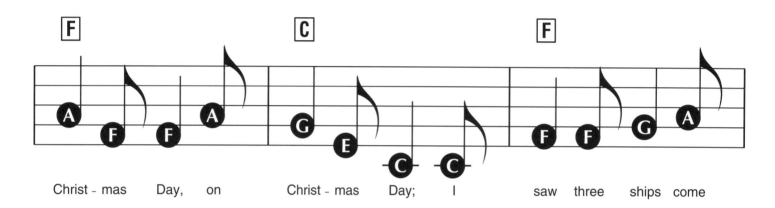

Christ - mas Day, on Christ - mas Day; I saw three ships come

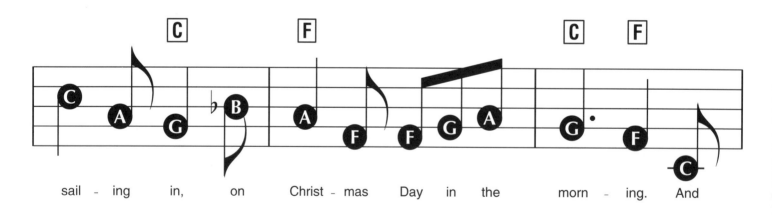

sail - ing in, on Christ - mas Day in the morn - ing. And

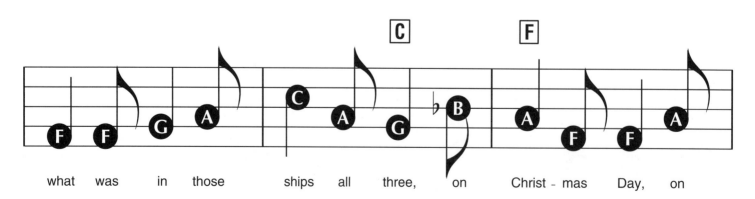

what was in those ships all three, on Christ - mas Day, on

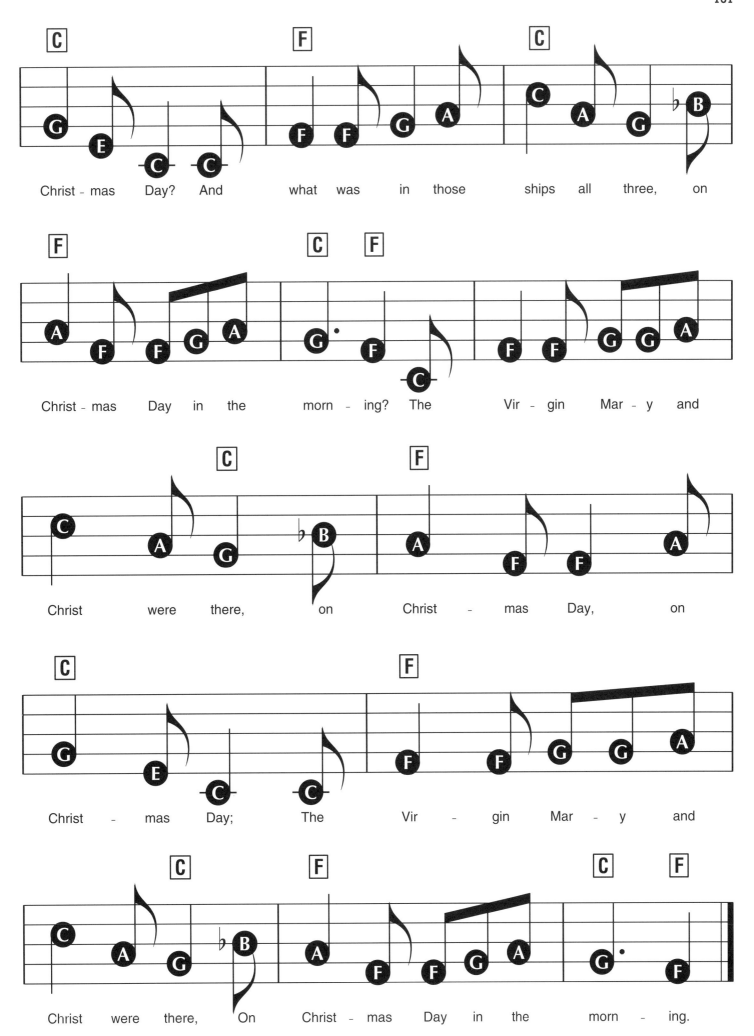

In the Bleak Midwinter

Registration 3
Rhythm: 8 Beat or Pops

Poem by Christina Rossetti
Music by Gustav Holst

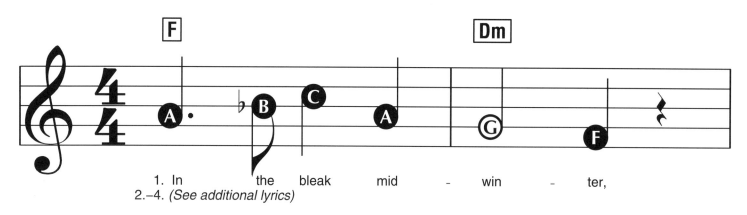

1. In the bleak mid - win - ter,
2.–4. *(See additional lyrics)*

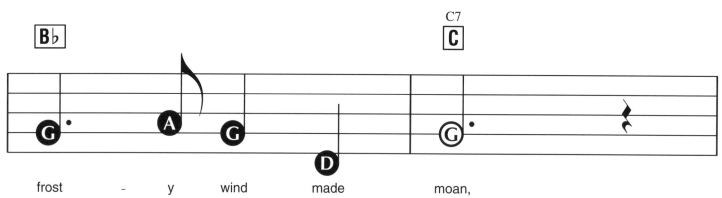

frost - y wind made moan,

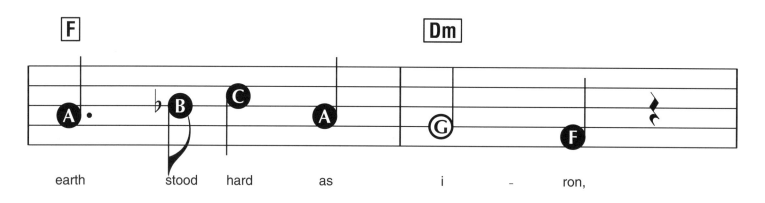

earth stood hard as i - ron,

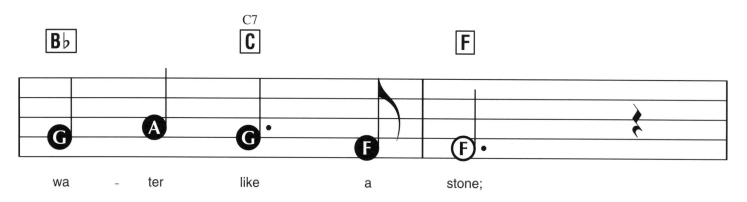

wa - ter like a stone;

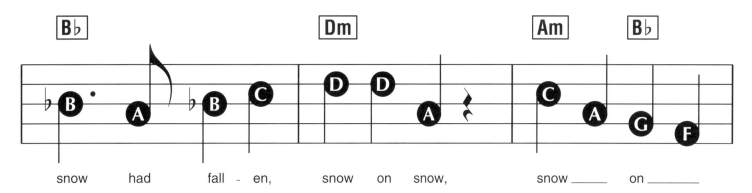

snow had fall - en, snow on snow, snow ___ on ___

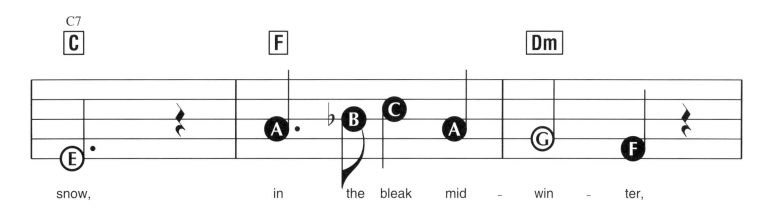

snow, in the bleak mid - win - ter,

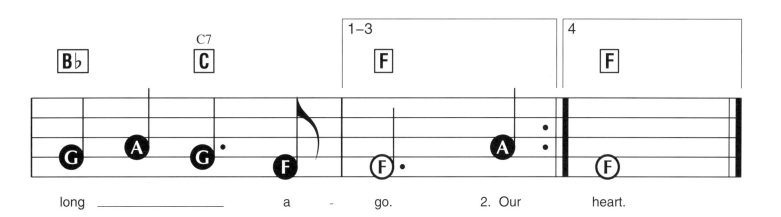

long ___ a - go. 2. Our heart.

Additional Lyrics

2. Our God, heaven cannot hold Him, nor earth sustain;
   Heaven and earth shall flee away when He comes to reign.
   In the bleak midwinter a stable place sufficed
   The Lord God Almighty, Jesus Christ.

3. Angels and archangels may have gathered there,
   Cherubim and seraphim thronged the air;
   But His mother only, in her maiden bliss,
   Worshiped the beloved with a kiss.

4. What can I give Him, poor as I am?
   If I were a shepherd, I would bring a lamb;
   If I were a Wise Man, I would do my part;
   Yet what I can I give Him: give my heart.

In the Field with Their Flocks Abiding

Registration 4
Rhythm: None

Traditional

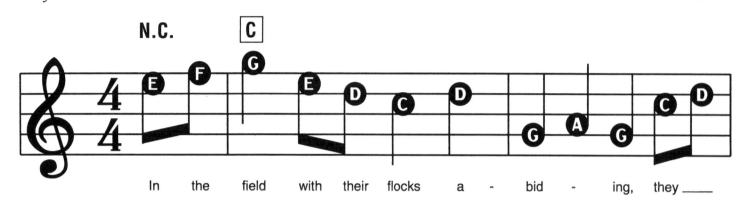

In the field with their flocks a - bid - ing, they ____

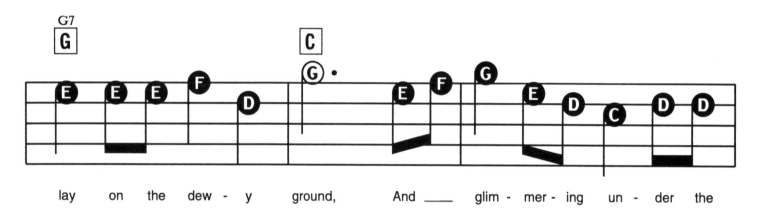

lay on the dew - y ground, And ____ glim - mer - ing un - der the

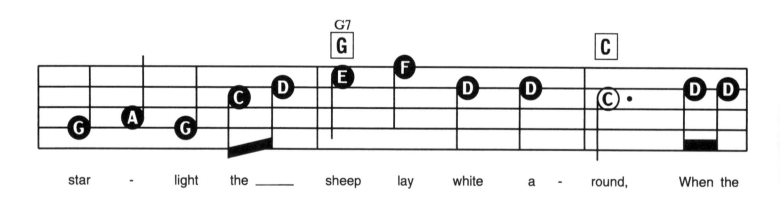

star - light the ____ sheep lay white a - round, When the

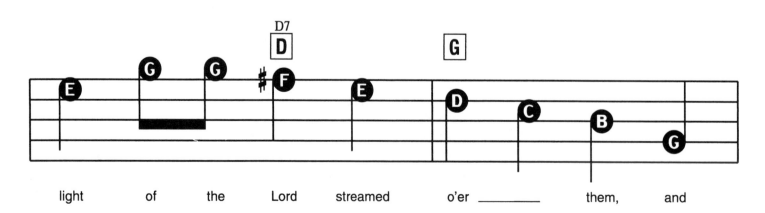

light of the Lord streamed o'er ____ them, and

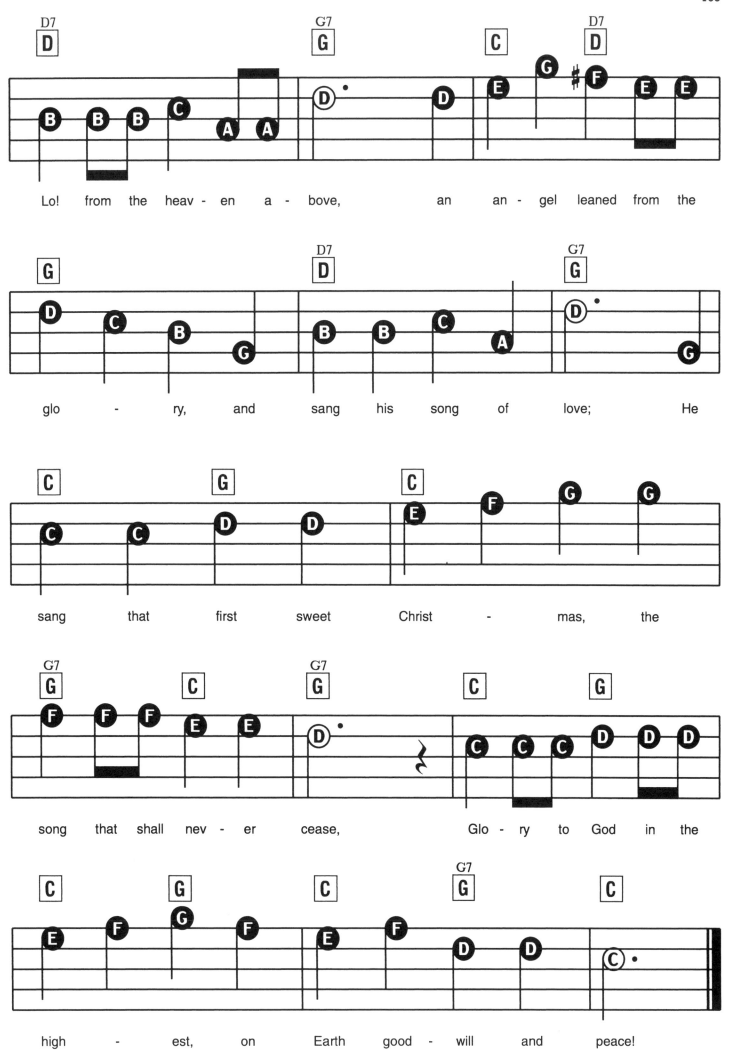

Infant Holy, Infant Lowly

Registration 4
Rhythm: Waltz

Traditional Polish Carol
Paraphrased by Edith M.G. Reed

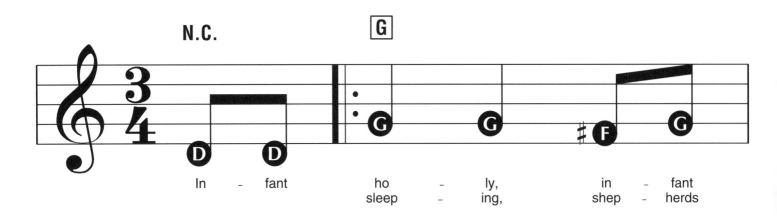

In - fant ho - ly, in - fant
sleep - ing, shep - herds

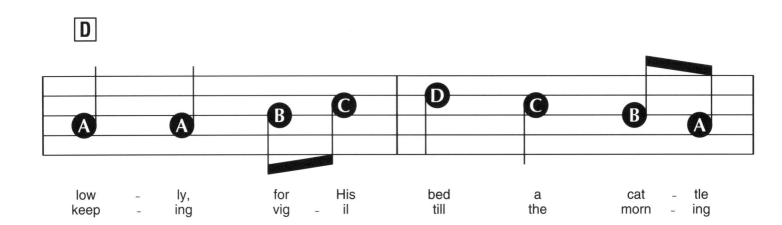

low - ly, for His bed a cat - tle
keep - ing vig - il till the morn - ing

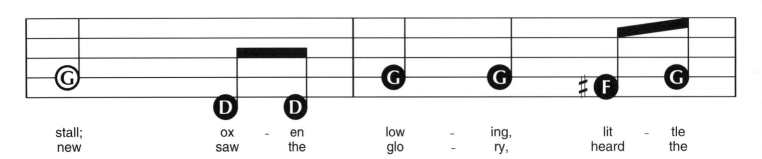

stall; ox - en low - ing, lit - tle
new saw the glo - ry, heard the

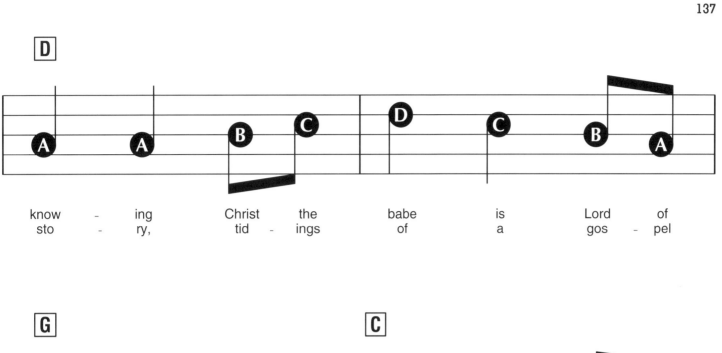

know - ing Christ the babe is Lord of
sto - ry, tid - ings of a gos - pel

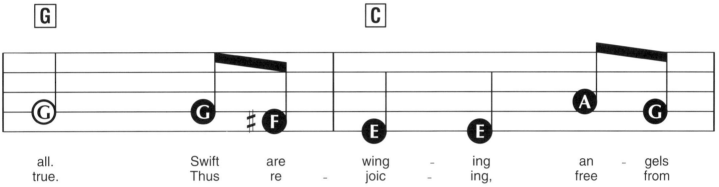

all. Swift are wing - ing an - gels
true. Thus re - joic - ing, free from

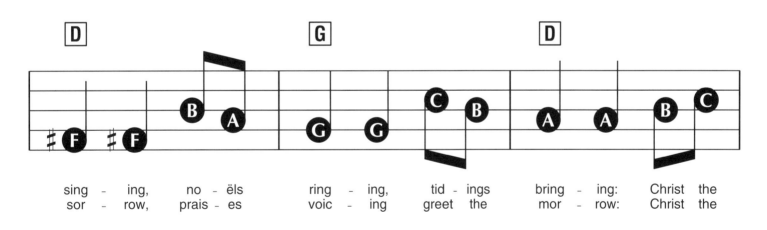

sing - ing, no - ëls ring - ing, tid - ings bring - ing: Christ the
sor - row, prais - es voic - ing greet the mor - row: Christ the

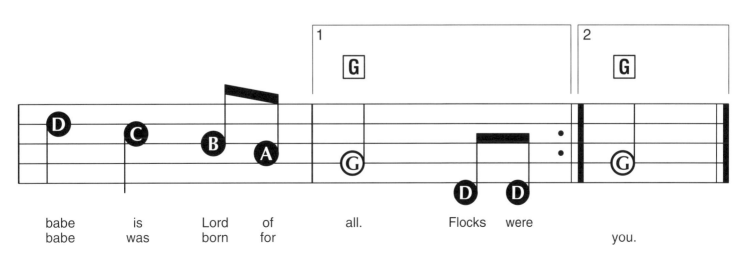

babe is Lord of all. Flocks were
babe is was born for you.

It Came Upon the Midnight Clear

Registration 1
Rhythm: None

Words by Edmund Hamilton Sears
Music by Richard Storrs Willis

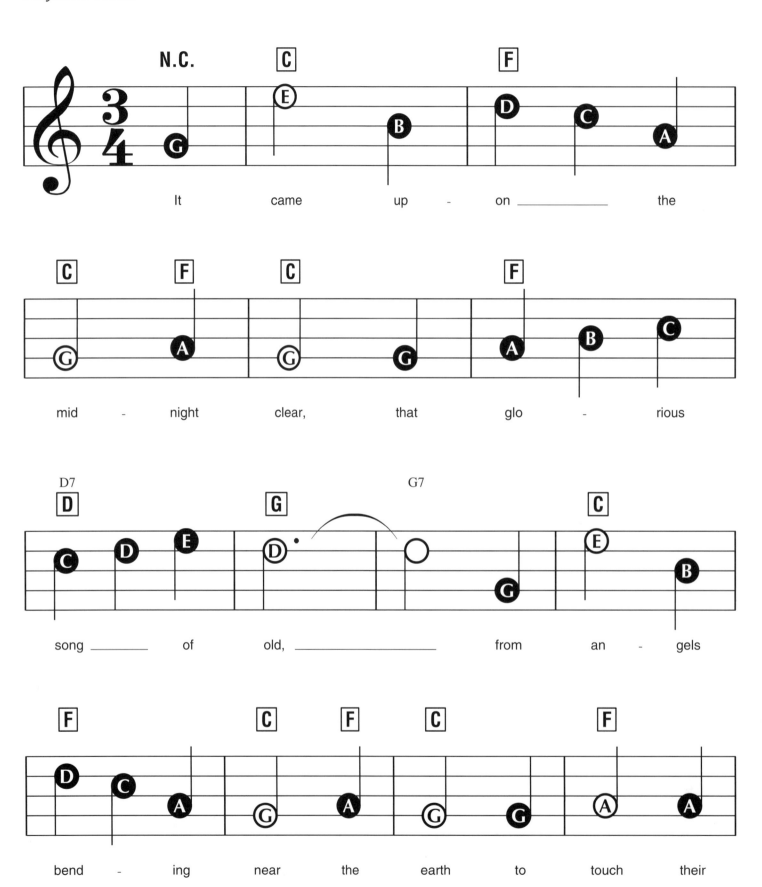

139

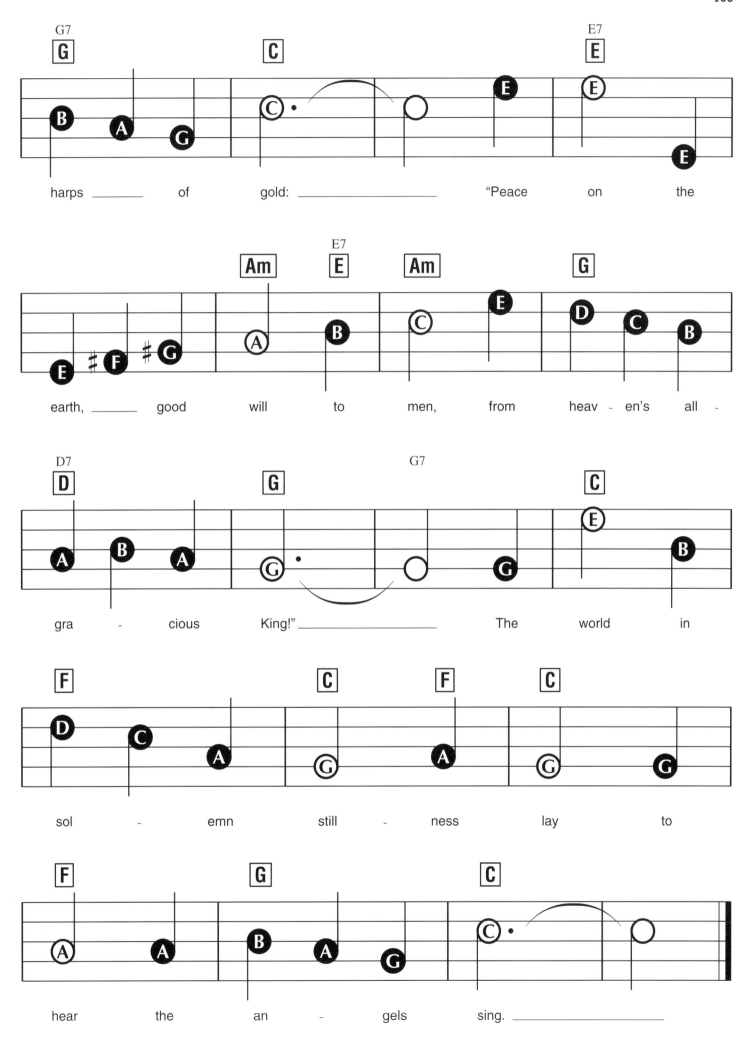

Jesu, Joy of Man's Desiring

Registration 2
Rhythm: None

By Johann Sebastian Bach

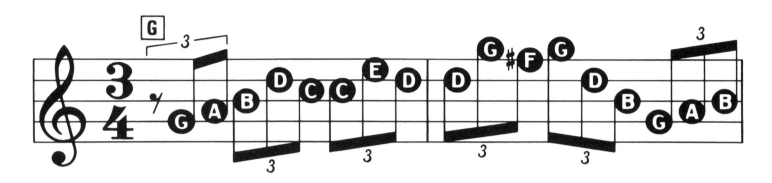

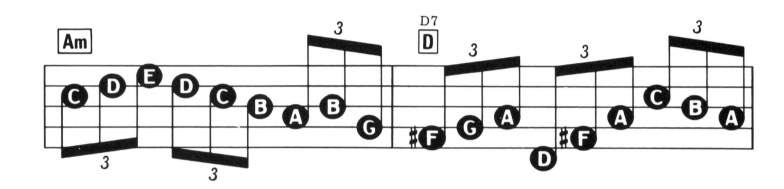

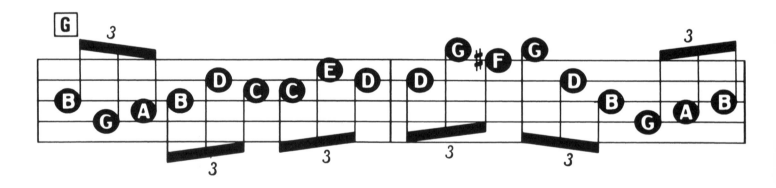

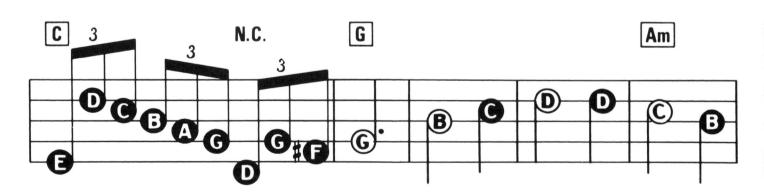

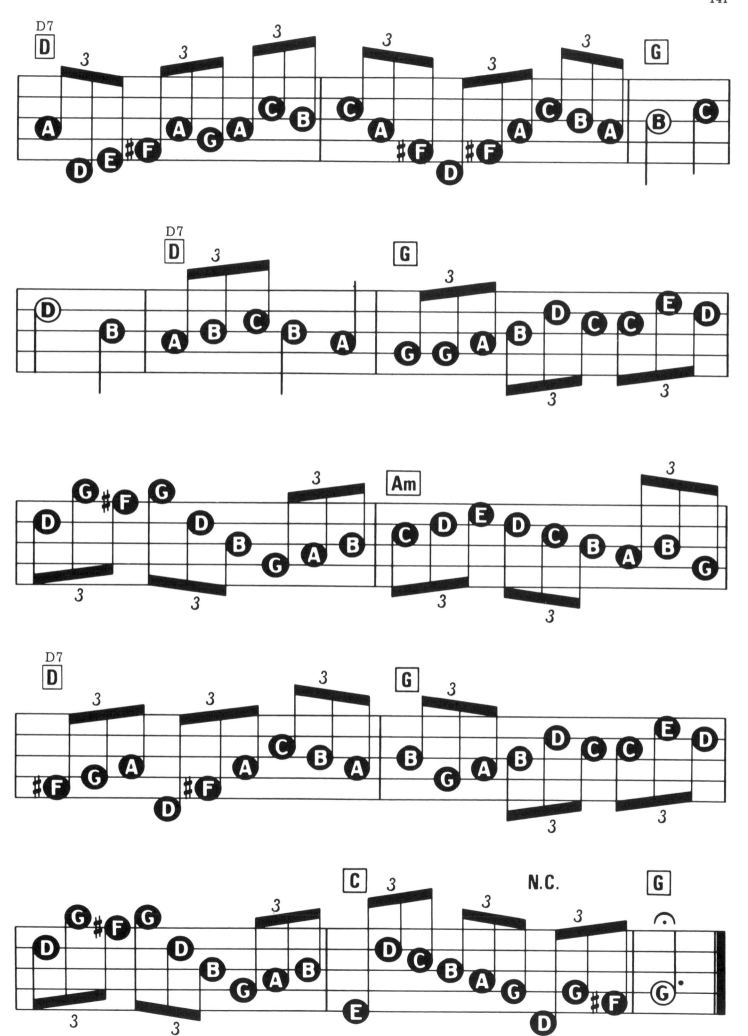

Jingle Bells

Registration 5
Rhythm: Fox Trot or Swing

Words and Music by
J. Pierpont

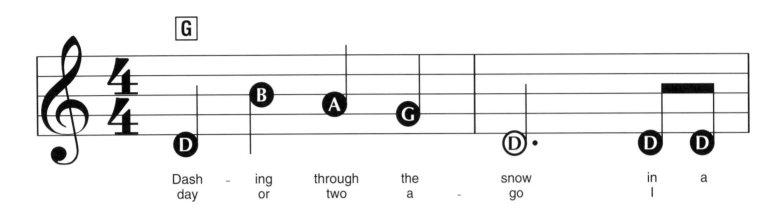

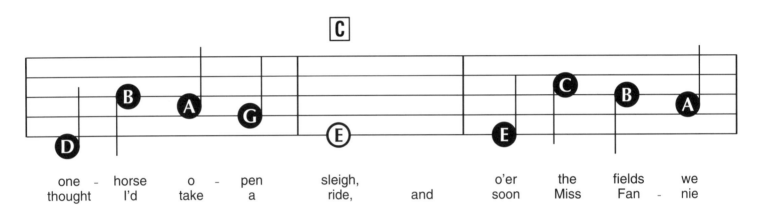

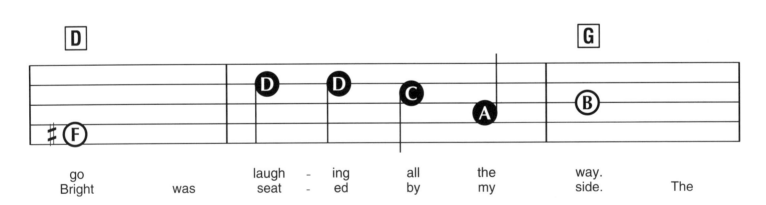

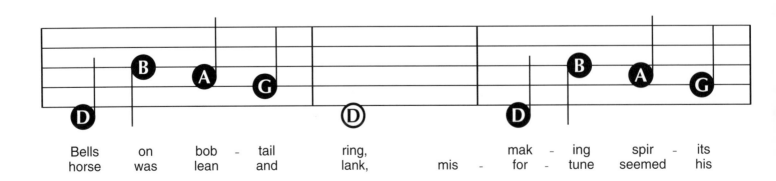

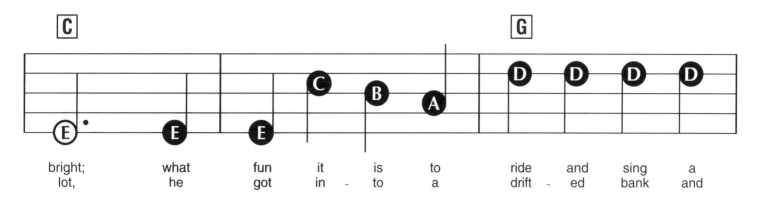

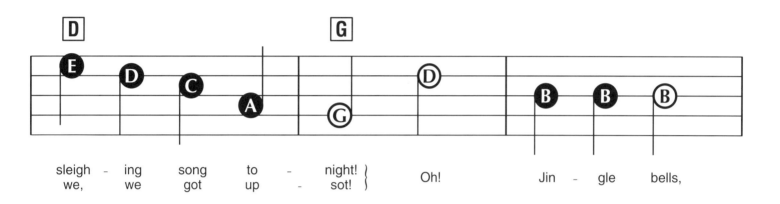

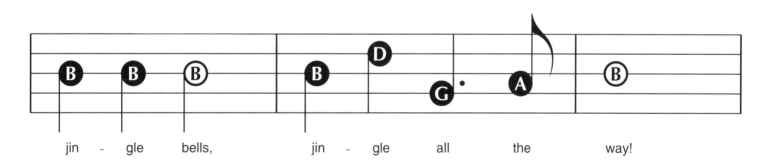

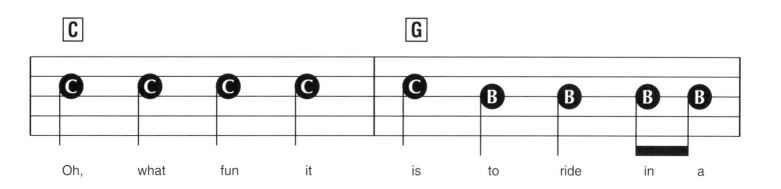

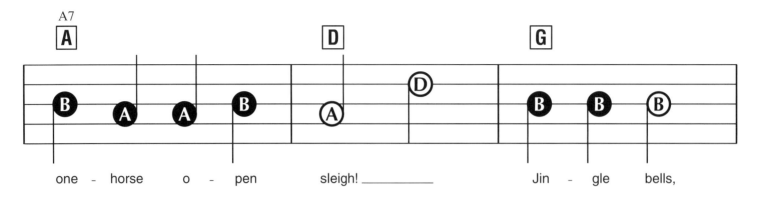

one - horse o - pen sleigh! _____ Jin - gle bells,

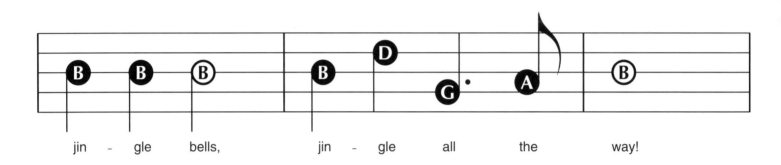

jin - gle bells, jin - gle all the way!

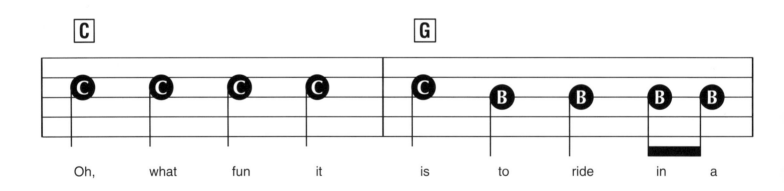

Oh, what fun it is to ride in a

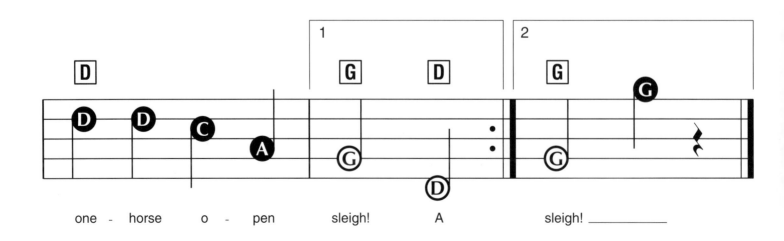

one - horse o - pen sleigh! A sleigh! _____

March of the Toys
from TOYLAND

Registration 5
Rhythm: 6/8 March

By Victor Herbert

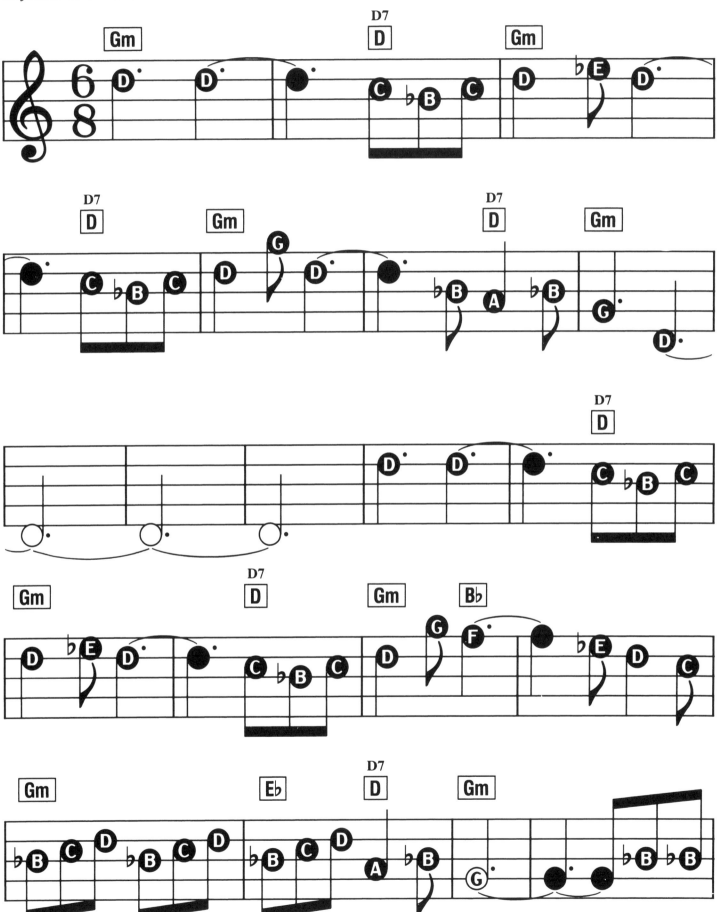

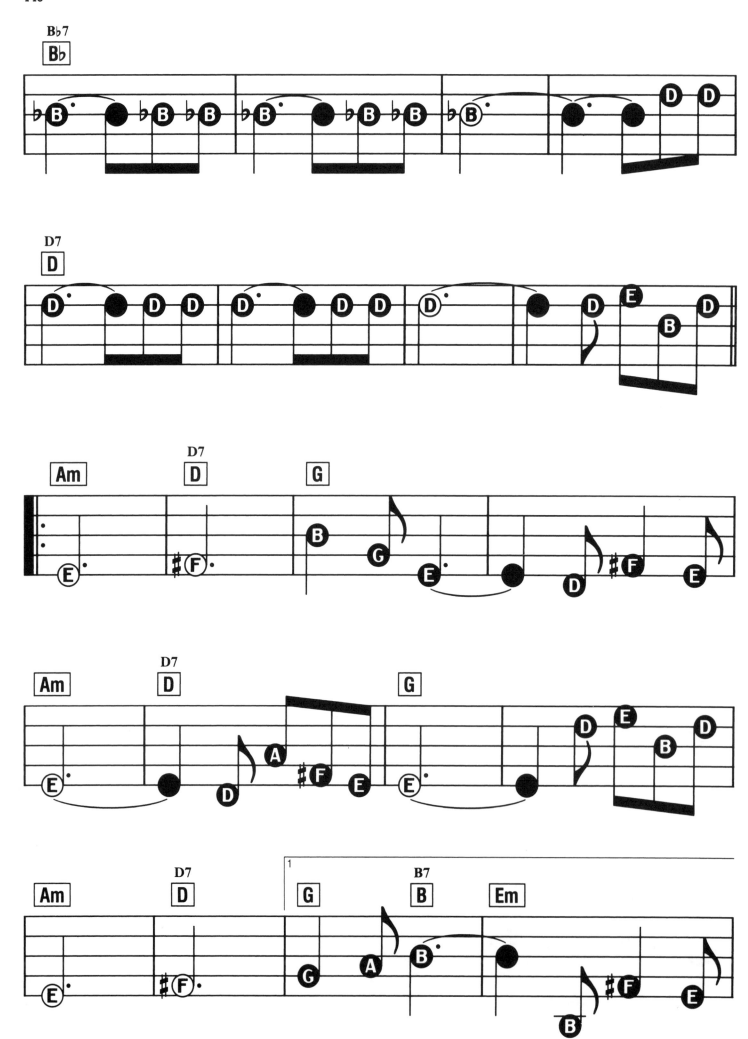

Jolly Old St. Nicholas

Registration 2
Rhythm: Fox Trot or Swing

Traditional 19th Century American Carol

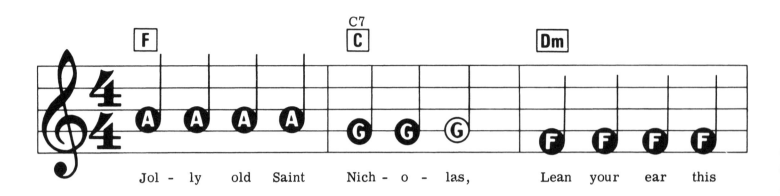

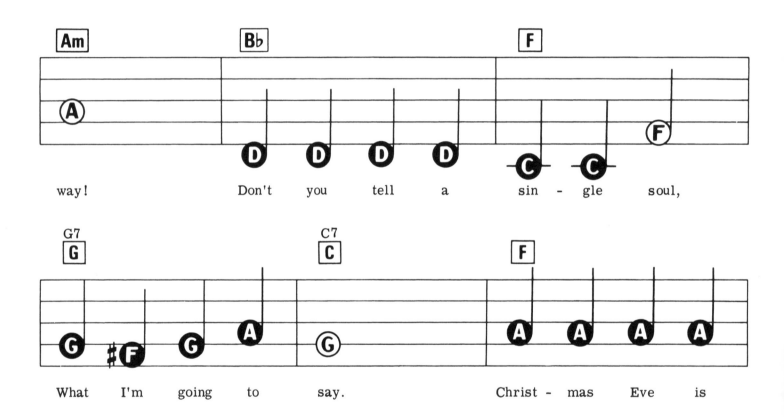

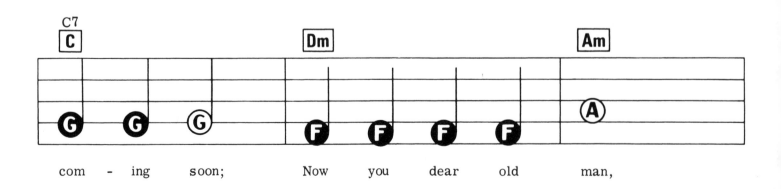

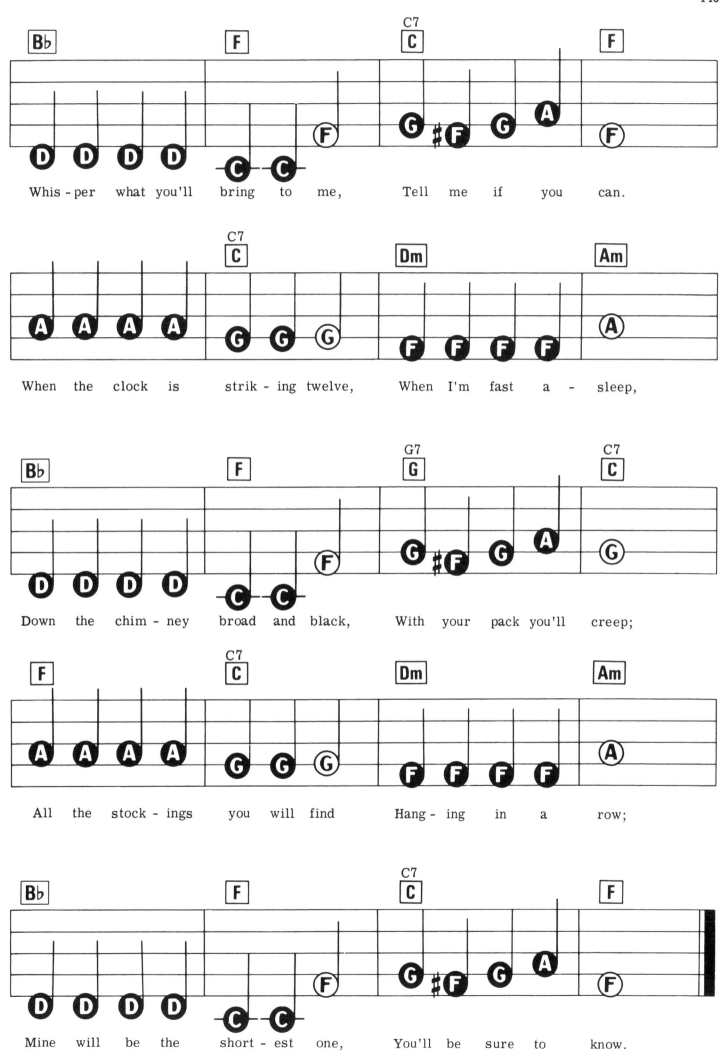

Joy to the World

Registration 2
Rhythm: None

Words by Isaac Watts
Music by George Frideric Handel
Arranged by Lowell Mason

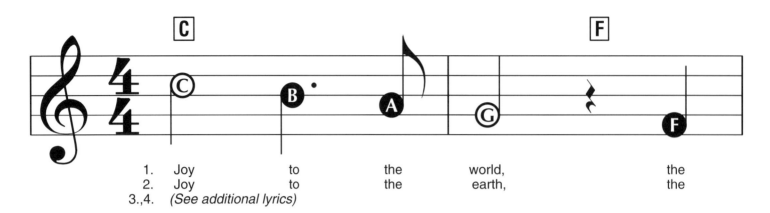

1. Joy   to   the   world,   the
2. Joy   to   the   earth,   the
3.,4. *(See additional lyrics)*

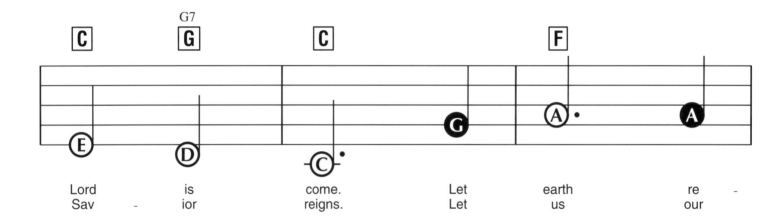

Lord   is   come.   Let   earth   re -
Sav -   ior   reigns.   Let   us   our

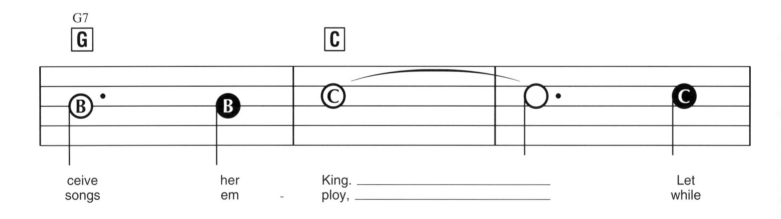

ceive   her   King. _____   Let
songs   em - ploy, _____   while

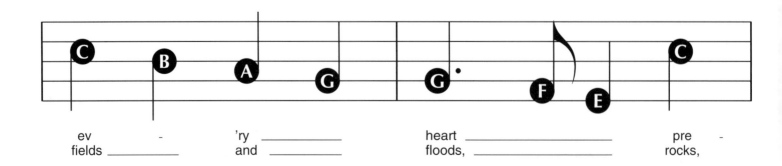

ev -   'ry _____   heart _____   pre -
fields _____ and _____   floods, _____   rocks,

151

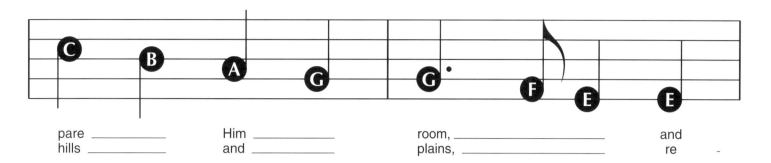

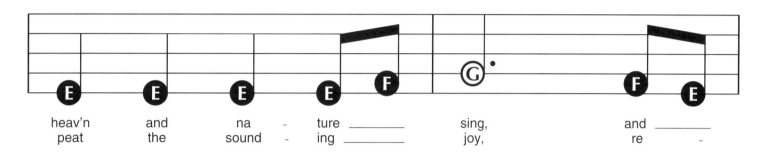

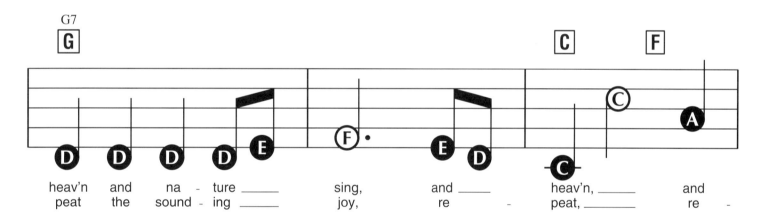

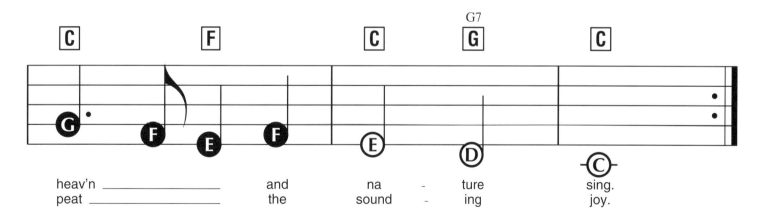

Additional Lyrics

3. No more let sins and sorrows grow,
Nor thorns infest the ground.
He comes to make His blessings flow
Far as the curse is found.

4. He rules the world with truth and grace,
And makes the nations prove
The glories of His righteousness,
And wonders of His love.

Little Children, Wake and Listen!

Registration 2
Rhythm: Waltz

Traditional French Carol

153

154

Lo, How a Rose E'er Blooming

Registration 2
Rhythm: None

15th Century German Carol
Translated by Theodore Baker
Music from *Alte Catholische Geistliche Kirchengesang*

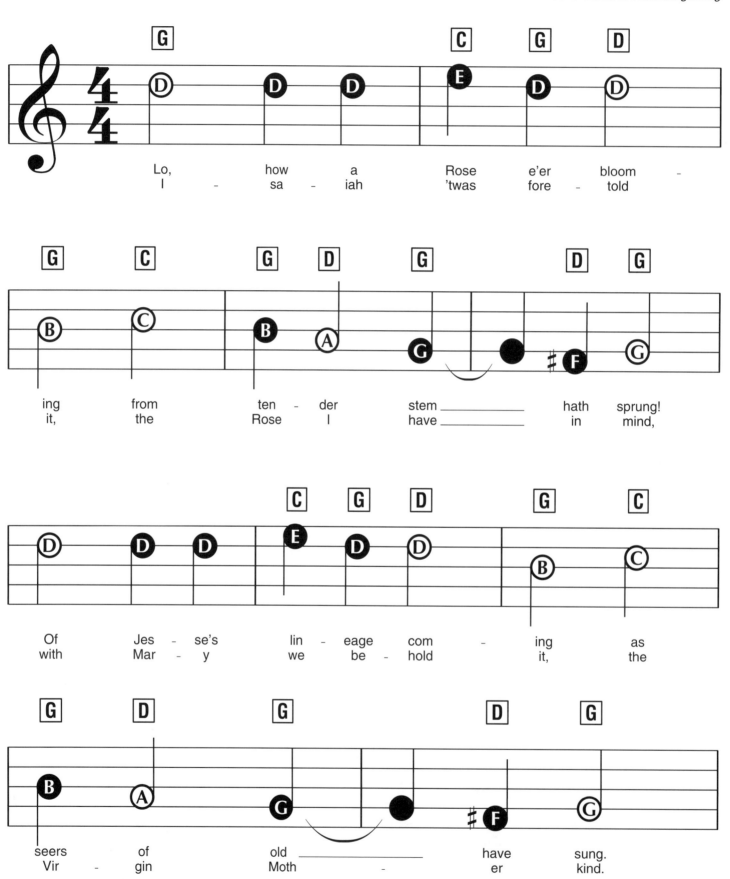

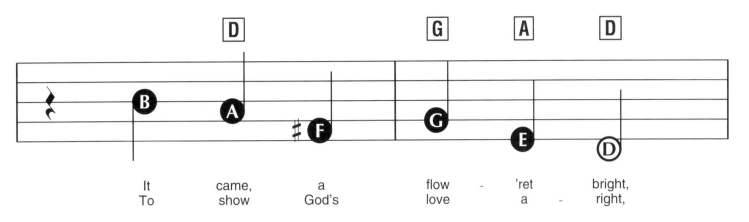

It   came,   a   flow - 'ret   bright,
To   show   God's   love   a - right,

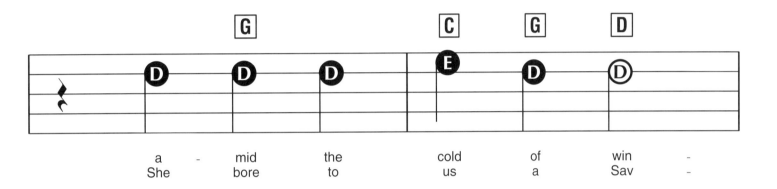

a - mid   the   cold   of   win -
She   bore   to   us   a   Sav -

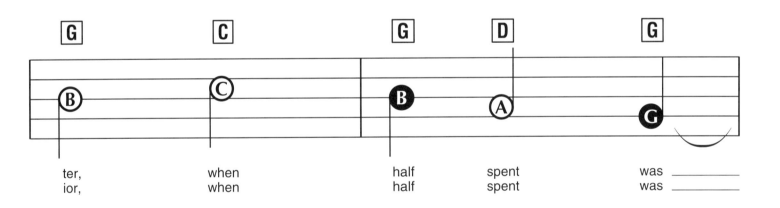

ter,   when   half   spent   was _____
ior,   when   half   spent   was _____

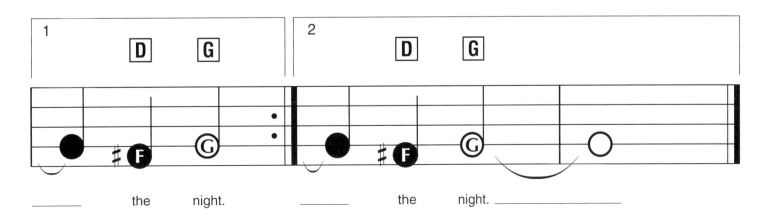

_____ the   night.   _____ the   night. _____

March of the Three Kings

Registration 2
Rhythm: None

Words by M.L. Hohman
Traditional French Melody

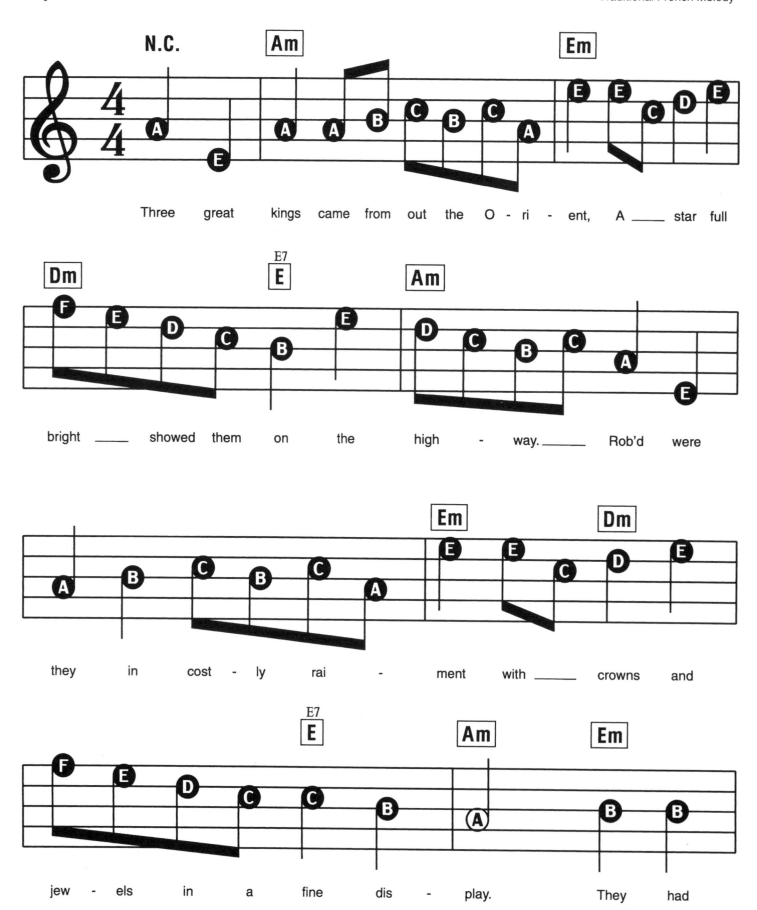

157

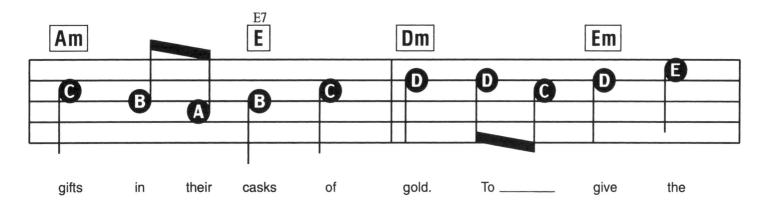

gifts in their casks of gold. To _____ give the

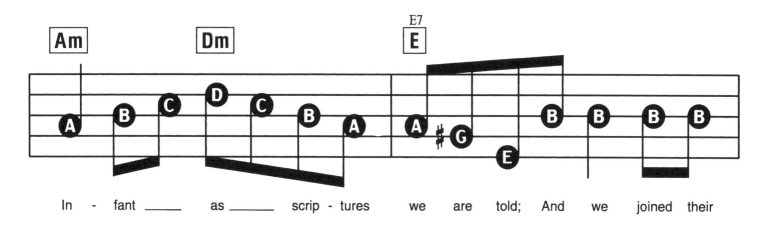

In - fant _____ as _____ scrip - tures we are told; And we joined their

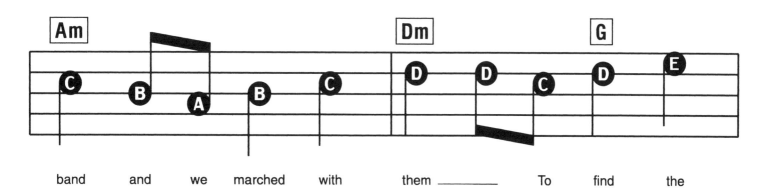

band and we marched with them _____ To find the

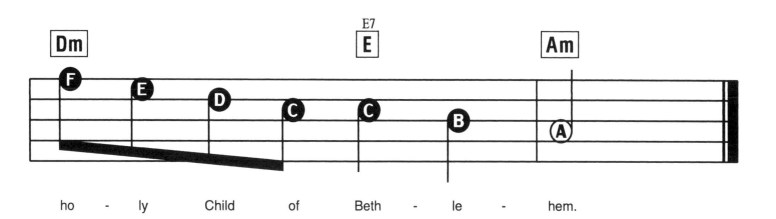

ho - ly Child of Beth - le - hem.

Mary Had a Baby

Registration 2
Rhythm: Calypso or Latin

African-American Spiritual

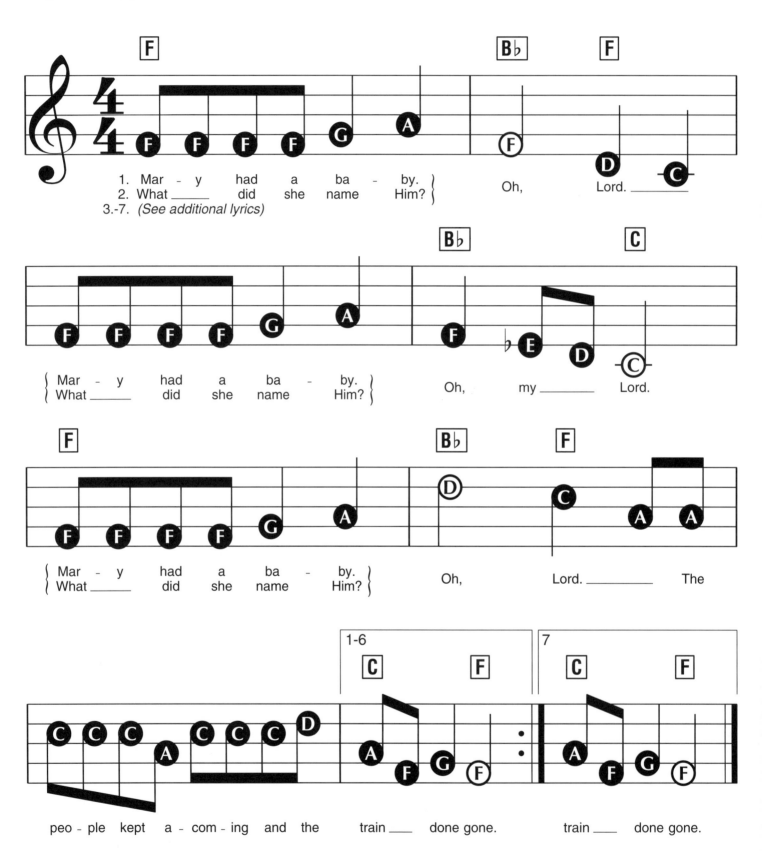

Additional Lyrics

3. She called Him Jesus.
4. Where was He born?
5. Born in a stable.

6. Where did they lay Him?
7. Laid Him in a manger.

O Little Town of Bethlehem

Registration 1
Rhythm: Fox Trot

Words by Phillips Brooks
Music by Lewis H. Redner

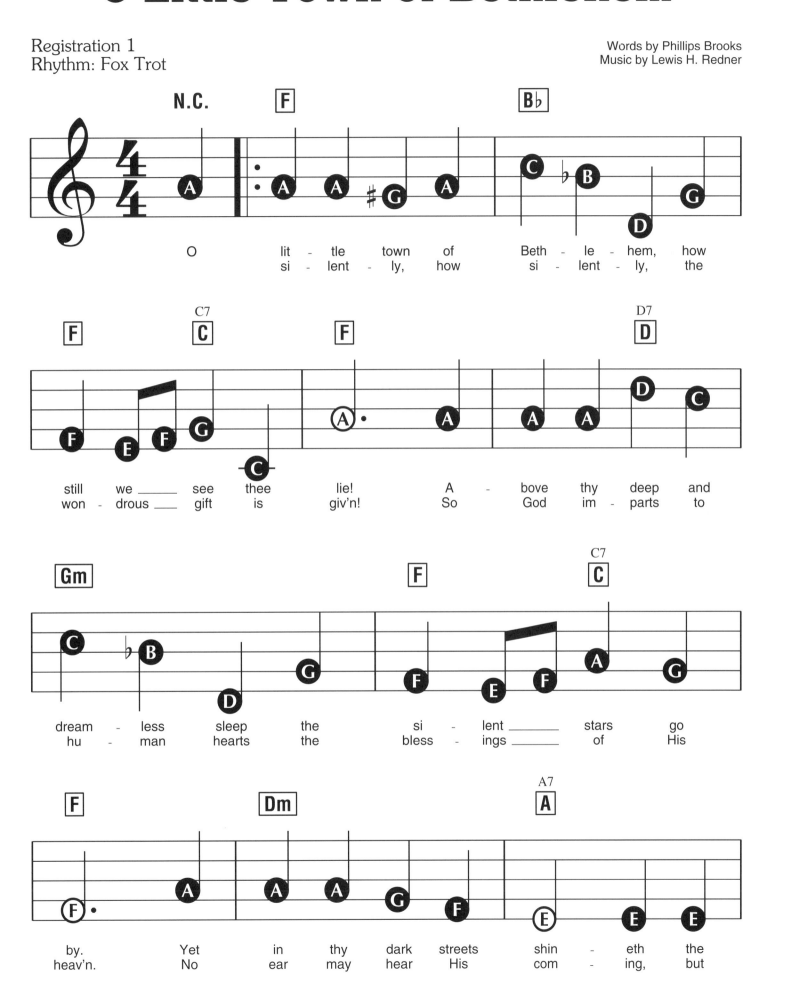

160

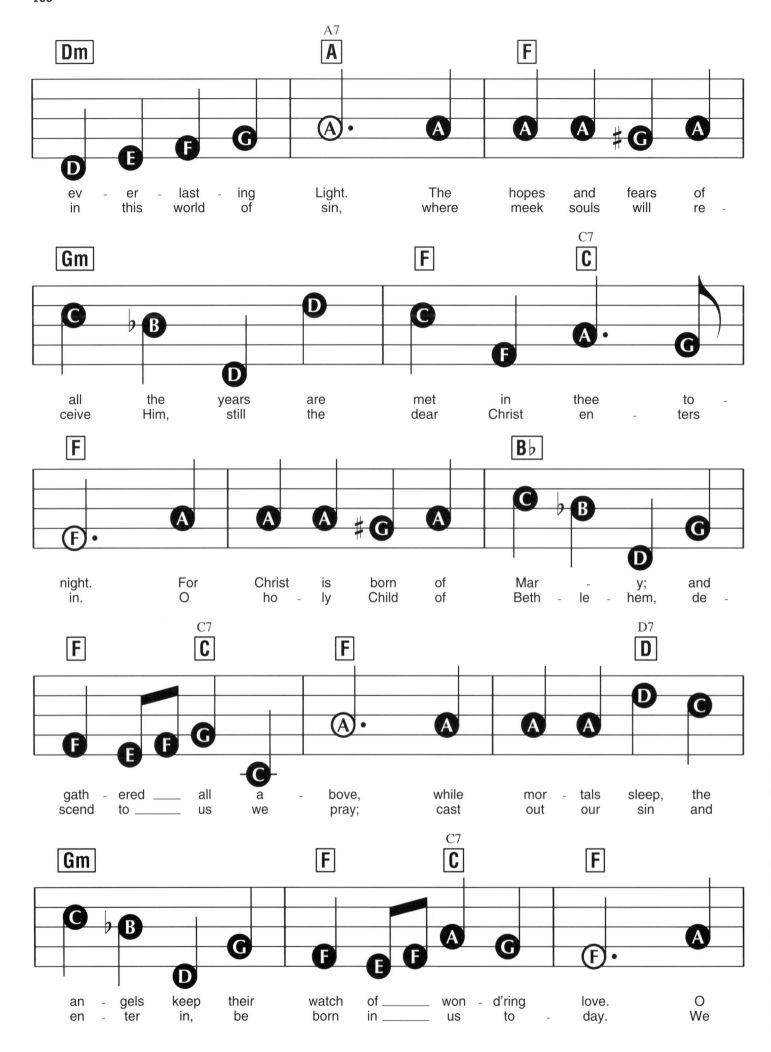

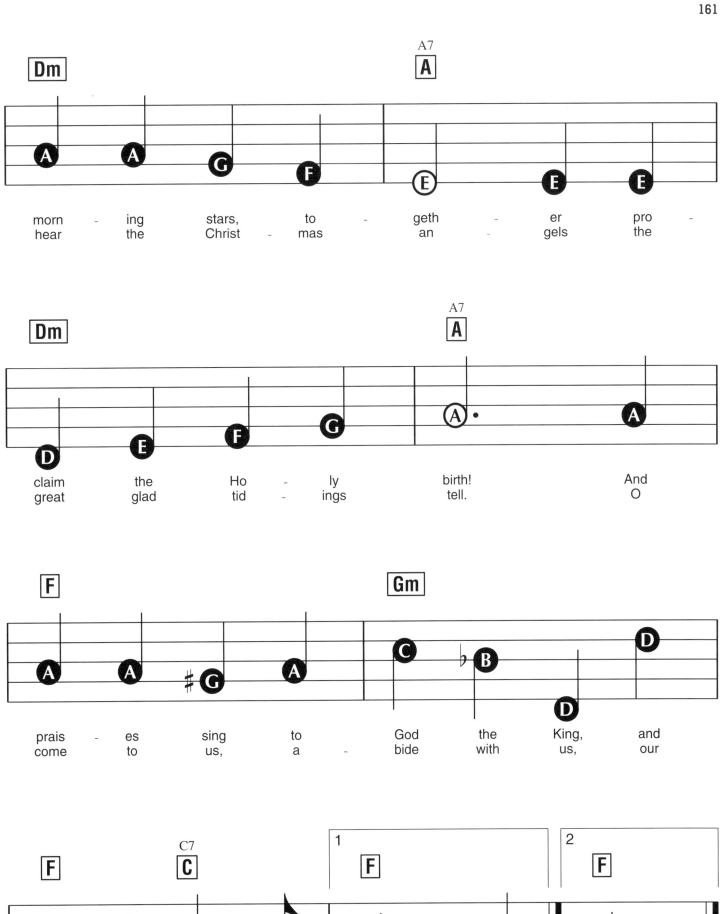

161

Masters in This Hall

Registration 4
Rhythm: Waltz

Traditional English

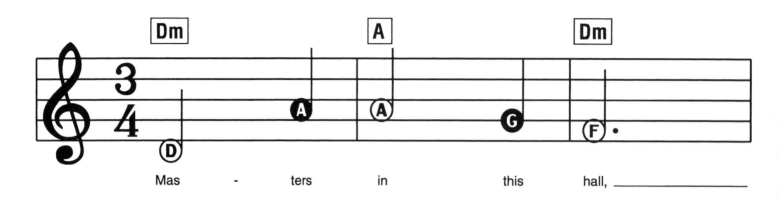

Mas - ters in this hall, _____

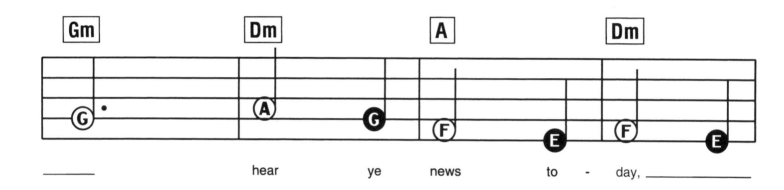

_____ hear ye news to - day, _____

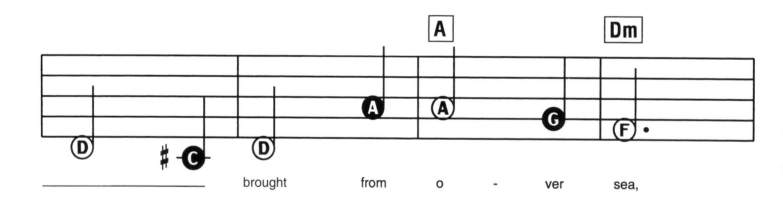

_____ brought from o - ver sea,

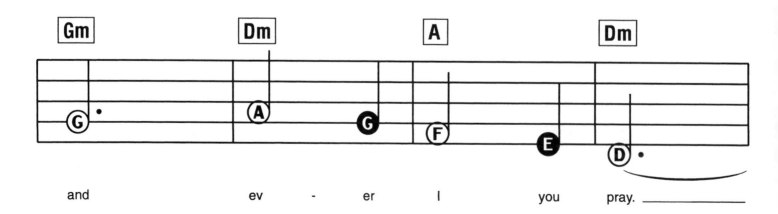

and ev - er I you pray. _____

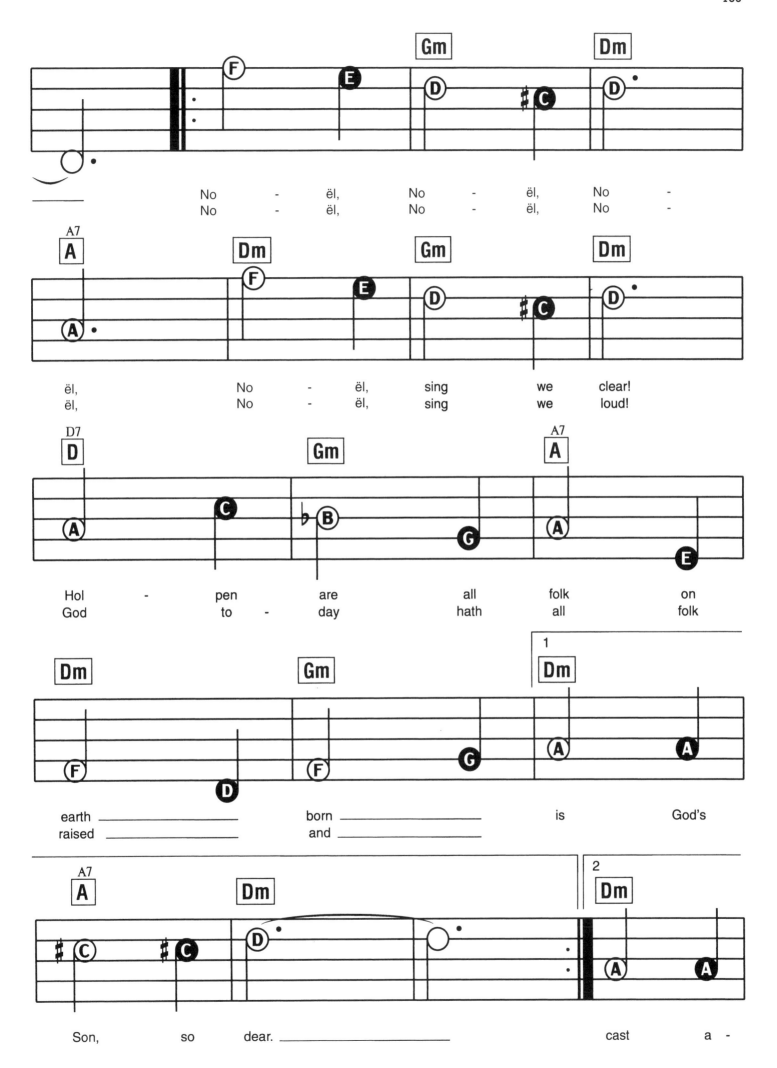

164

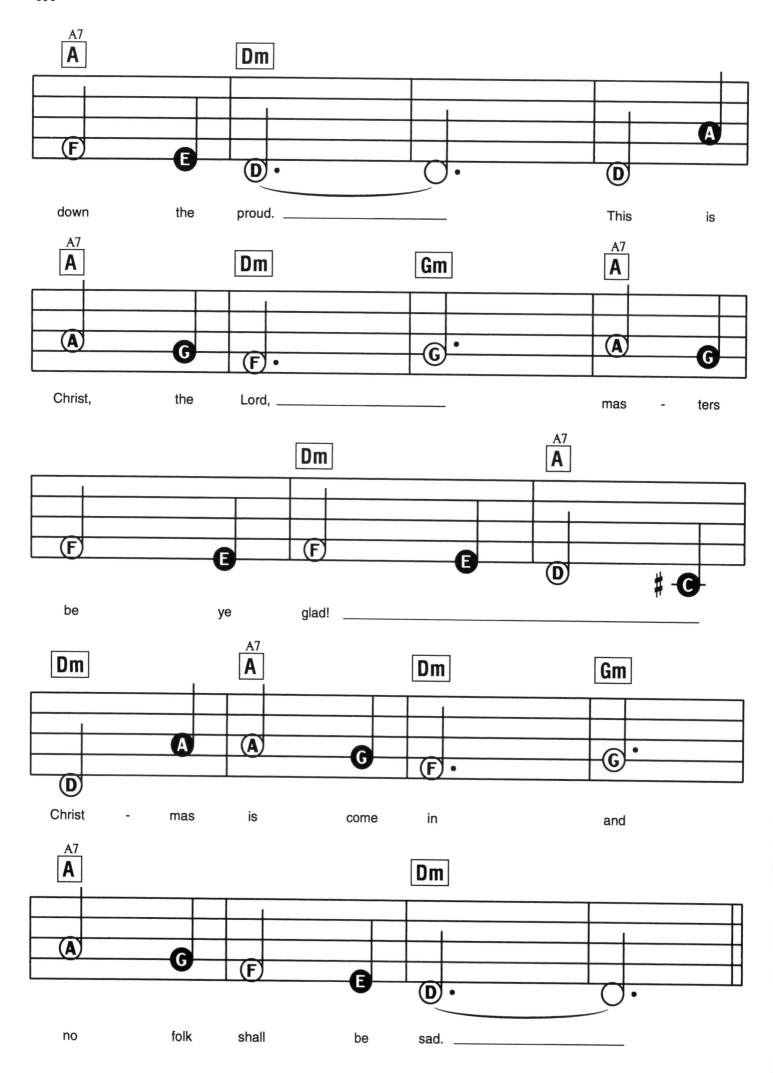

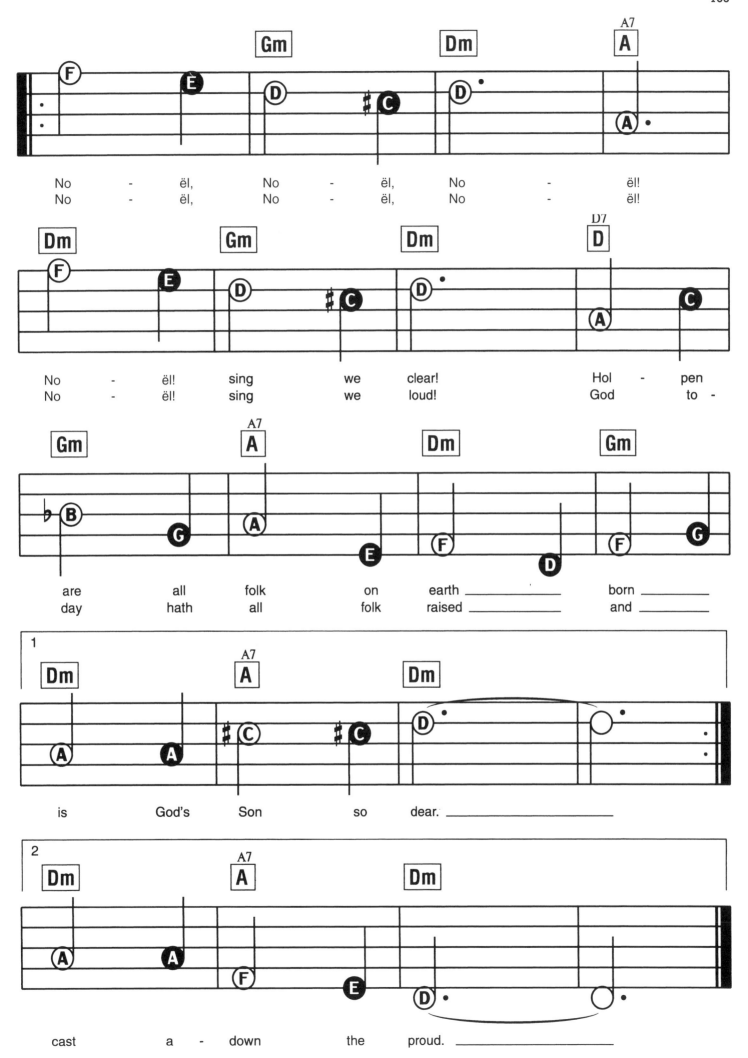

Neighbor, What Has You So Excited?

Registration 8
Rhythm: Waltz

Traditional French

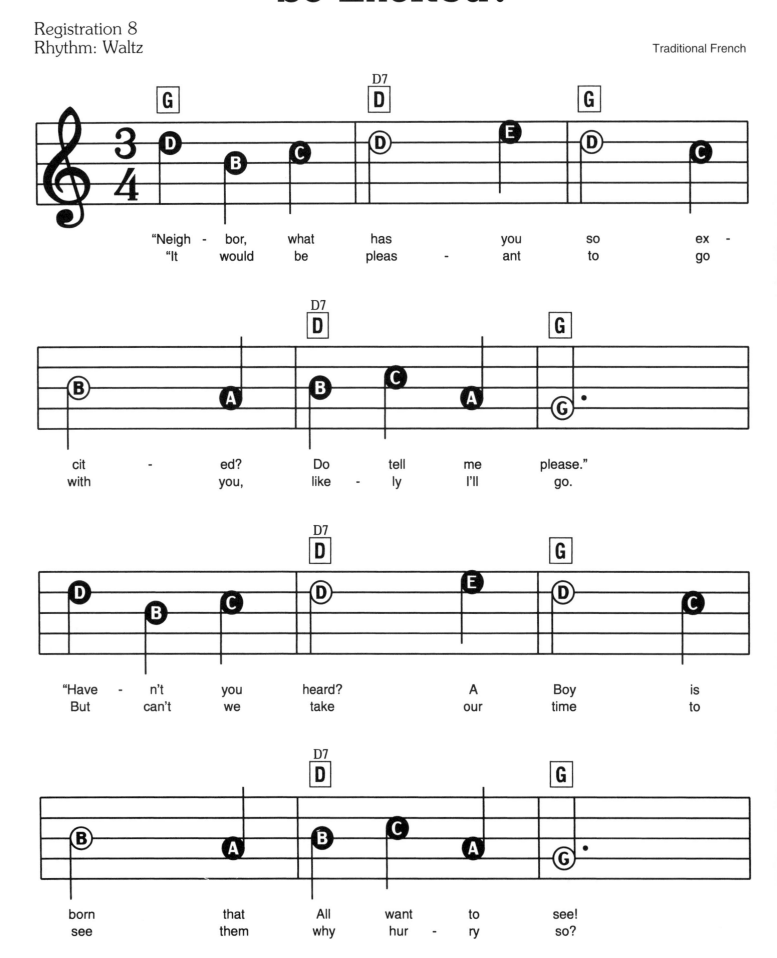

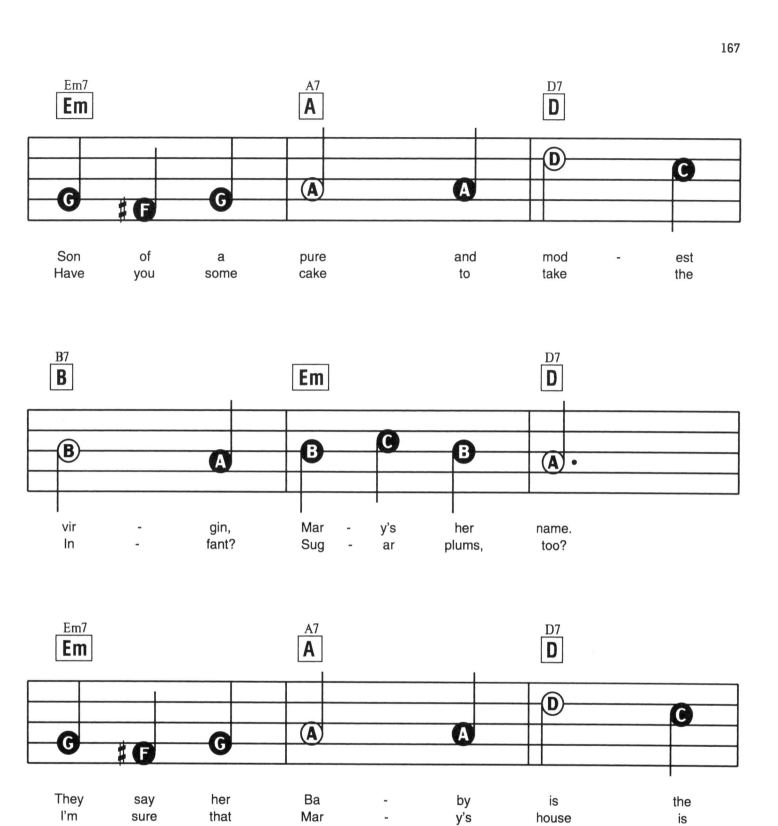

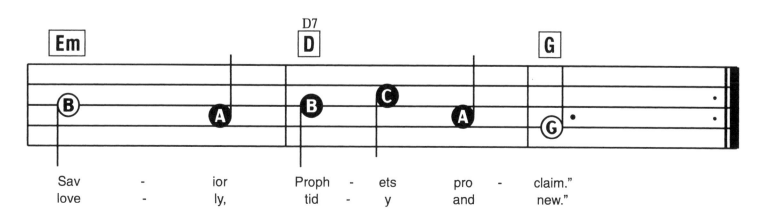

Noël! Noël!

Registration 2
Rhythm: None

French-English Carol

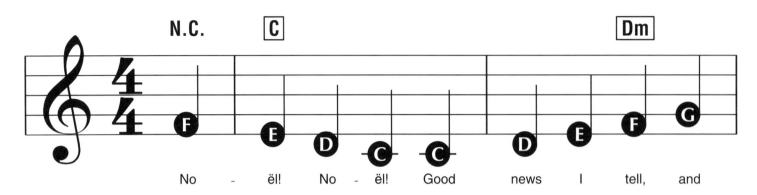

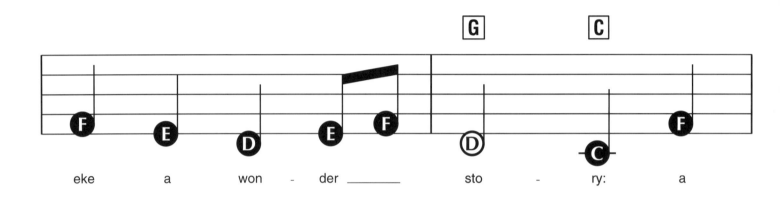

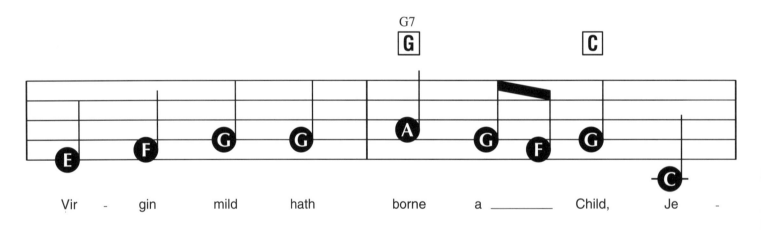

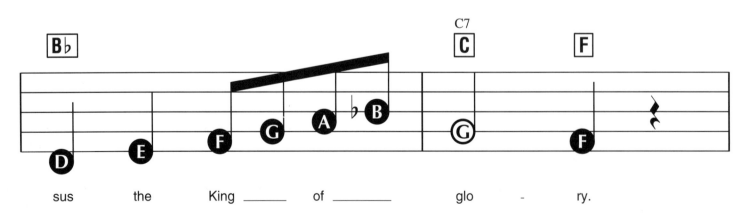

169

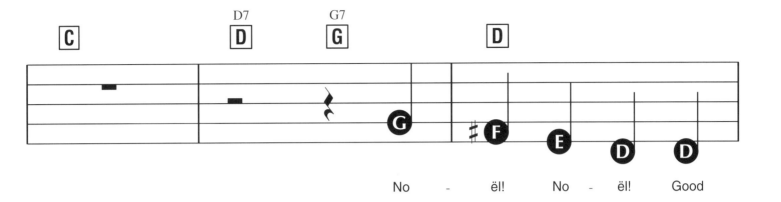

No - ël! No - ël! Good

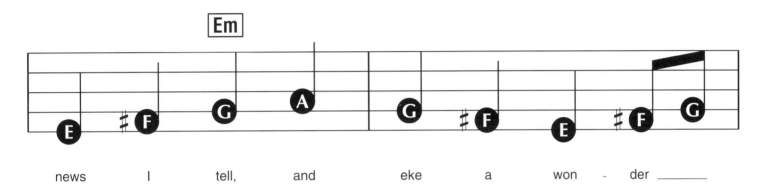

news I tell, and eke a won - der _____

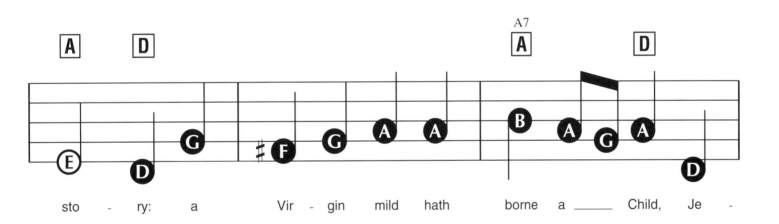

sto - ry: a Vir - gin mild hath borne a _____ Child, Je -

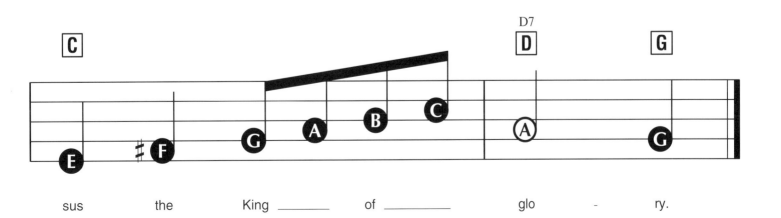

sus the King _____ of _____ glo - ry.

O Bethlehem

Registration 6
Rhythm: Waltz

Traditional Spanish

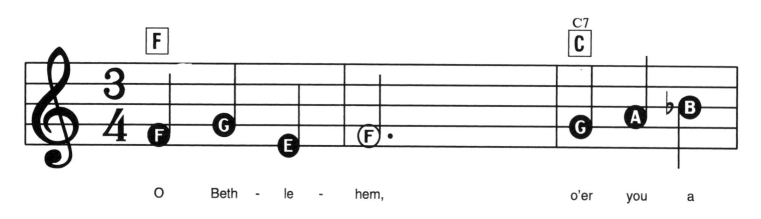

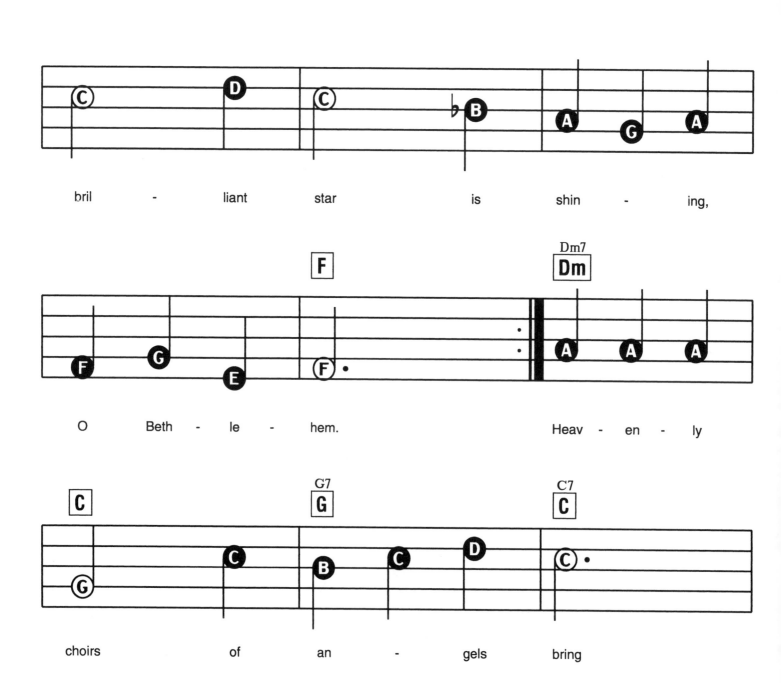

171

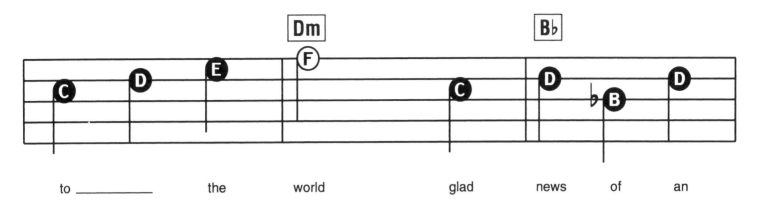

to _____ the world glad news of an

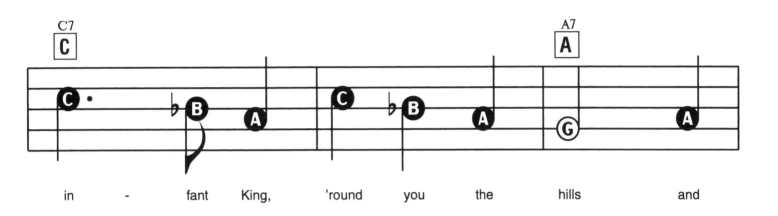

in - fant King, 'round you the hills and

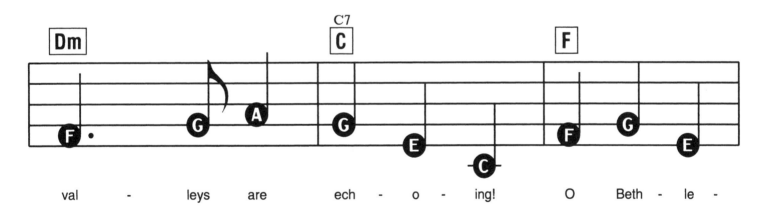

val - leys are ech - o - ing! O Beth - le -

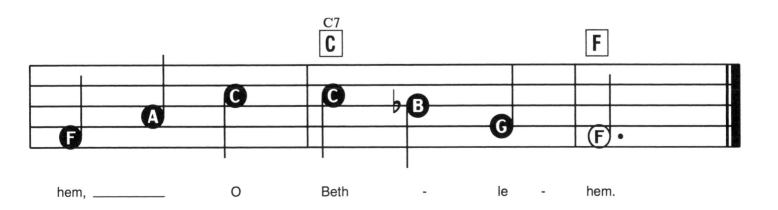

hem, _____ O Beth - le - hem.

O Christmas Tree

Registration 3
Rhythm: None

Traditional German Carol

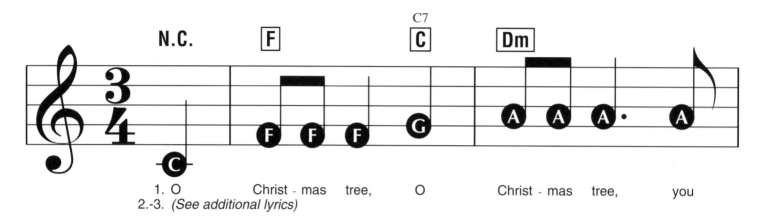

1. O   Christ - mas   tree,   O   Christ - mas   tree,   you
2.-3. *(See additional lyrics)*

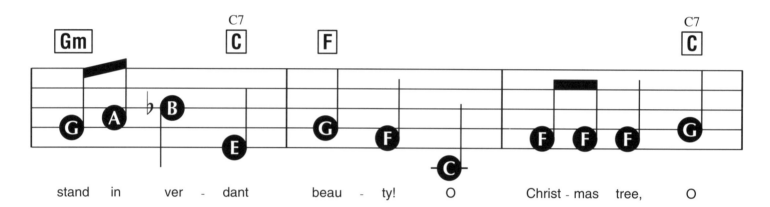

stand   in   ver - dant   beau - ty!   O   Christ - mas   tree,   O

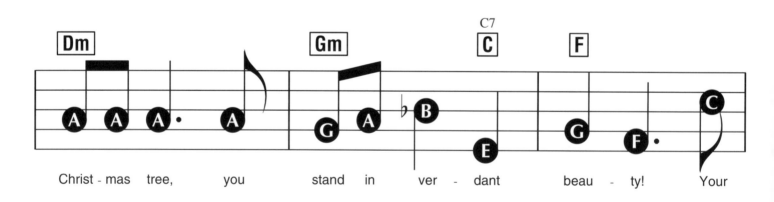

Christ - mas   tree,   you   stand   in   ver - dant   beau - ty!   Your

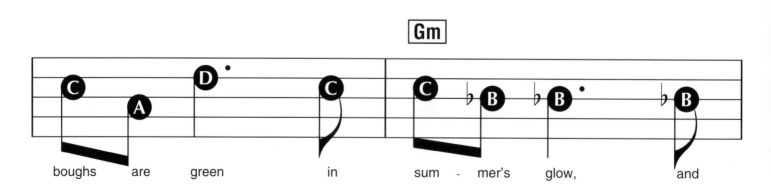

boughs   are   green   in   sum - mer's   glow,   and

173

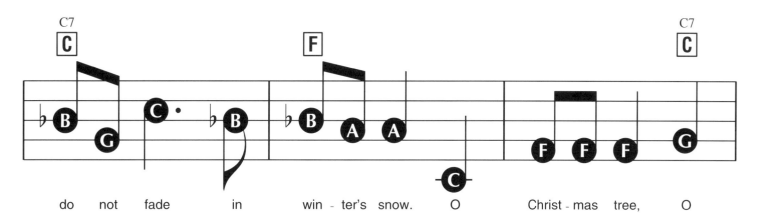

do not fade in win - ter's snow. O Christ - mas tree, O

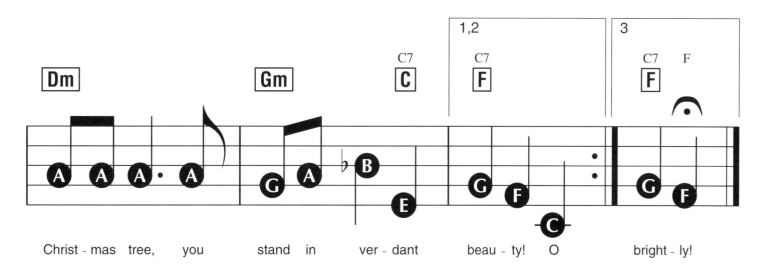

Christ - mas tree, you stand in ver - dant beau - ty! O bright - ly!

Additional Lyrics

2. O Christmas tree, O Christmas tree,
Much pleasure doth thou bring me!
O Christmas tree, O Christmas tree,
Much pleasure doth thou bring me!
For ev'ry year the Christmas tree
Brings to us all both joy and glee.
O Christmas tree, O Christmas tree,
Much pleasure doth thou bring me!

3. O Christmas tree, O Christmas tree,
Thy candles shine out brightly!
O Christmas tree, O Christmas tree,
Thy candles shine out brightly!
Each bough doth hold its tiny light
That makes each toy to sparkle bright.
O Christmas tree, O Christmas tree,
Thy candles shine out brightly!

O Come, All Ye Faithful
(Adeste fideles)

Registration 6
Rhythm: None

Words and Music by John Francis Wade
Latin Words translated by Frederick Oakeley

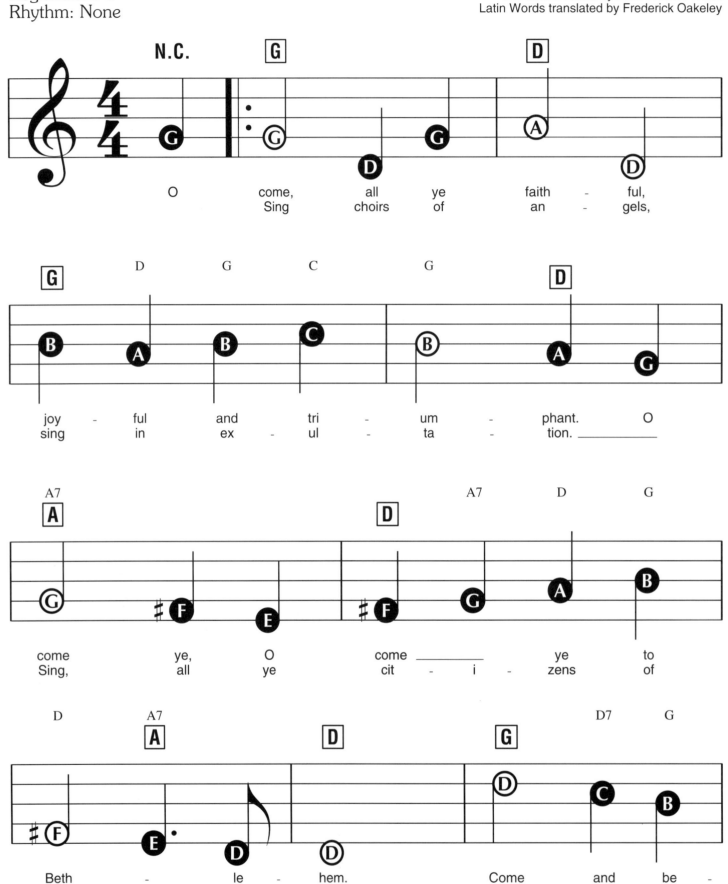

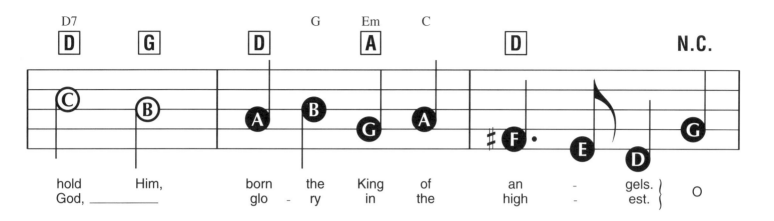

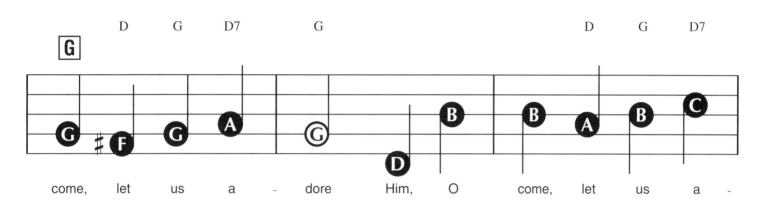

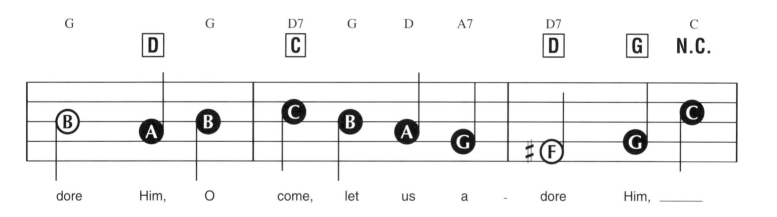

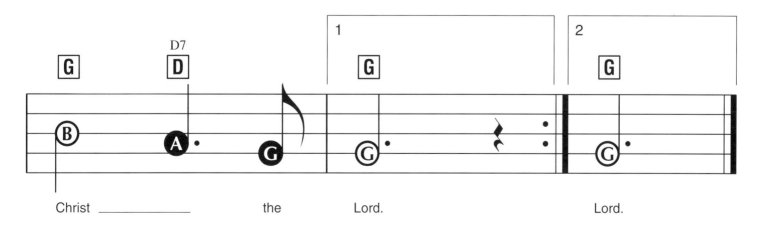

O Come Away, Ye Shepherds

Registration 6
Rhythm: None

18th Century French Text
Tune from Air "Nanon Dormait"

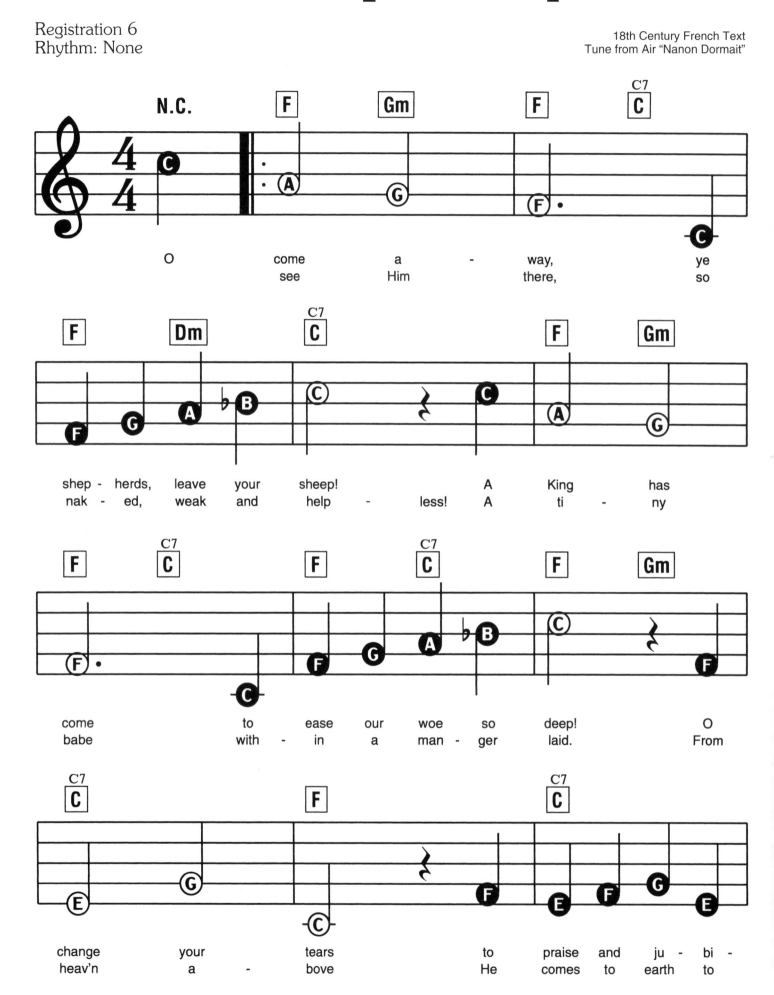

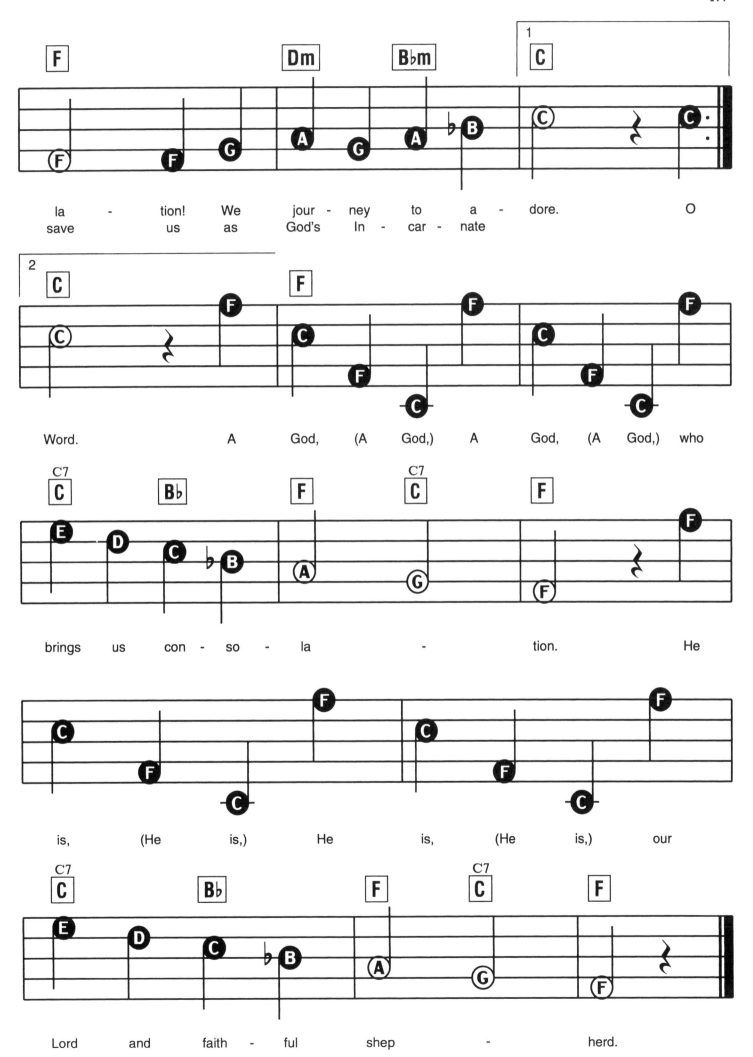

O Come, Little Children

Registration 1
Rhythm: 4/4 Ballad

Words by C. von Schmidt
Music by J.P.A. Schulz

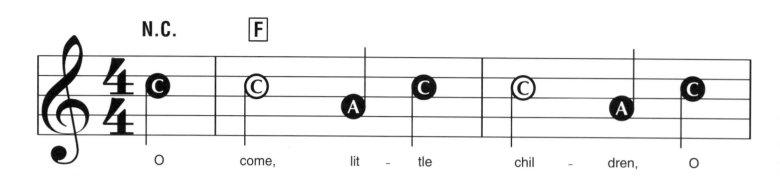

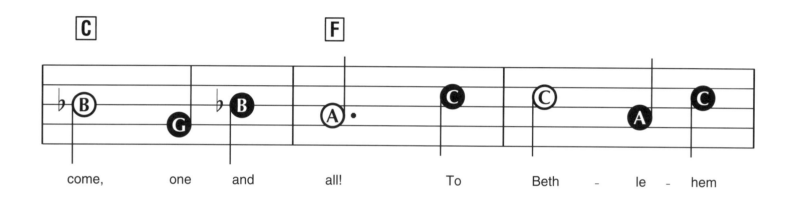

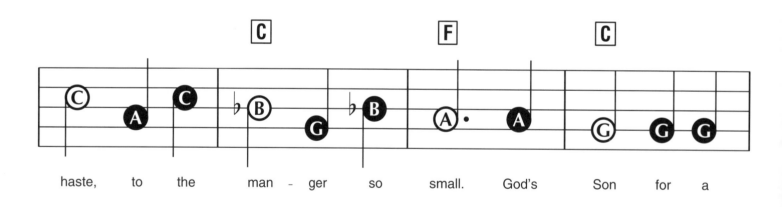

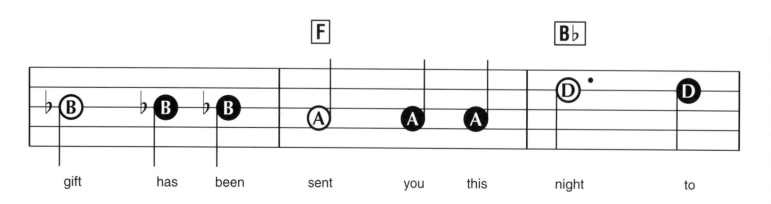

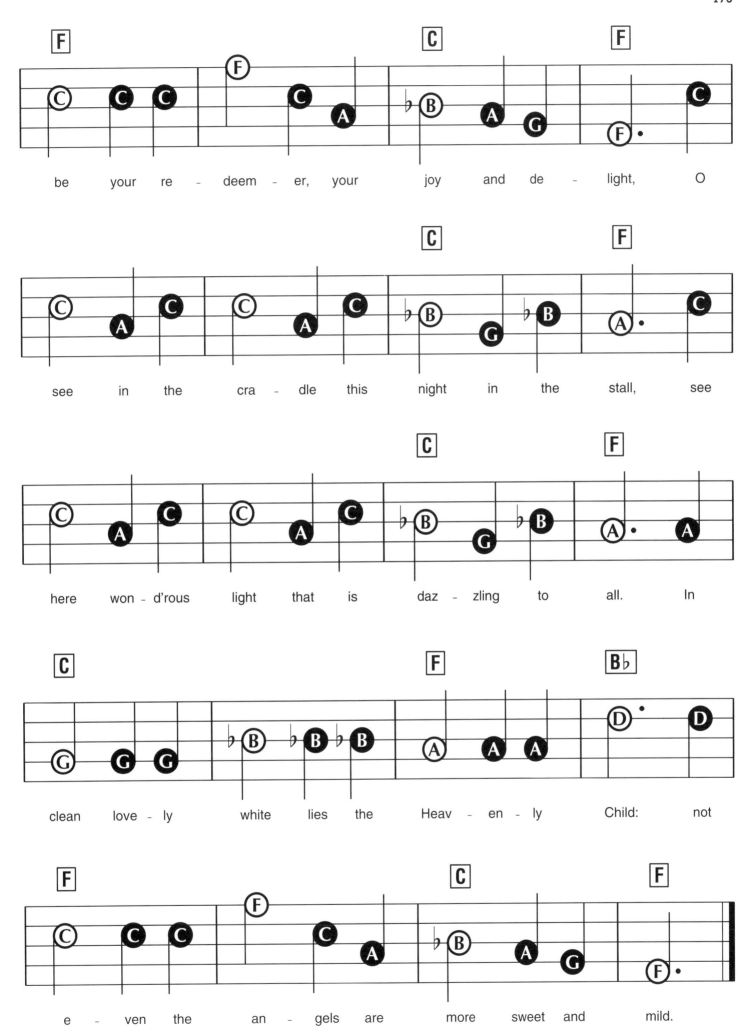

179

O Come, O Come, Emmanuel

Registration 8
Rhythm: None

Traditional Latin Text
v. 1, 2 translated by John M. Neale
v. 3, 4 translated by Henry S. Coffin
15th Century French Melody
Adapted by Thomas Helmore

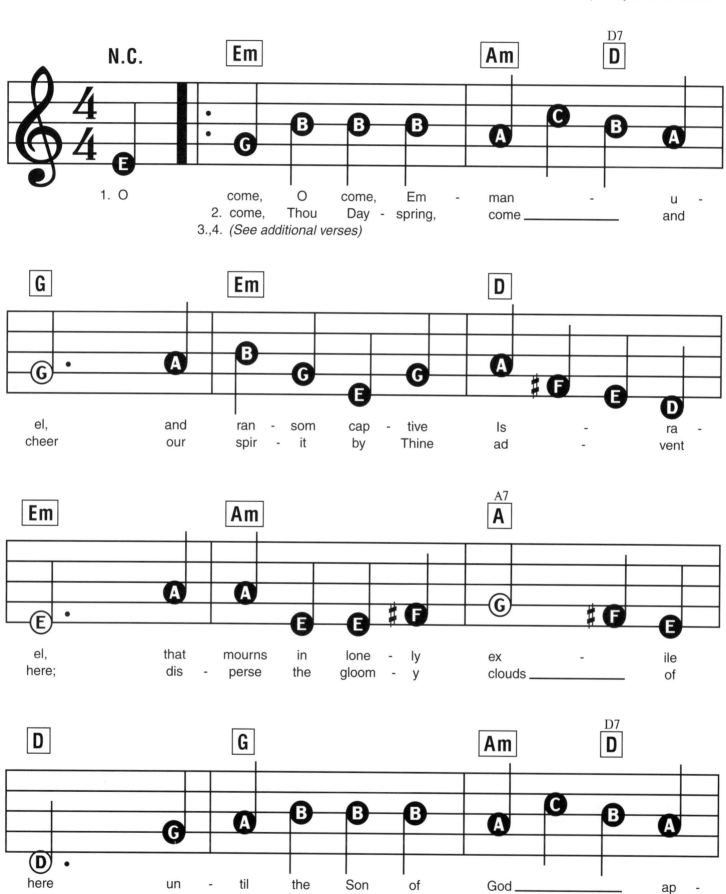

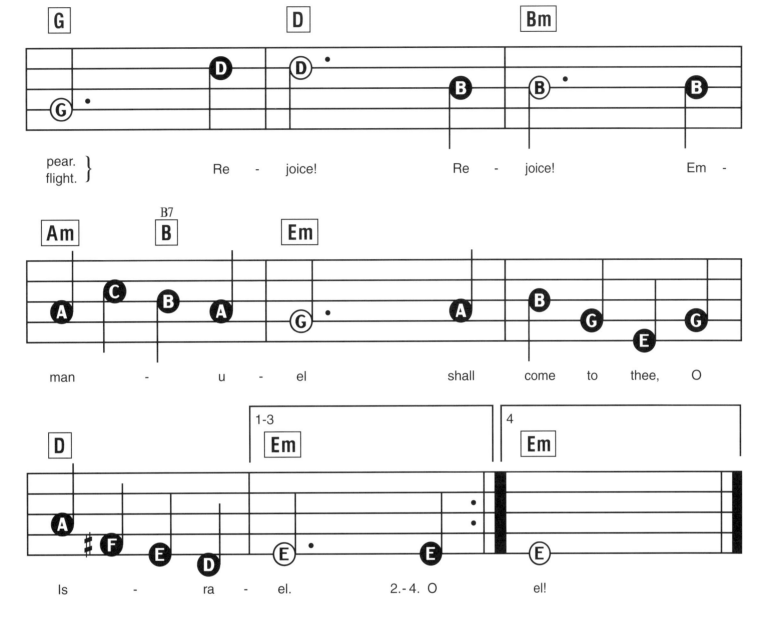

pear.
flight. } Re - joice! Re - joice! Em -

man - u - el shall come to thee, O

Is - ra - el. 2.-4. O el!

Additional Verses

3. O come, Thou wisdom from on high,
And order all things, far and nigh;
To us the path of knowledge show,
And cause us in her ways to go.
Refrain

4. O come, Desire of nations, bind
All peoples in one heart and mind;
Bid envy, strife and quarrels cease,
Fill all the world with heaven's peace.
Refrain

O Come Rejoicing

Registration 6
Rhythm: Waltz

Traditional Polish Carol

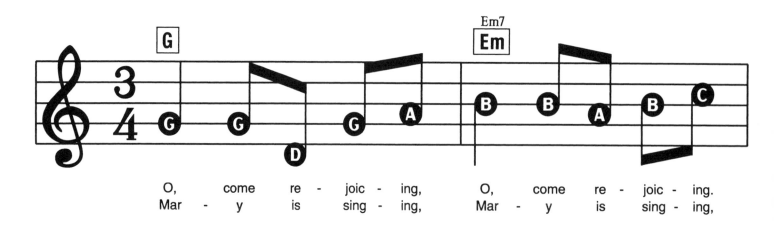

O, come re - joic - ing, O, come re - joic - ing.
Mar - y is sing - ing, Mar - y is sing - ing,

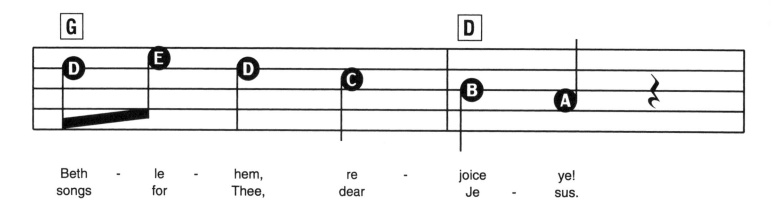

Beth - le - hem, re - joice ye!
songs for Thee, dear Je - sus.

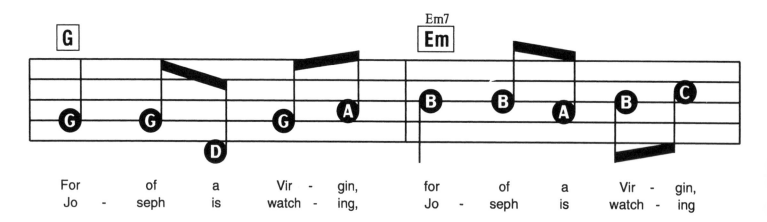

For of a Vir - gin, for of a Vir - gin,
Jo - seph is watch - ing, Jo - seph is watch - ing

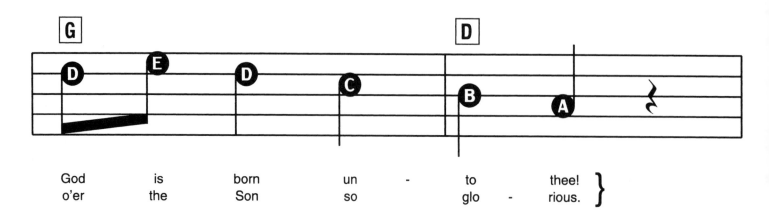

God is born un - to thee!
o'er the Son so glo - rious.

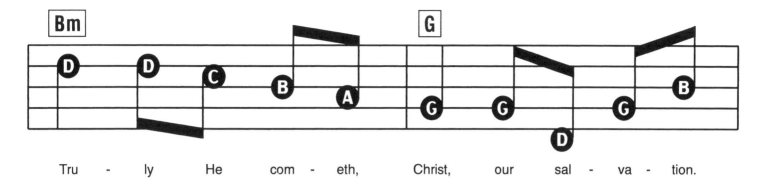

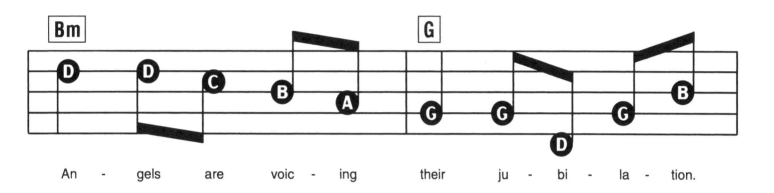

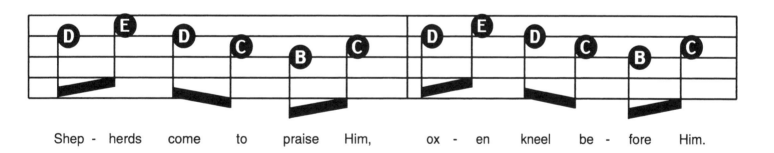

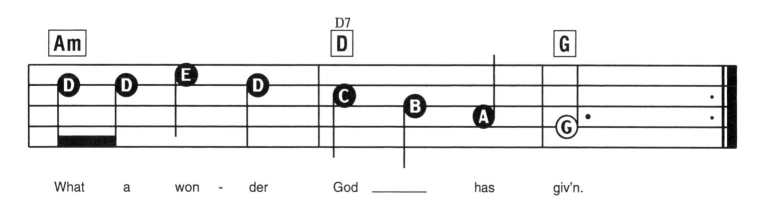

O Holy Night

Registration 6
Rhythm: None

French Words by Placide Cappeau
English Words by John S. Dwight
Music by Adolphe Adam

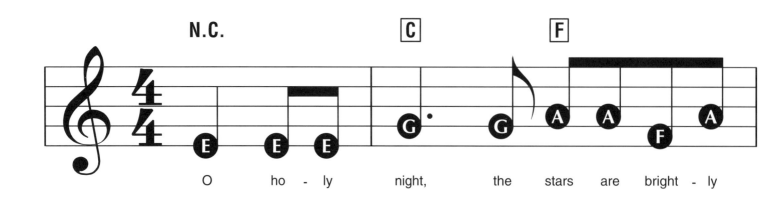

O ho - ly night, the stars are bright - ly

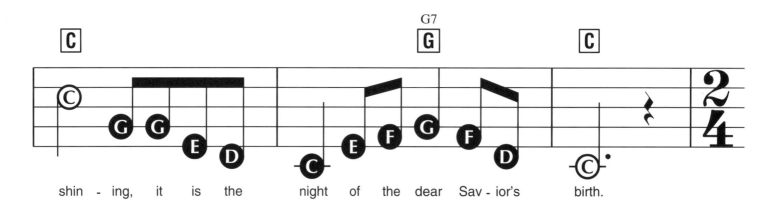

shin - ing, it is the night of the dear Sav - ior's birth.

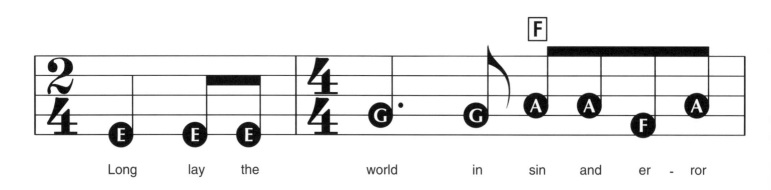

Long lay the world in sin and er - ror

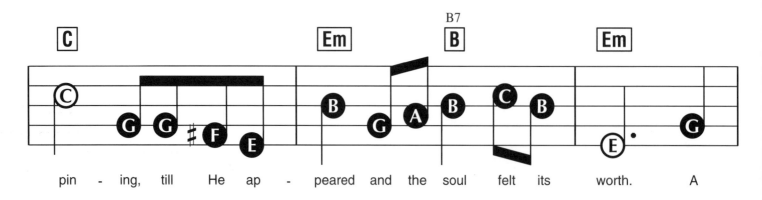

pin - ing, till He ap - peared and the soul felt its worth. A

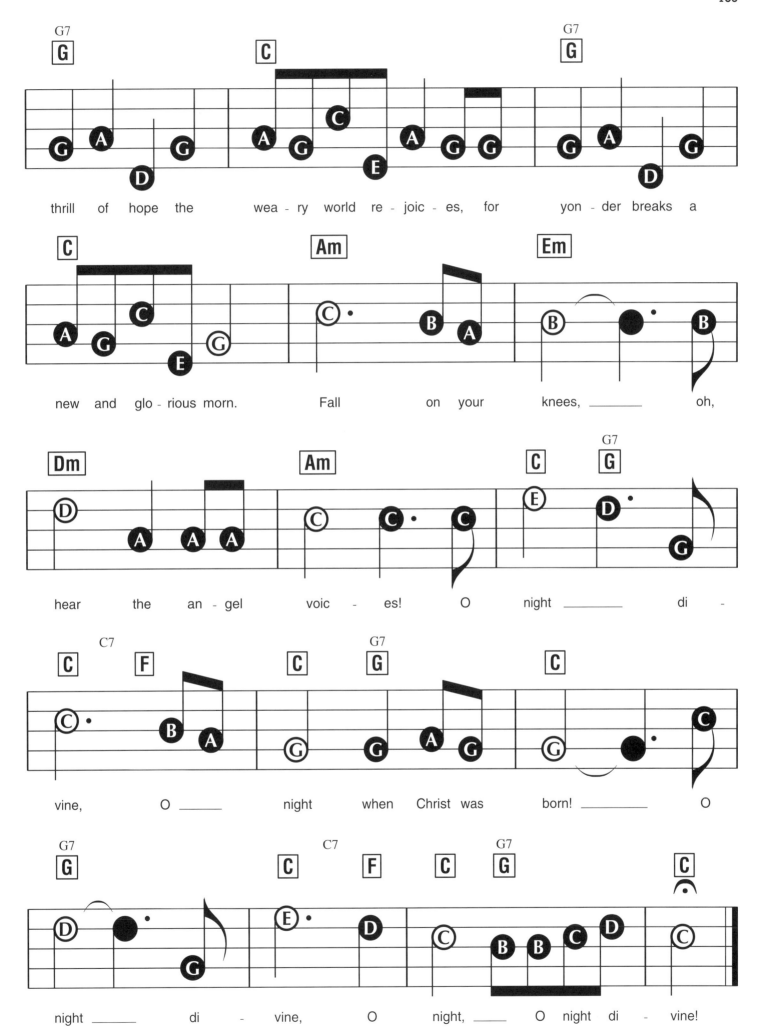

O Let Us All Be Glad Today

Registration 6
Rhythm: None

Words and Music by
Martin Luther

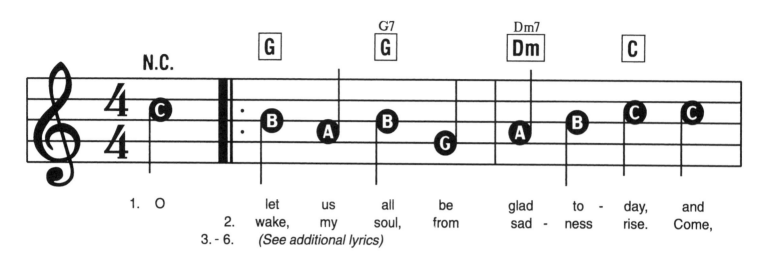

1. O   let us all be glad to - day, and
2. wake, my soul, from sad - ness rise. Come,
3. - 6. *(See additional lyrics)*

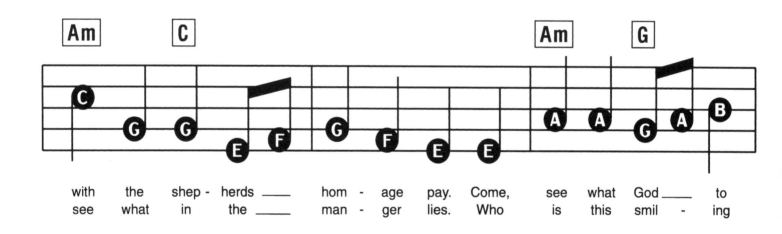

with the shep - herds ____ hom - age pay. Come, see what God ____ to
see what in the ____ man - ger lies. Who is this smil - ing

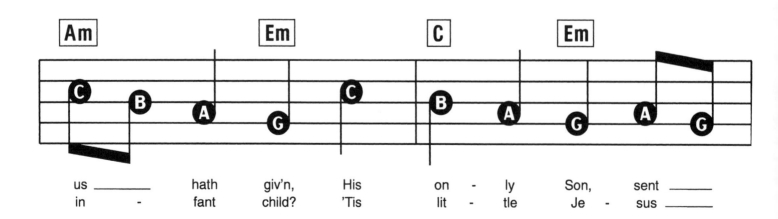

us ____ hath giv'n, His on - ly Son, sent ____
in - fant child? 'Tis lit - tle Je - sus ____

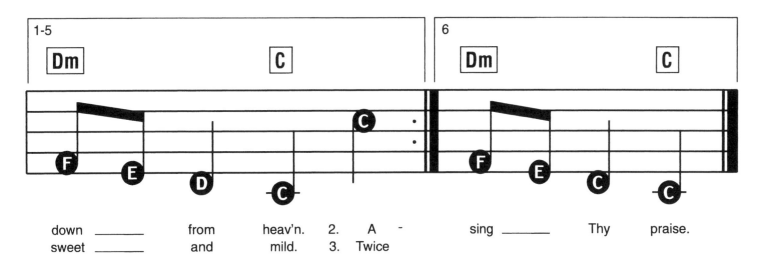

down _____ from heav'n. 2. A - sing _____ Thy praise.
sweet _____ and mild. 3. Twice

Additional Lyrics

3. Twice welcome, O Thou heavenly guest,
   To save a world with sin distressed;
   Com'st Thou in lowly guise for me?
   What homage shall I give to Thee?

4. Ah! Lord eternal, heavenly King.
   Hast Thou become so mean a thing?
   And hast Thou left blissful seat,
   To rest where colts and oxen eat?

5. Jesus, my Savior, come to me,
   Make here a little crib for Thee;
   A bed make in this heart of mine,
   That I may ay remember Thine.

6. Then from my soul glad songs shall ring;
   Of Thee each day I'll gladly sing;
   Then glad hosannas will I raise,
   From heart that loves to sing Thy praise.

O Sanctissima

Registration 6
Rhythm: None

Sicilian Carol

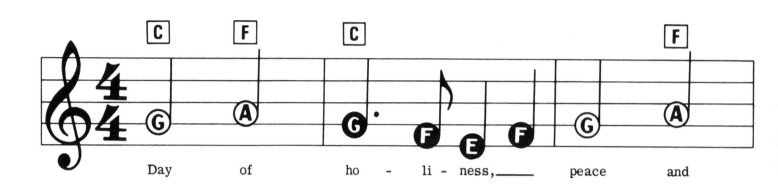

Day of ho - li - ness,_____ peace and

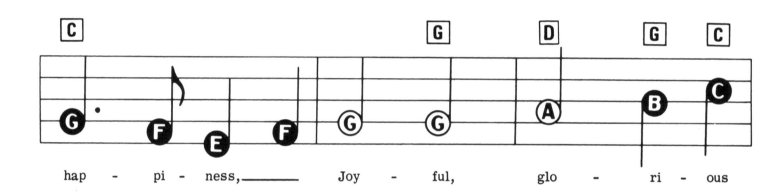

hap - pi - ness,_____ Joy - ful, glo - ri - ous

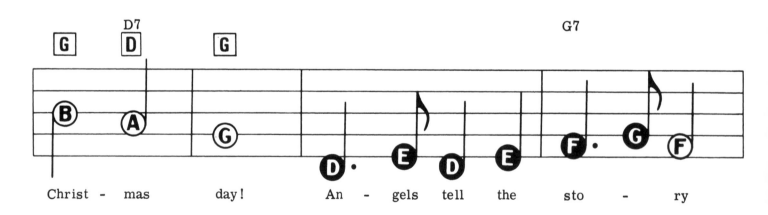

Christ - mas day! An - gels tell the sto - ry

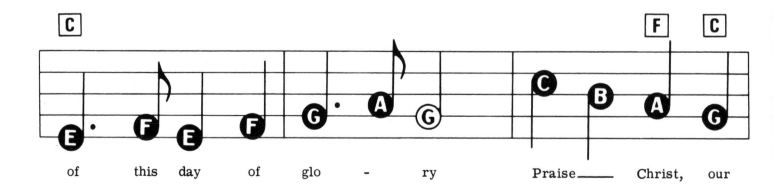

of this day of glo - ry Praise_____ Christ, our

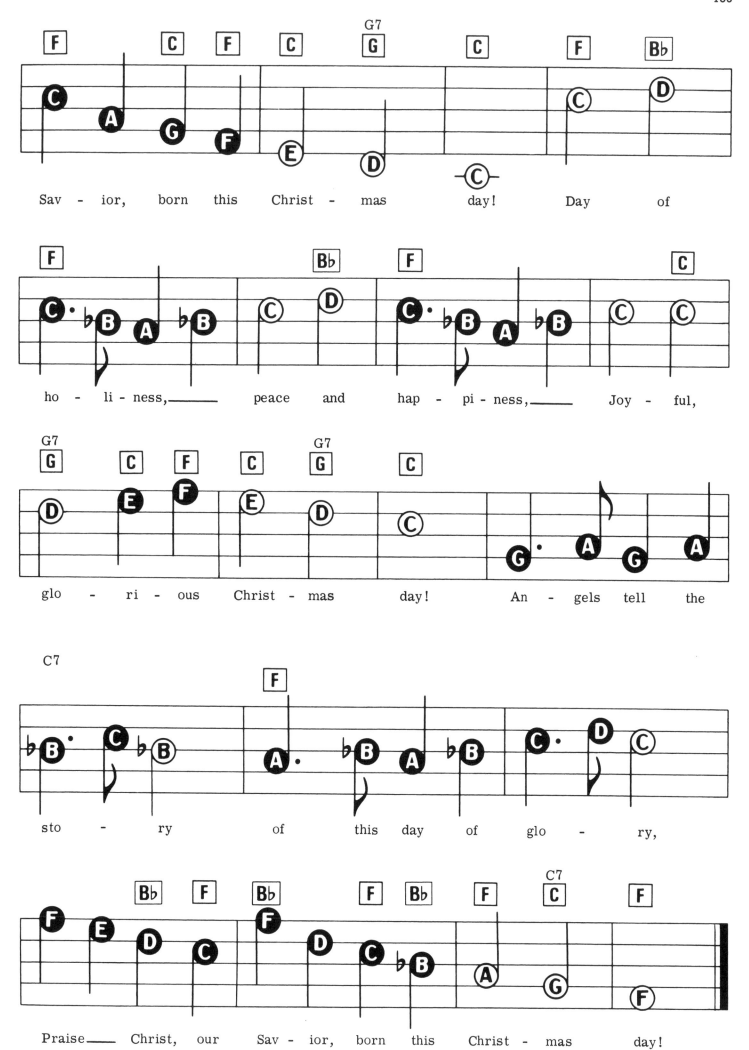

On Christmas Night

Registration 8
Rhythm: Waltz

Sussex Carol

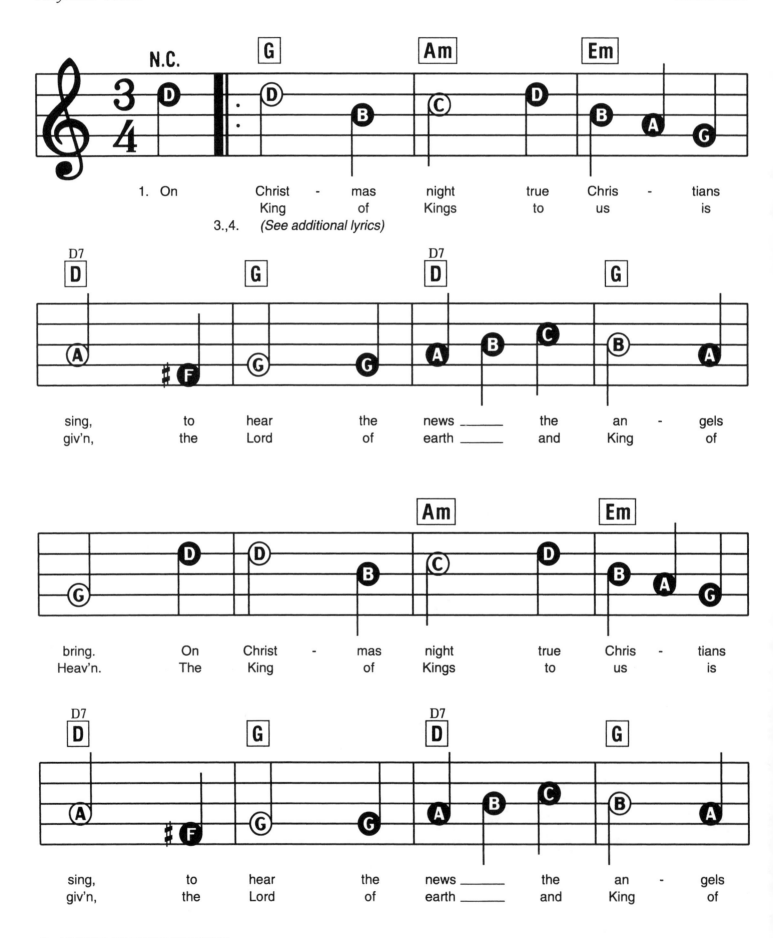

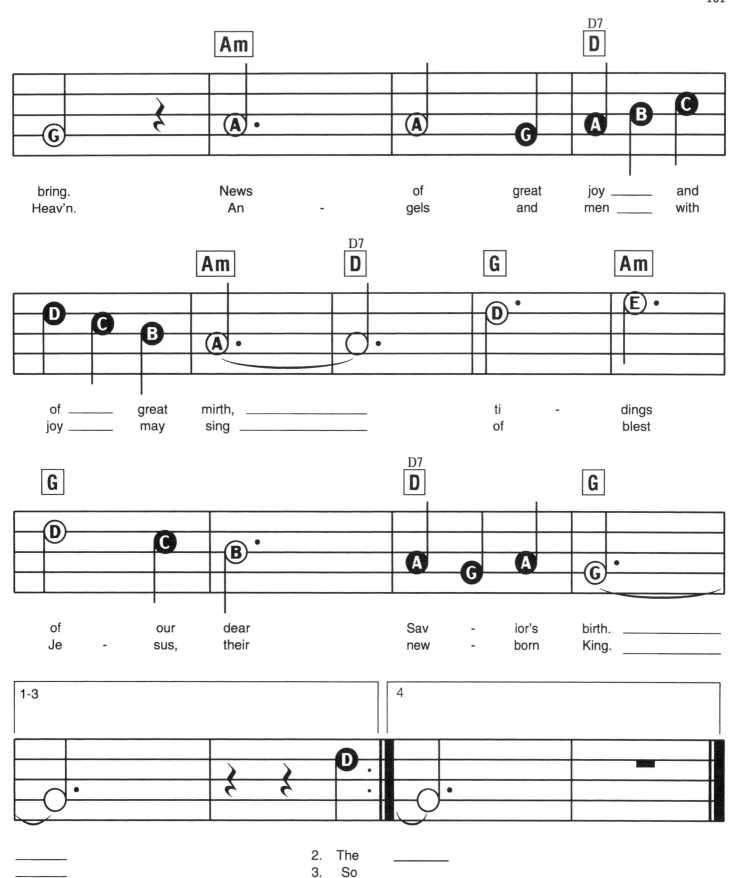

Additional Lyrics

3. So how on earth can men be sad,
When Jesus comes to make us glad?
So how on earth can men be sad,
When Jesus comes to make us glad?
From all our sins to set us free,
Buying for us our liberty.

4. From out the darkness have we light,
Which makes the angels sing this night;
From out the darkness have we light,
Which makes the angels sing this night;
"Glory to God, His peace to men,
And good will, evermore! Amen!"

Once in Royal David's City

Registration 10
Rhythm: Pops

Words by Cecil F. Alexander
Music by Henry J. Gauntlett

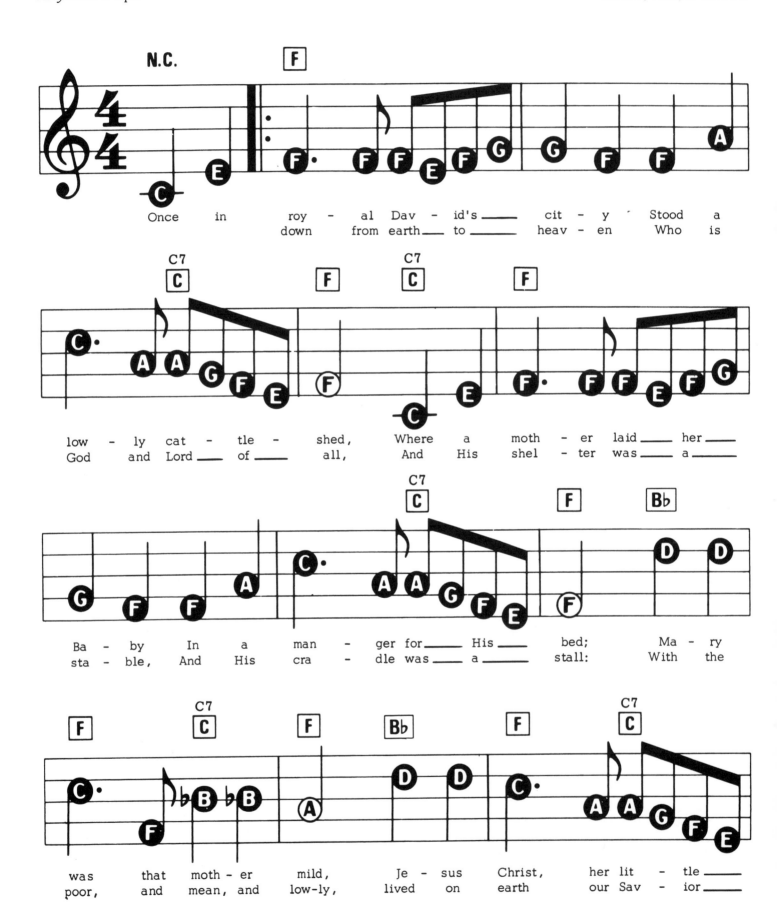

193

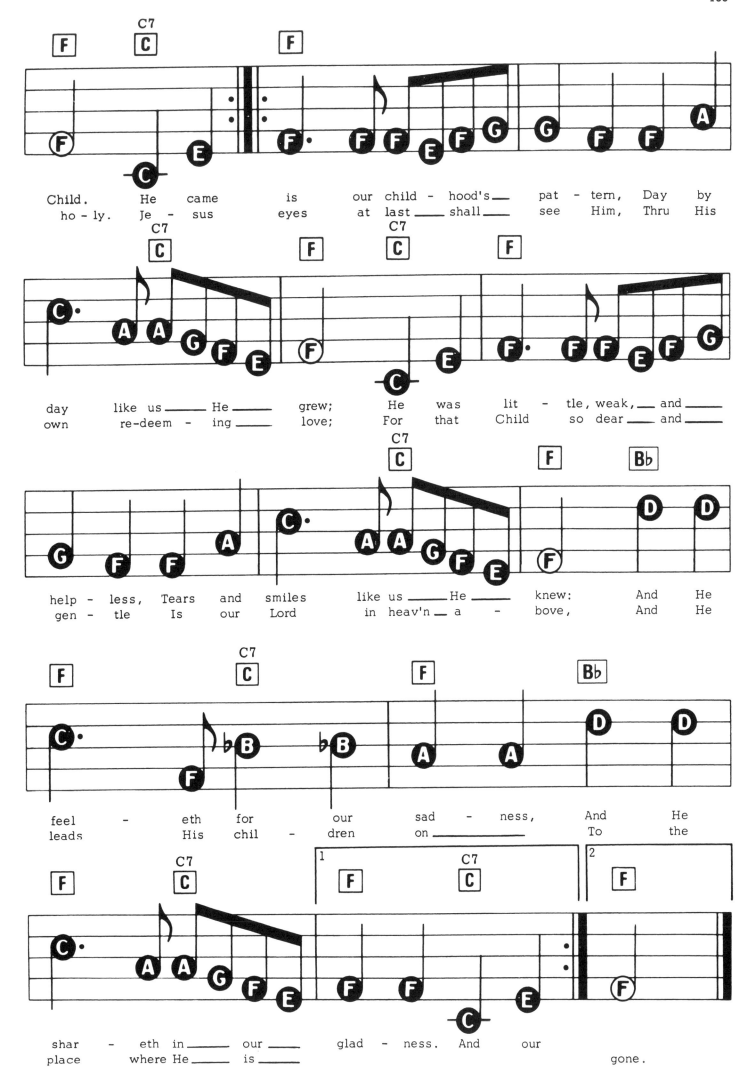

Pat-a-Pan
(Willie, Take Your Little Drum)

Registration 7
Rhythm: March

Words and Music by
Bernard de la Monnoye

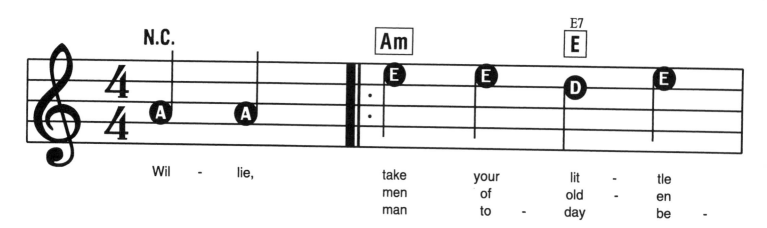

Wil - lie,   take   your   lit - tle
men   of   old - en
man   to - day   be -

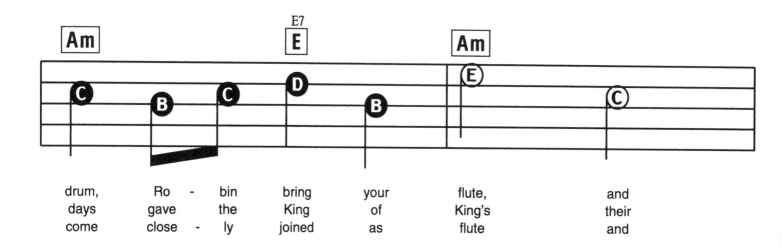

drum,   Ro - bin   bring   your   flute,   and
days   gave   the   King   of   King's   their
come   close - ly   joined   as   flute   and

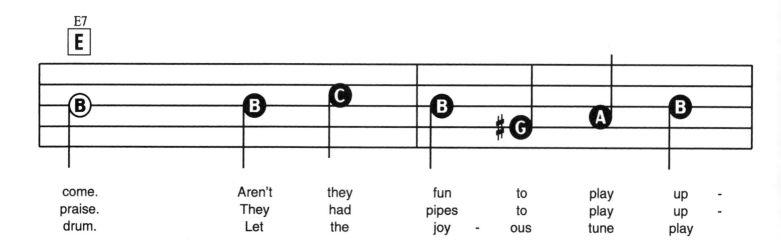

come.   Aren't   they   fun   to   play   up -
praise.   They   had   fun   pipes   to   play   up -
drum.   Let   the   joy - ous   tune   play

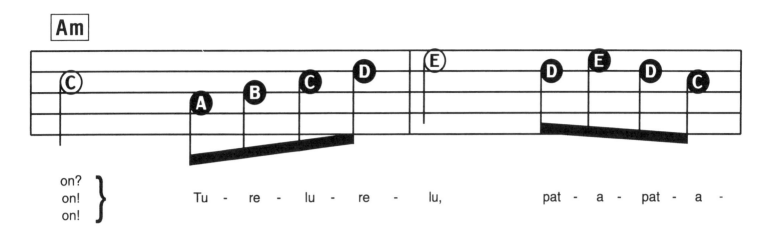

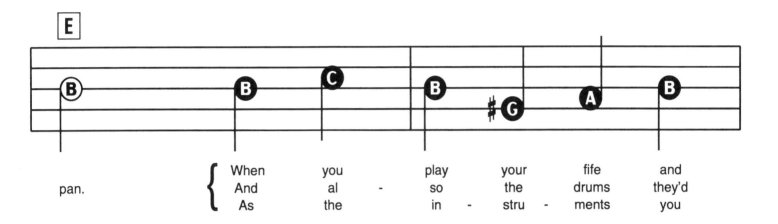

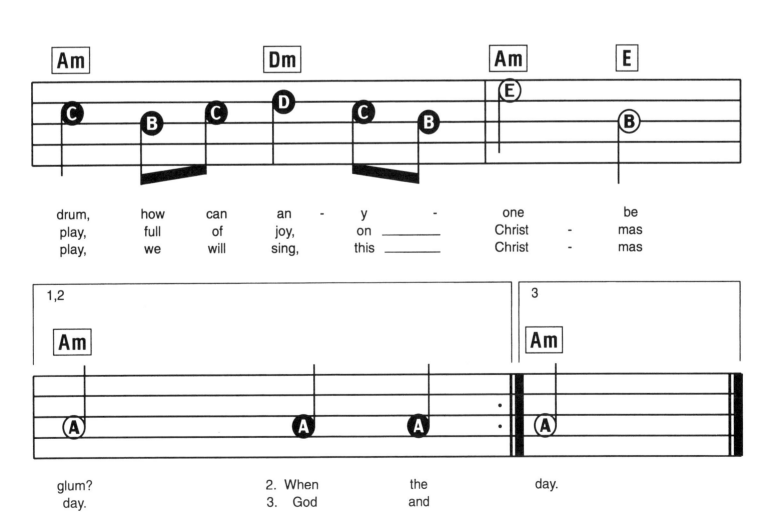

Rejoice and Be Merry

Registration 2
Rhythm: Waltz

Gallery Carol

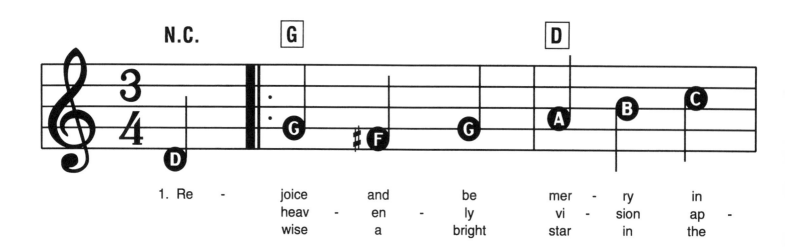

1. Re - joice and be mer - ry in
heav - en - ly vi - sion ap -
wise a bright star in the

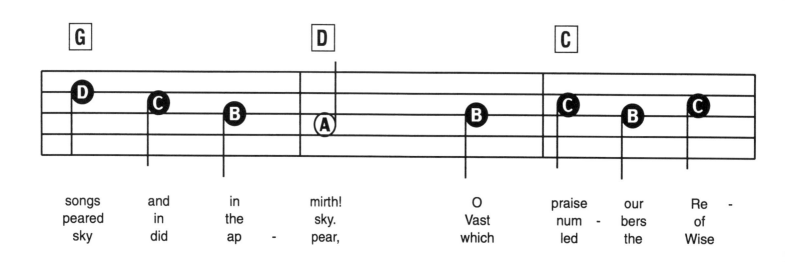

songs and in mirth! O praise our Re -
peared in the sky. Vast num - bers of
sky did ap - pear, which led the Wise

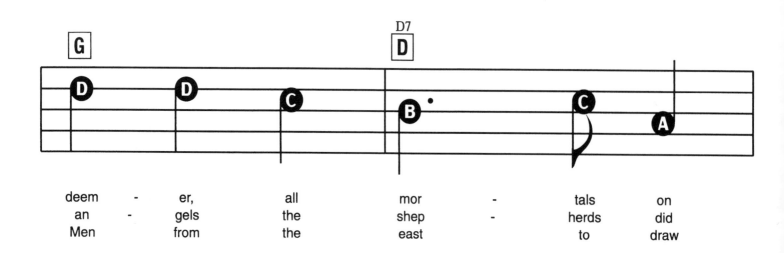

deem - er, all mor - tals on
an - gels from the shep - herds did
Men from the east to draw

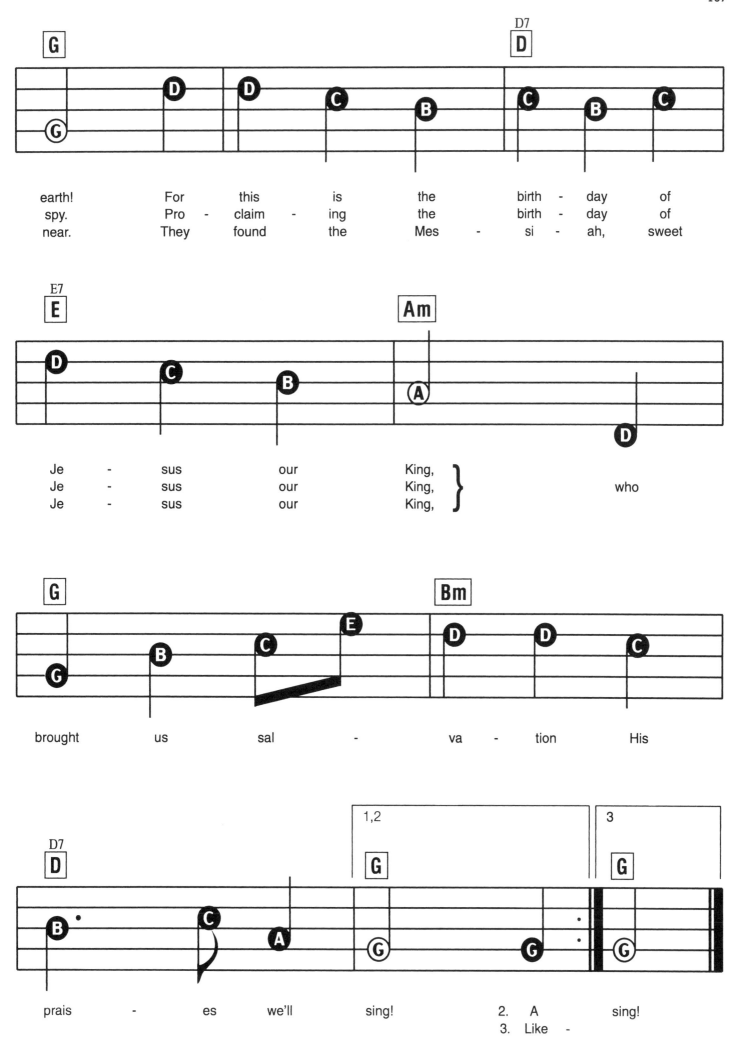

Ring Out, Ye Wild and Merry Bells

Registration 9
Rhythm: Waltz

Words and Music by
C. Maitland

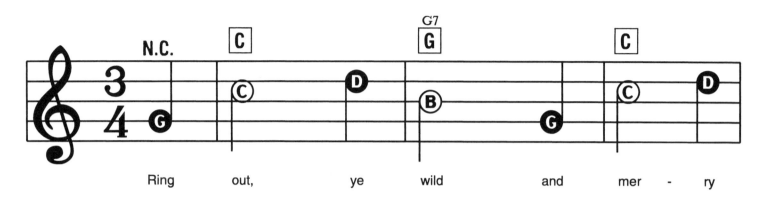

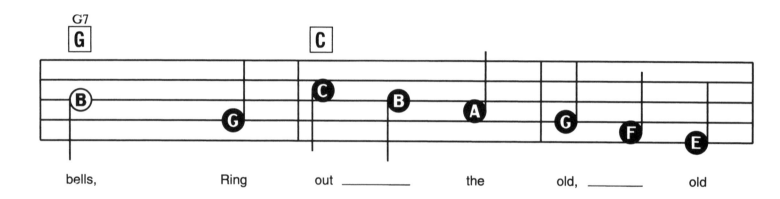

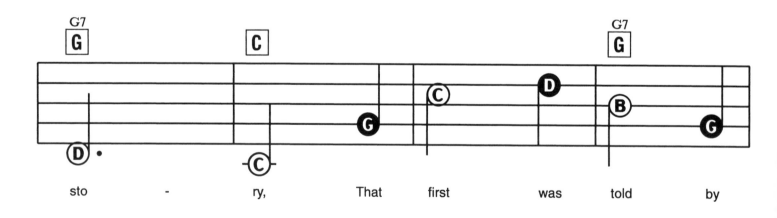

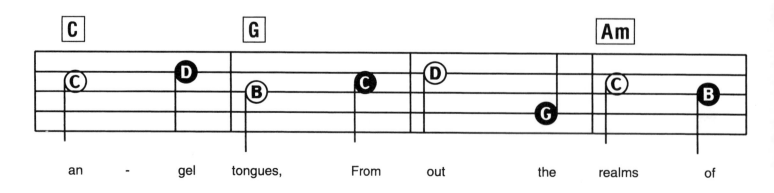

199

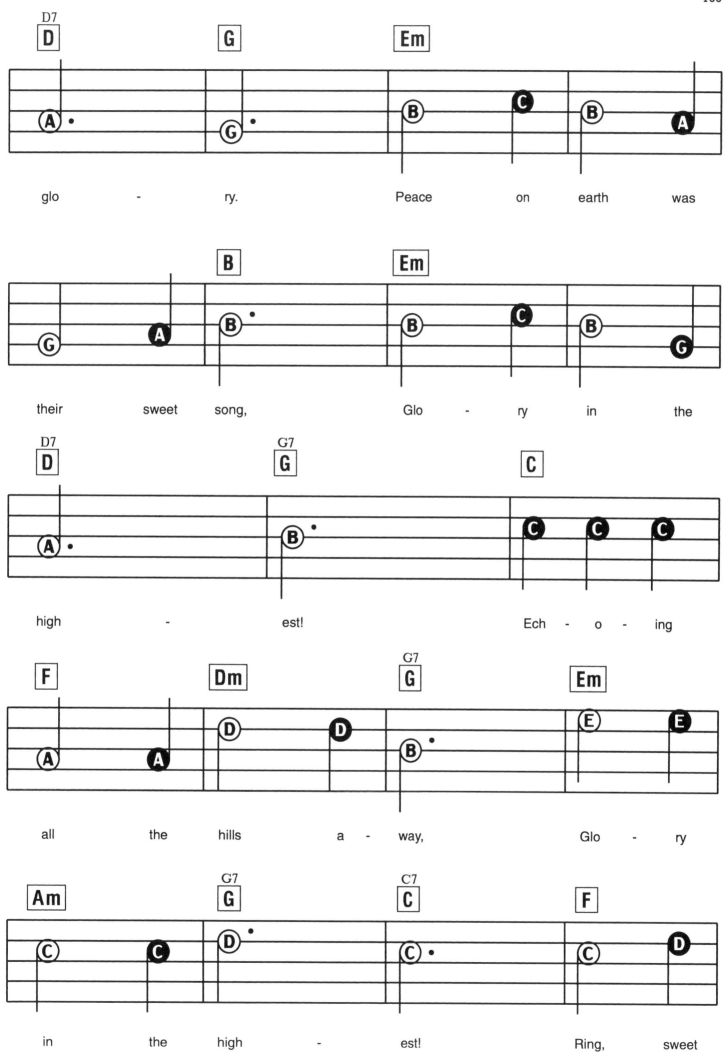

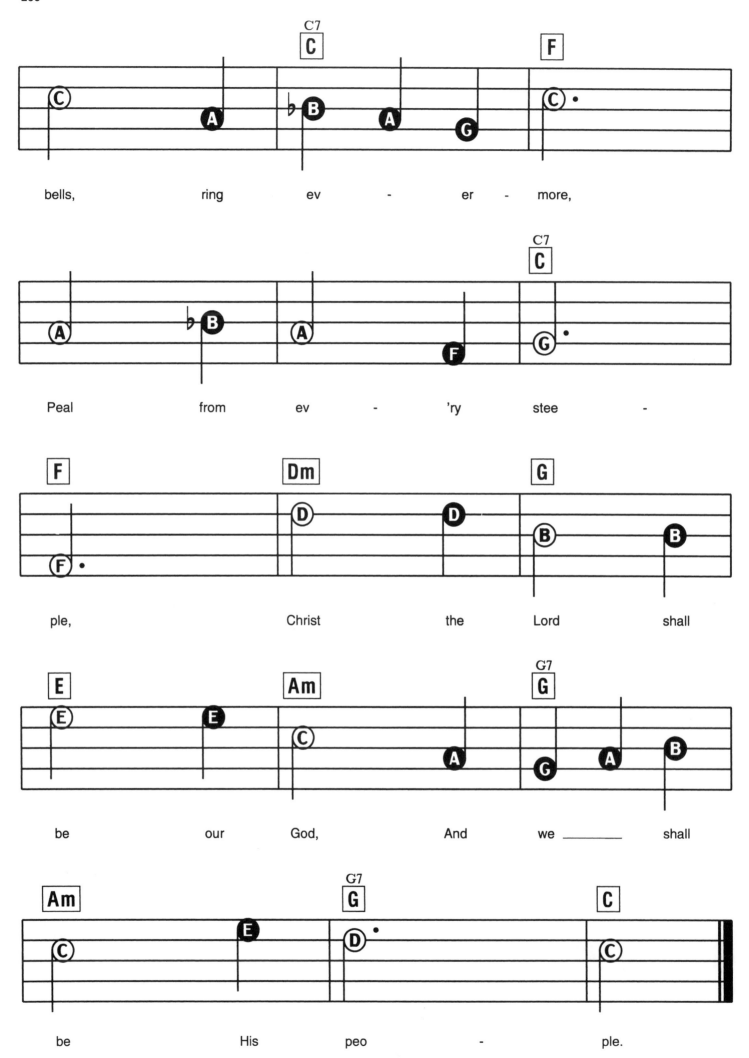

Sing We Now of Christmas

Registration 2
Rhythm: None

Traditional French Carol

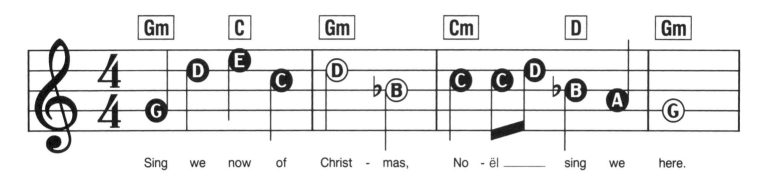

Sing we now of Christ - mas, No - ël ____ sing we here.

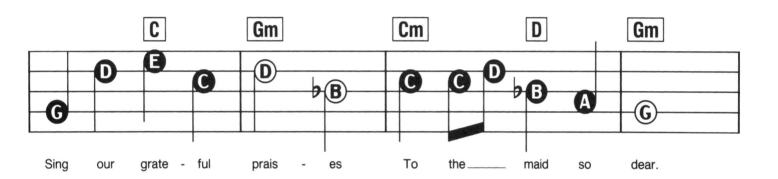

Sing our grate - ful prais - es To the ____ maid so dear.

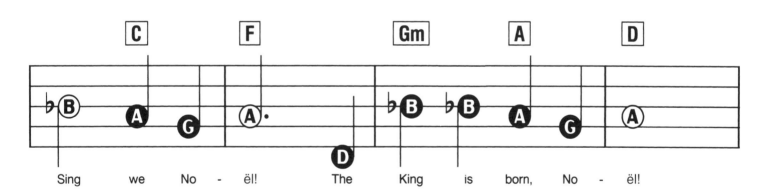

Sing we No - ël! The King is born, No - ël!

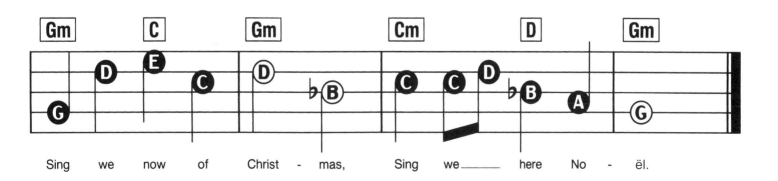

Sing we now of Christ - mas, Sing we ____ here No - ël.

Rise Up, Shepherd, and Follow

Registration 4
Rhythm: March

African-American Spiritual

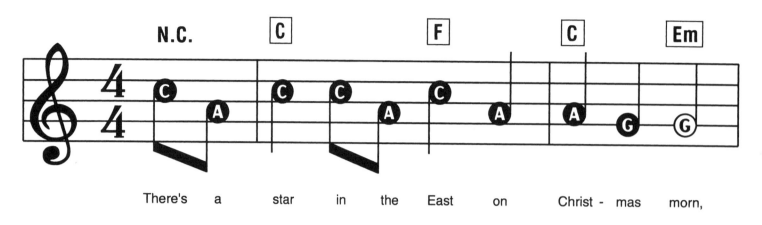

There's a star in the East on Christ - mas morn,

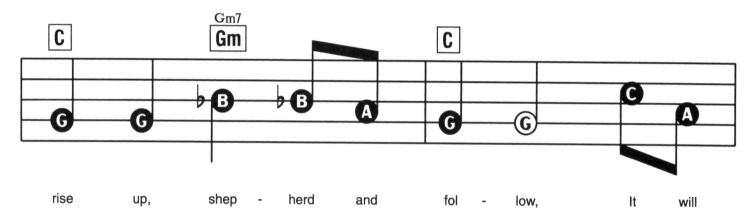

rise up, shep - herd and fol - low, It will

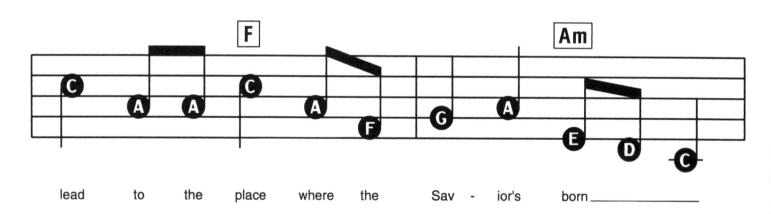

lead to the place where the Sav - ior's born_____

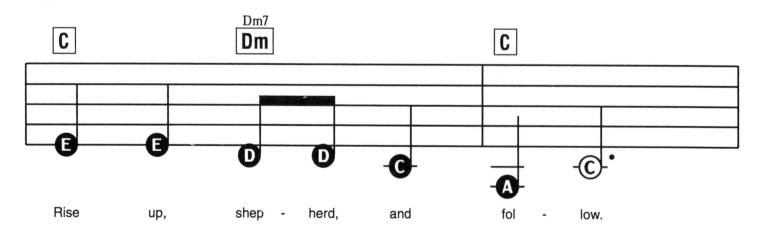

Rise up, shep - herd, and fol - low.

203

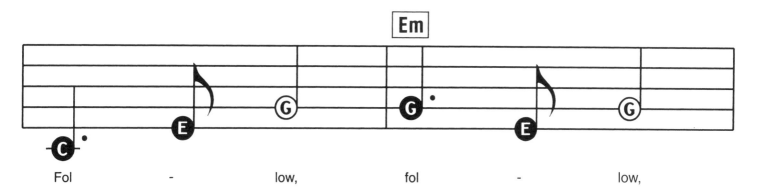

Fol - low, fol - low,

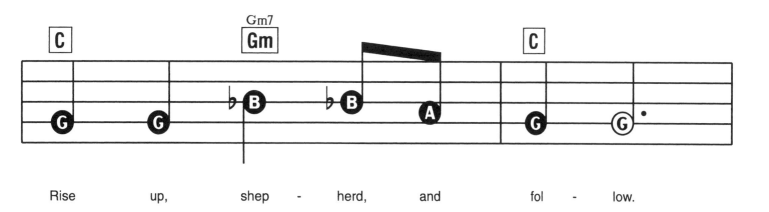

Rise up, shep - herd, and fol - low.

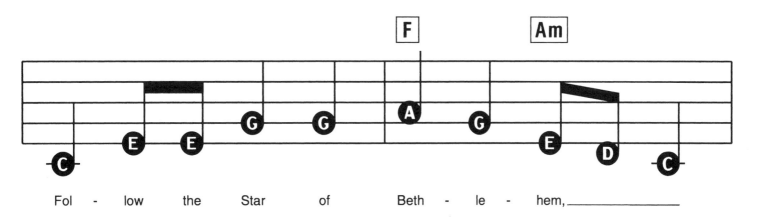

Fol - low the Star of Beth - le - hem,_____

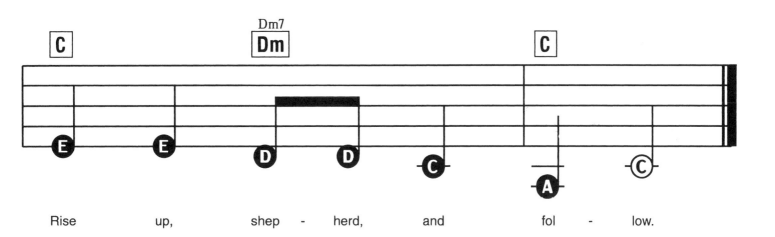

Rise up, shep - herd, and fol - low.

Shepherds' Cradle Song

Registration 3
Rhythm: Waltz

Words and Music by
C.D. Schubert

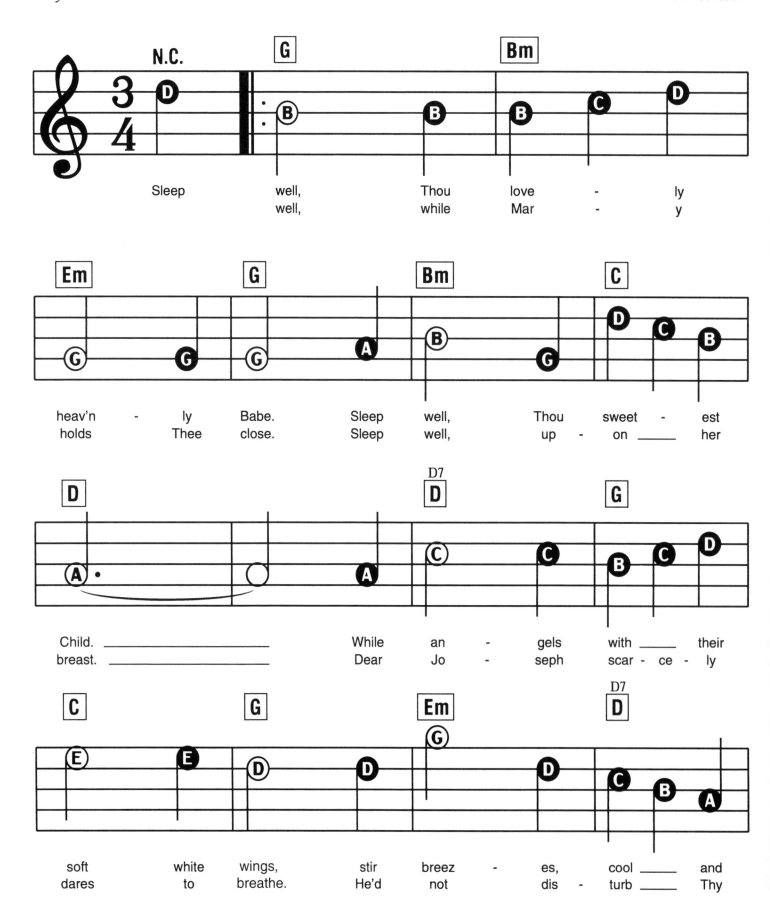

205

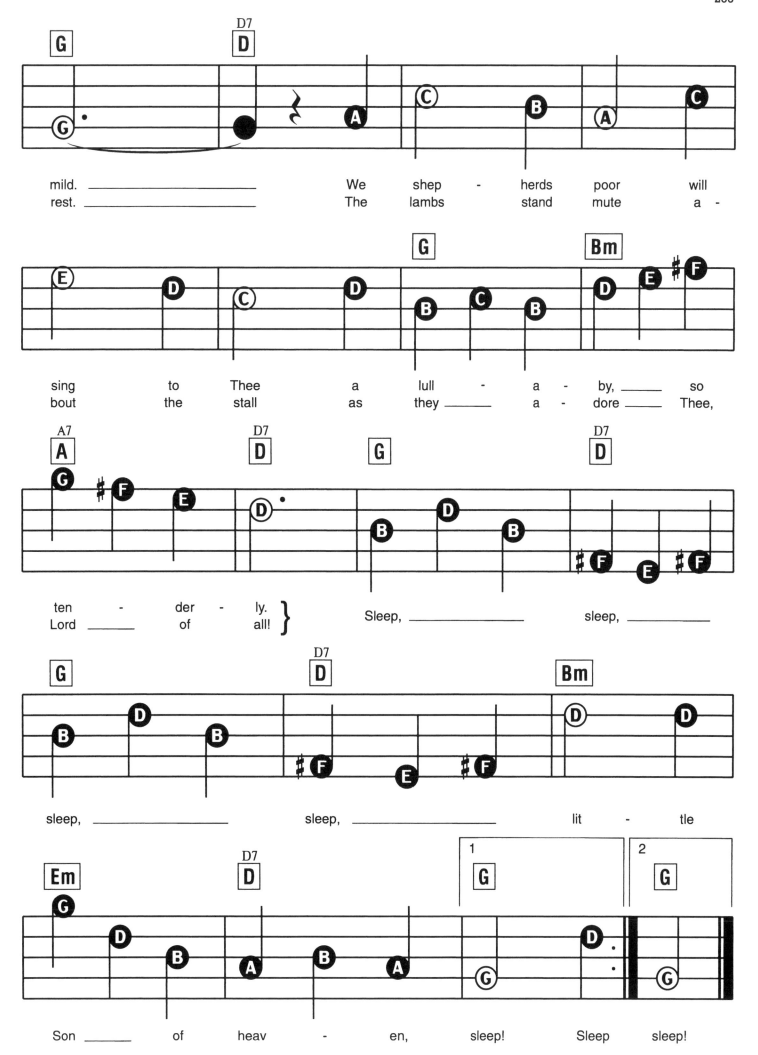

Shepherds, Shake Off
Your Drowsy Sleep

Registration 4
Rhythm: None

Traditional French Carol

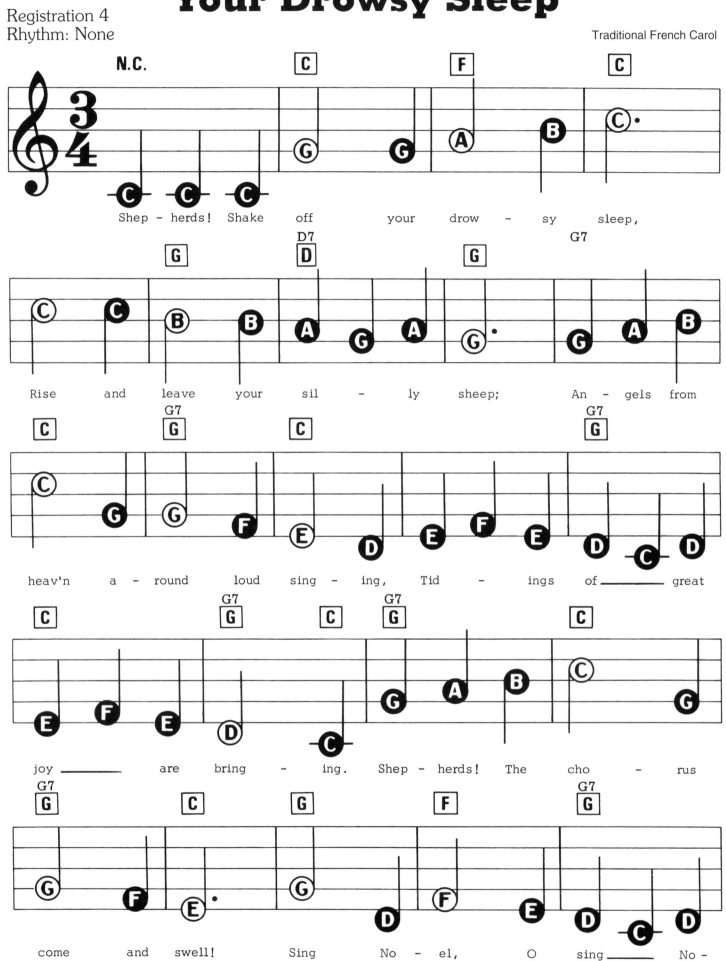

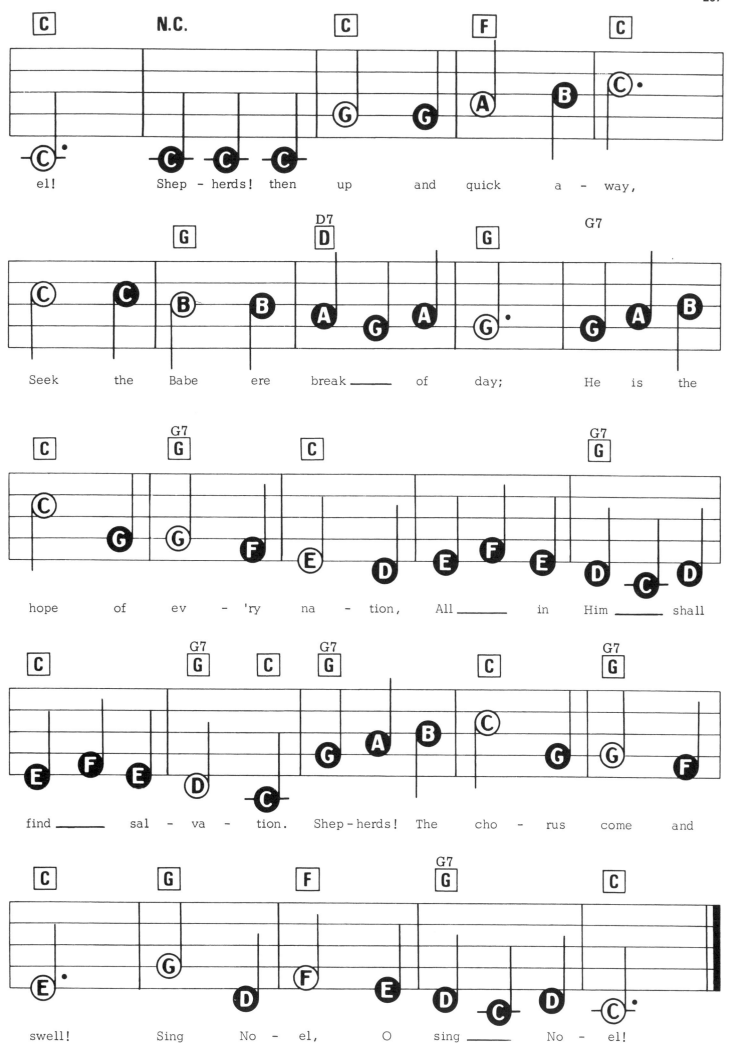

Shout the Glad Tidings

Registration 9
Rhythm: Waltz

Traditional

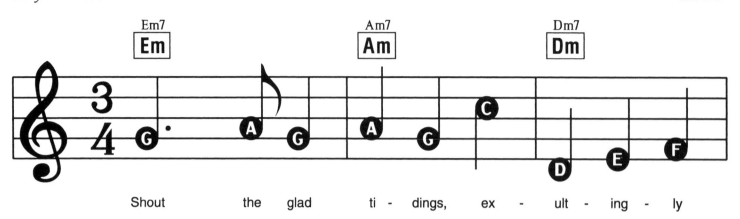

Shout   the   glad   ti - dings,   ex - ult - ing - ly

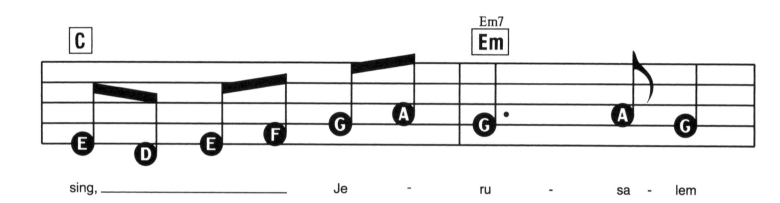

sing, _____ Je - ru - sa - lem

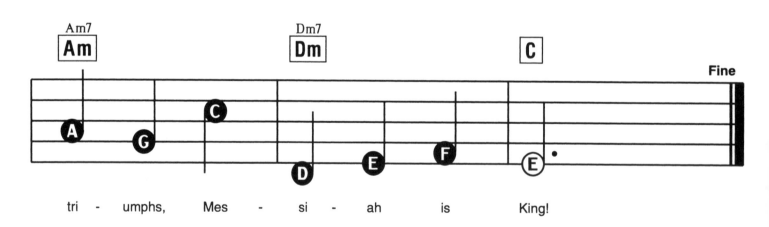

tri - umphs,   Mes - si - ah   is   King!

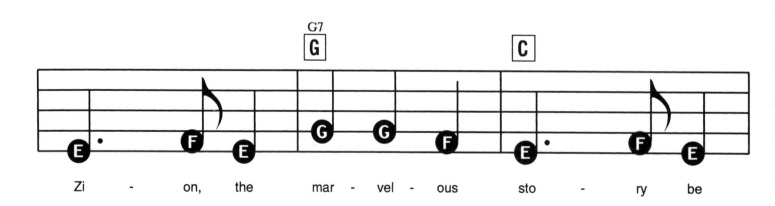

Zi - on,   the   mar - vel - ous   sto - ry   be

209

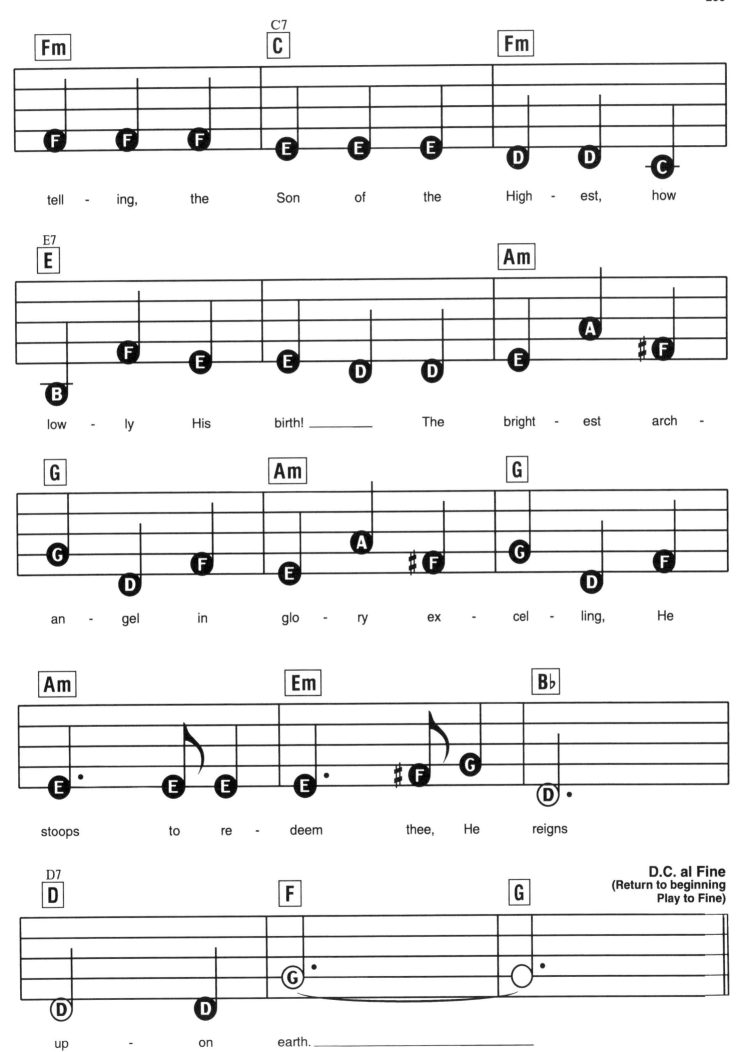

Silent Night

Registration 1
Rhythm: Waltz

Words by Joseph Mohr
Translated by John F. Young
Music by Franz X. Grüber

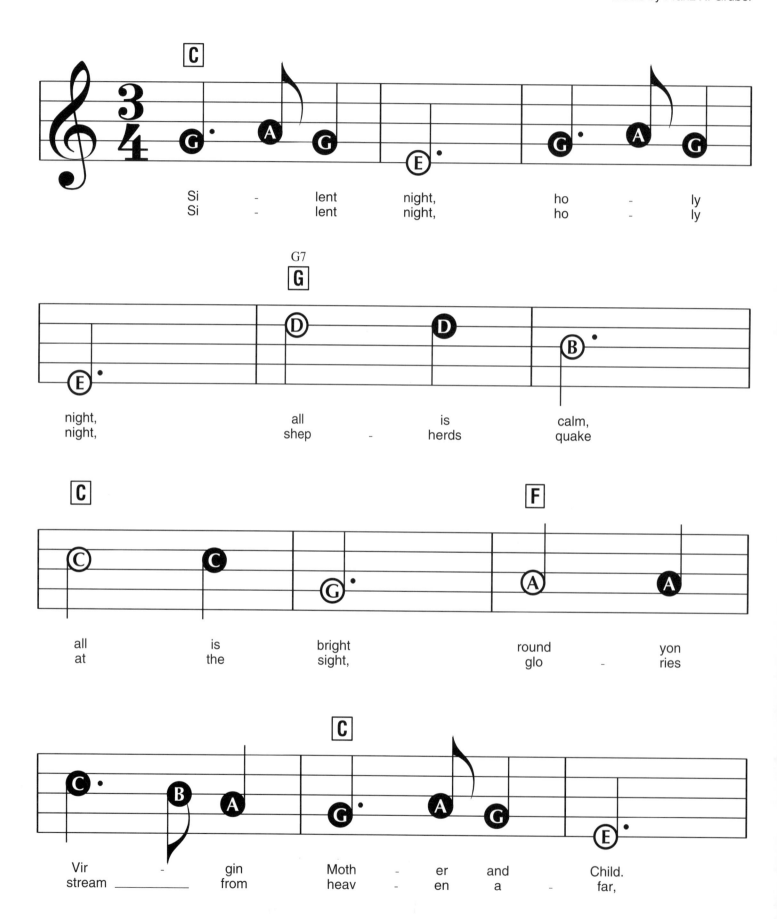

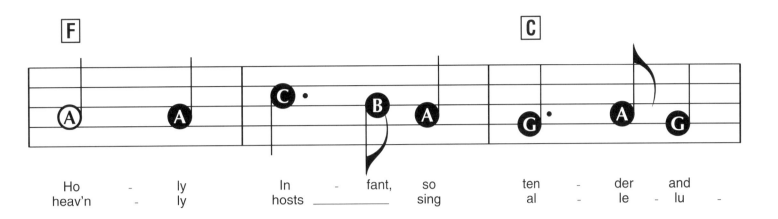

Ho - ly In - fant, so ten - der and
heav'n - ly hosts _____ sing al - le - lu -

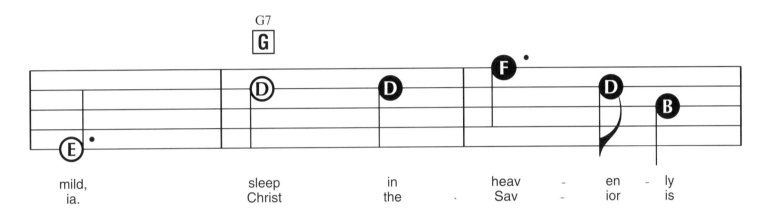

mild, sleep in heav - en - ly
ia. Christ in the Sav - ior is

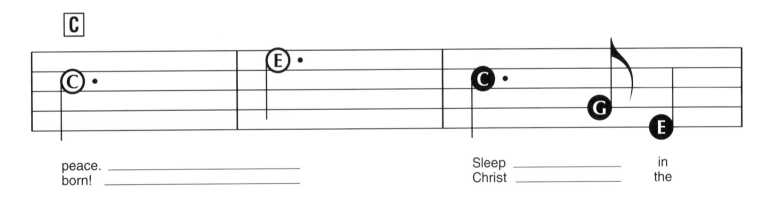

peace. _____
born! _____ Sleep _____ in
Christ _____ the

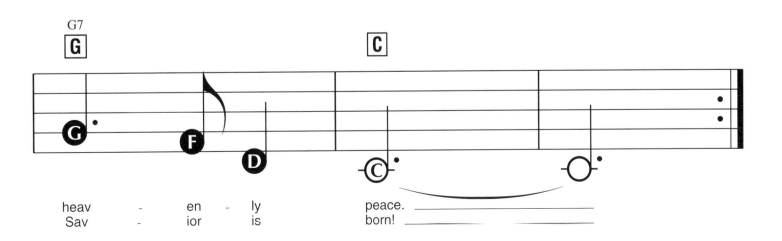

heav - en - ly peace. _____
Sav - ior is born! _____

The Simple Birth

Registration 3
Rhythm: Waltz

Traditional Flemish Carol

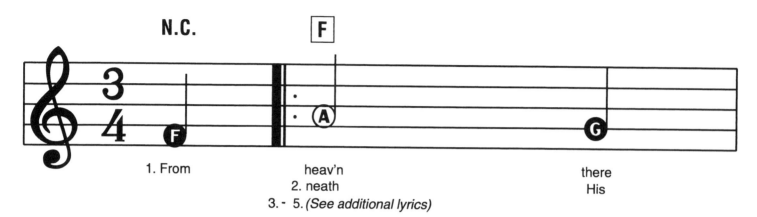

1. From heav'n there
2. neath His
3. - 5. *(See additional lyrics)*

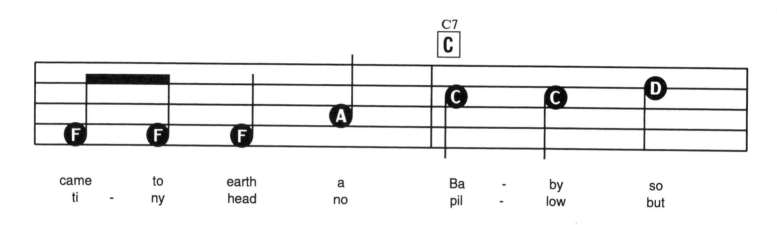

came to earth a Ba - by so
ti - ny head a no pil - low so

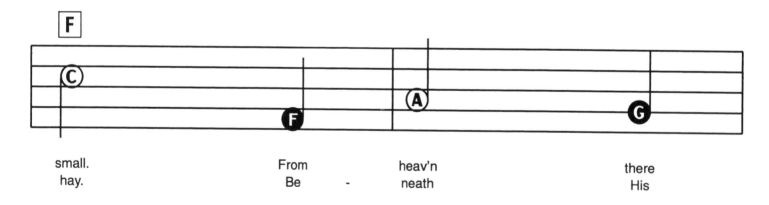

small. From heav'n there
hay. Be - neath His

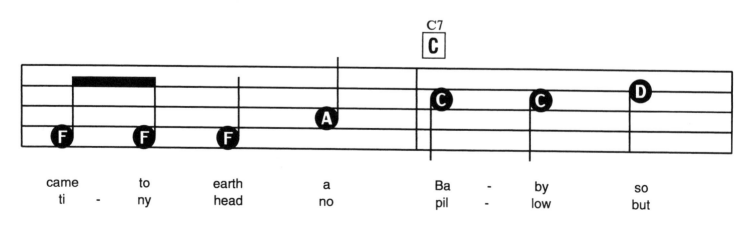

came to earth a Ba - by so
ti - ny head a no pil - low but

213

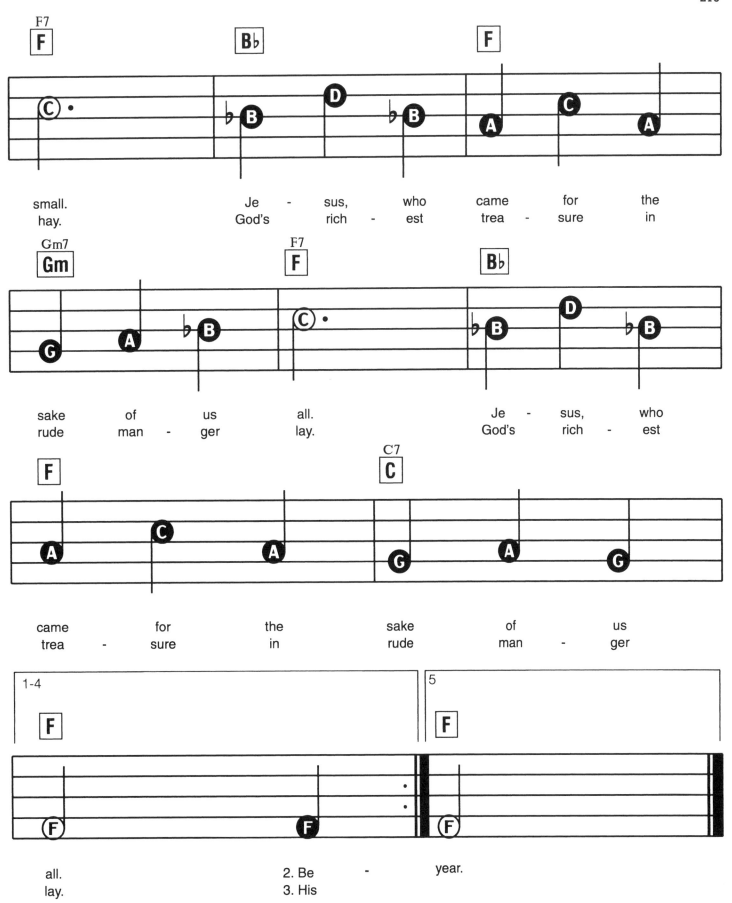

small.
hay.

Je - sus, who came for the
God's rich - est trea - sure in

sake of us all.
rude man - ger lay.

Je - sus, who
God's rich - est

came for the sake of us
trea - sure in rude man - ger

all.
lay.

2. Be - year.
3. His

Additional Lyrics

3. His eyes of blackest jet were sparkling with light,
   Rosy cheeks bloomed on His face fair and bright.

4. And from His lovely mouth, the laughter did swell,
   When He saw Mary, whom He loved so well.

5. He came to weary earth, so dark and so drear,
   To wish to mankind a blessed New Year.

Sing, O Sing, This Blessed Morn

Registration 6
Rhythm: None

Words by Christopher Wordsworth
Traditional German Tune

1. Sing, O sing, this bless - ed morn,
2. God with us, Im - man - u - el,
3.,4. *(See additional lyrics)*

un - to us _____ a Child is born.
deigns for ev - er now to dwell.

Un - to us a Son is _____ giv'n,
And on Ad - am's fall - en _____ race,

God Him - self comes down from heav'n. }
sheds the full - ness of His grace. }

215

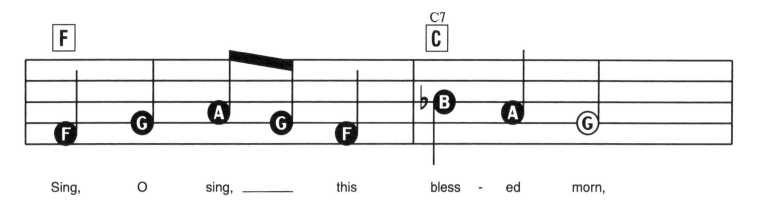

Sing, O sing, _____ this bless - ed morn,

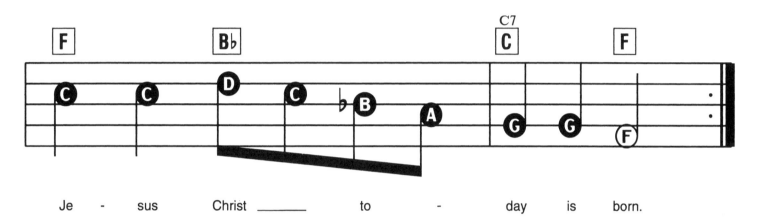

Je - sus Christ _____ to - day is born.

Additional Lyrics

3. God comes down that man may rise,
   Lifted by Him to the skies;
   Christ is Son of Man that we
   Sons of God in Him may be:
   Chorus

4. O renew us, Lord, we pray,
   With Thy spirit day by day;
   That we ever one may be
   With the Father and with Thee:
   Chorus

Sleep, Holy Babe

Registration 3
Rhythm: None

Words by Edward Caswell
Music by J.B. Dykes

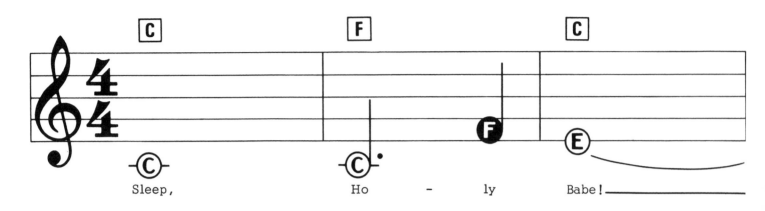

Sleep, Ho - ly Babe! _____

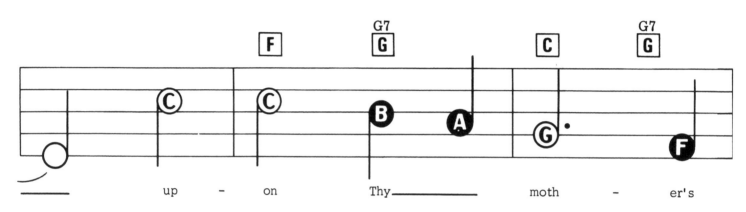

___ up - on Thy _____ moth - er's

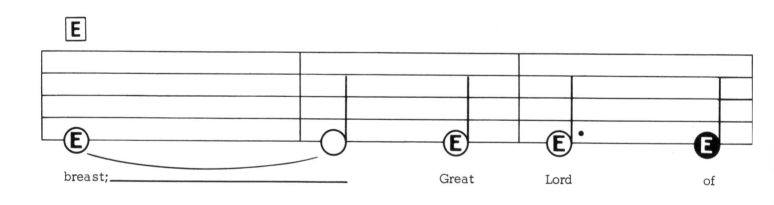

breast; _____ Great Lord of

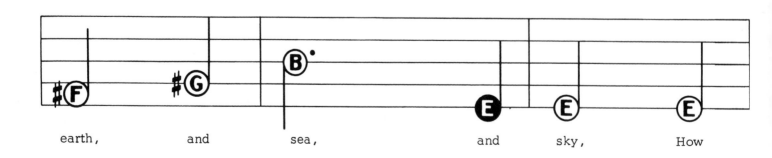

earth, and sea, and sky, How

217

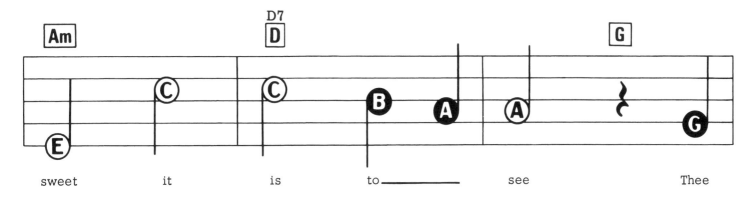

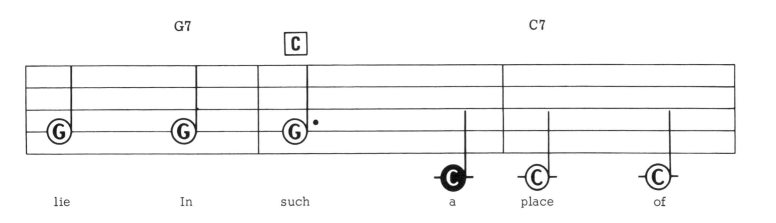

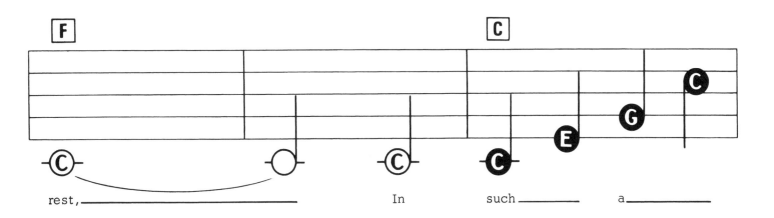

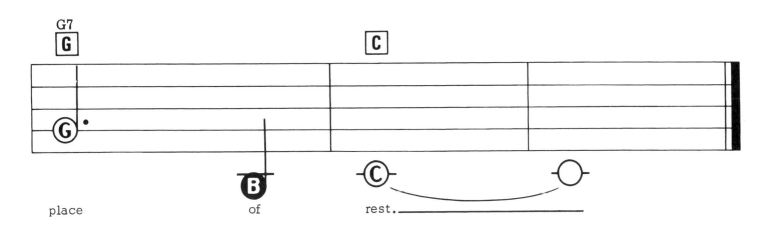

Sleep, O Sleep, My Lovely Child

Registration 2
Rhythm: None

Traditional Italian Carol

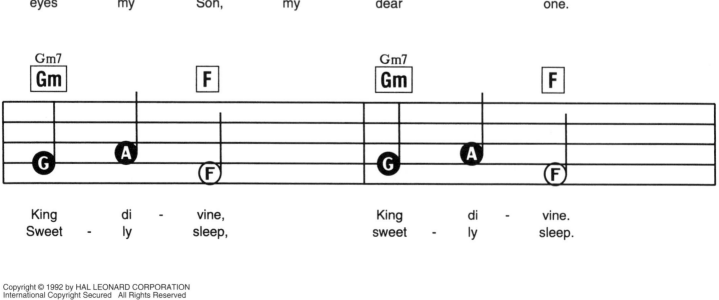

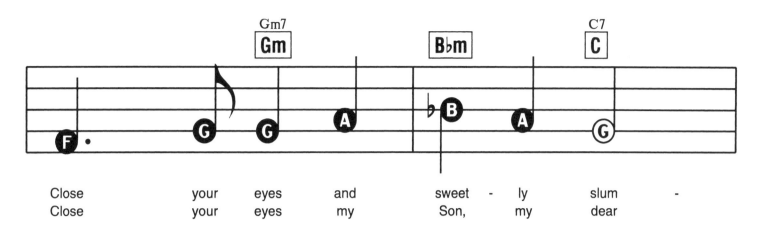

Close   your   eyes   and   sweet -   ly   slum -
Close   your   eyes   my   Son,   my   dear

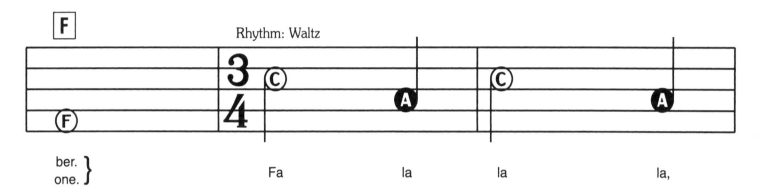

Rhythm: Waltz

ber. }
one. }   Fa   la   la   la,

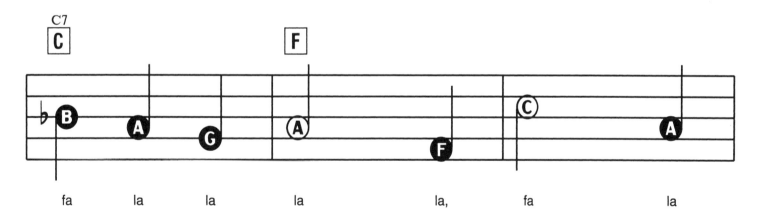

fa   la   la   la   la,   fa   la

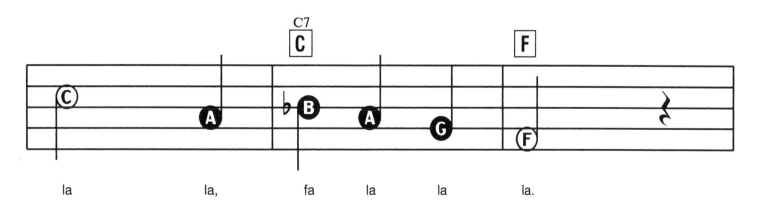

la   la,   fa   la   la   la.

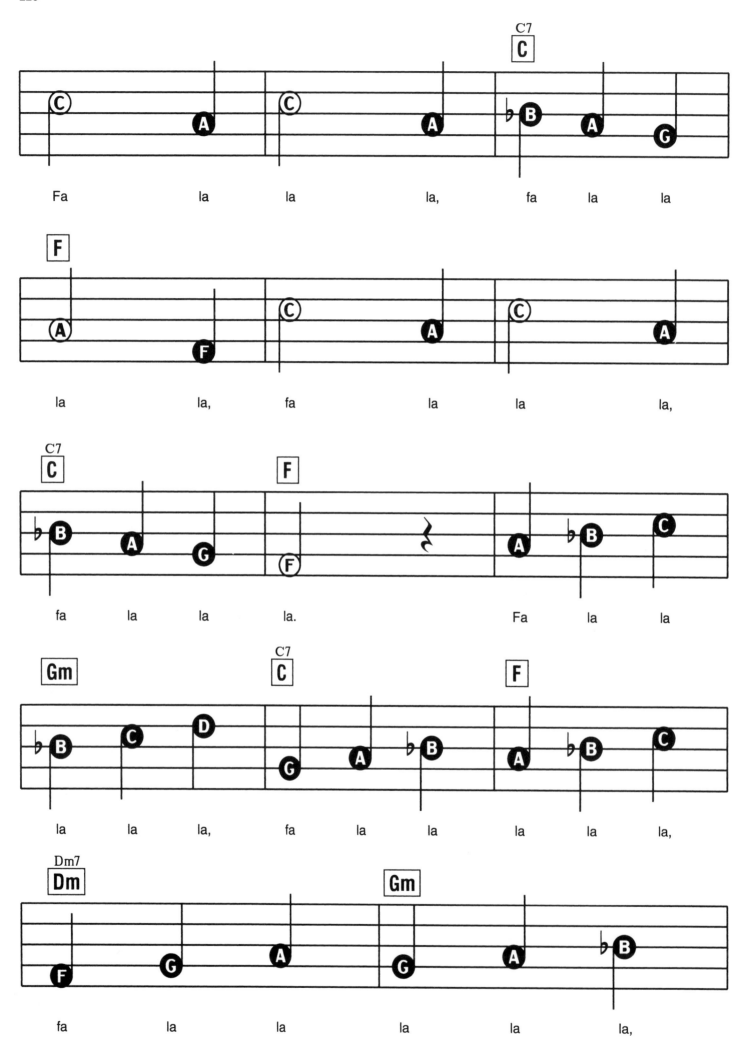

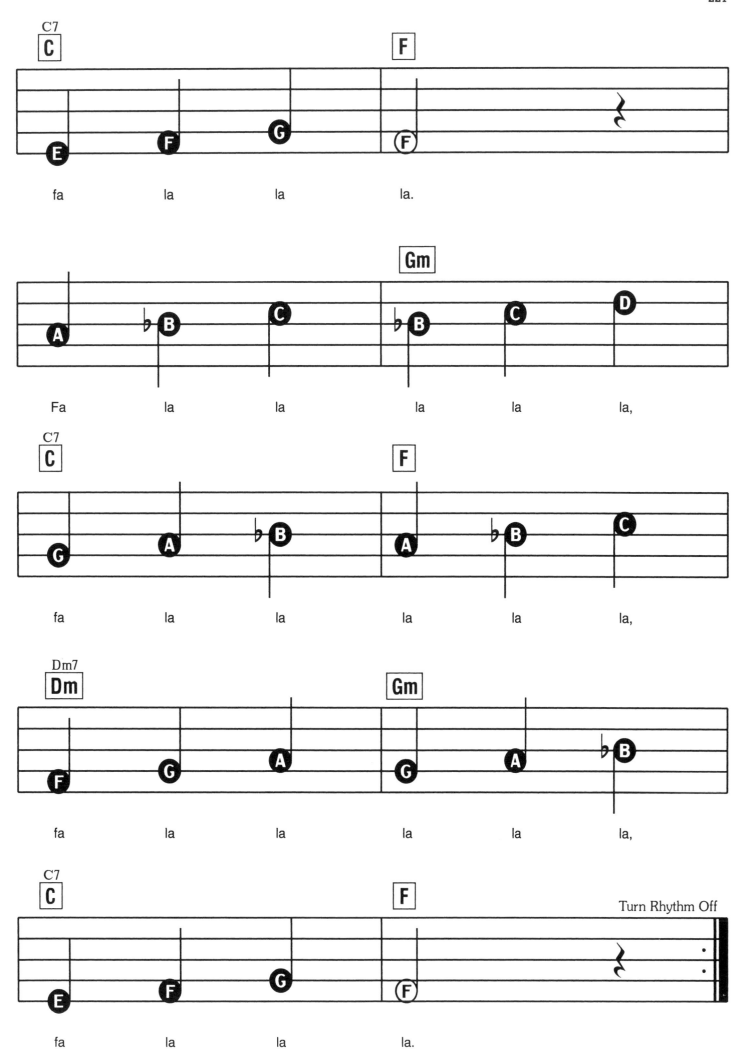

The Snow Lay on the Ground

Registration 9
Rhythm: March

Traditional Irish Carol

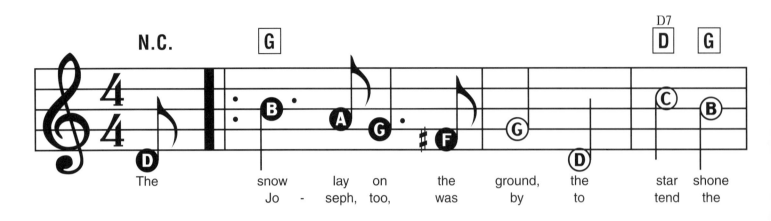

The | snow lay on the ground, the | star shone
Jo - seph, too, was by to | tend the

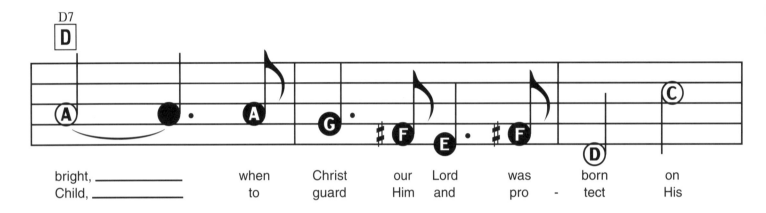

bright, _____ when Christ our Lord was born on
Child, _____ to guard Him and was pro - tect on His

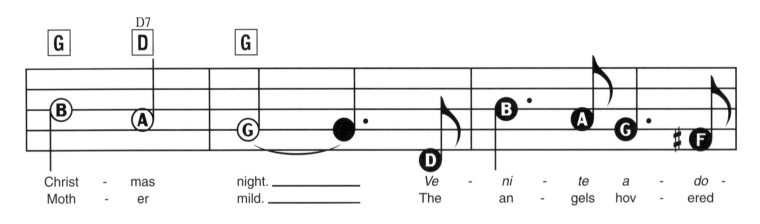

Christ - mas night. _____ Ve - ni - te a - do -
Moth - er mild. _____ The an - gels hov - ered

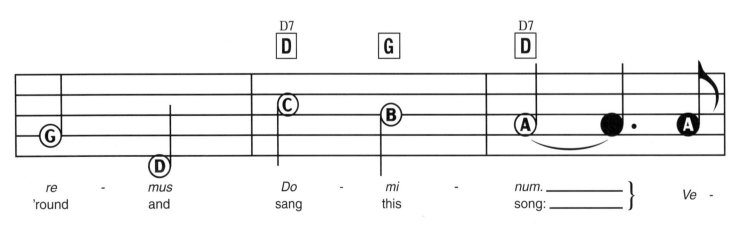

re - mus and Do - mi - num. _____ } Ve -
'round and sang this song: _____

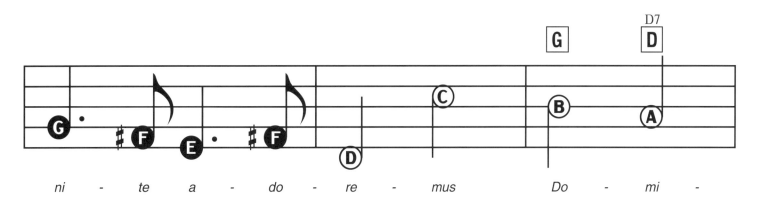

ni - te a - do - re - mus Do - mi -

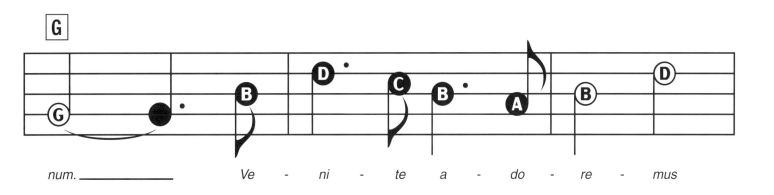

num. _____ Ve - ni - te a - do - re - mus

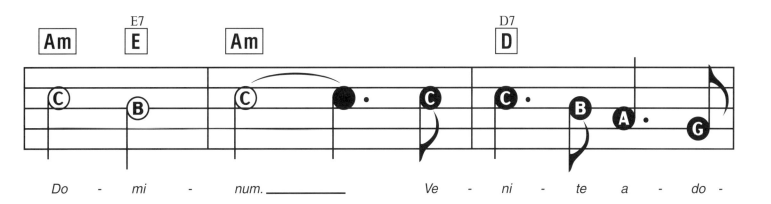

Do - mi - num. _____ Ve - ni - te a - do -

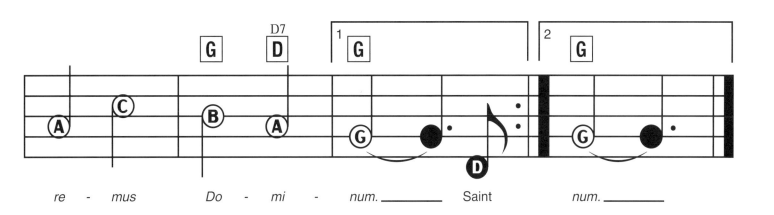

re - mus Do - mi - num. _____ Saint num. _____

The Star of Christmas Morning

Registration 9
Rhythm: Waltz

Traditional

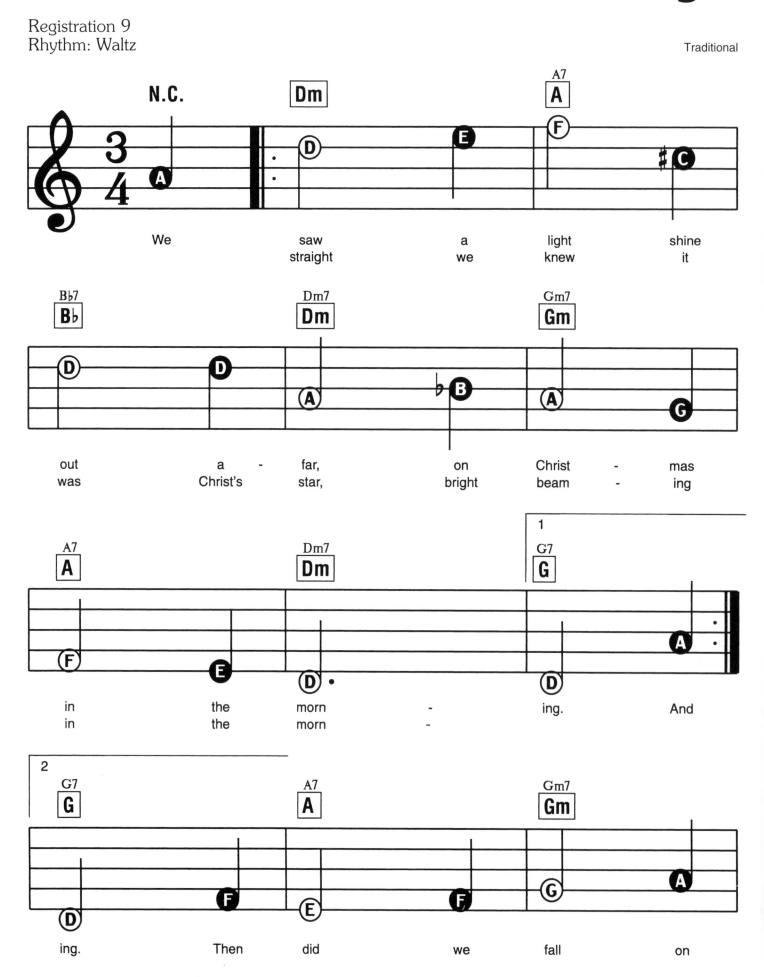

225

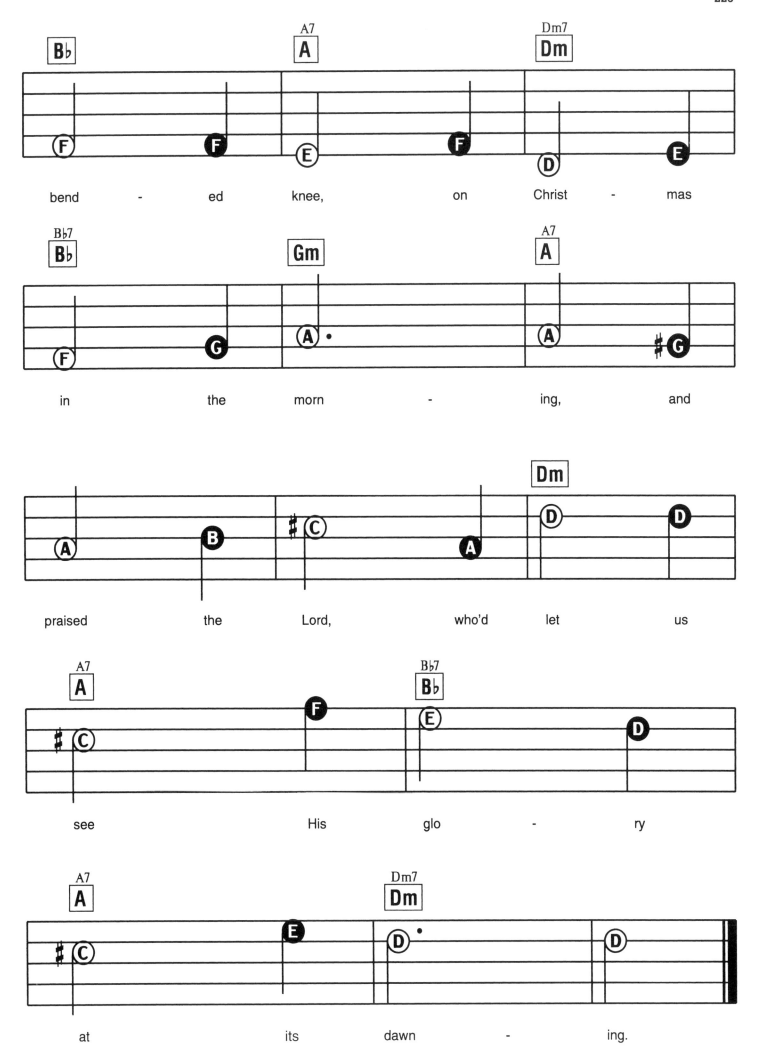

Star of the East

Registration 9
Rhythm: Waltz

Words by George Cooper
Music by Amanda Kennedy

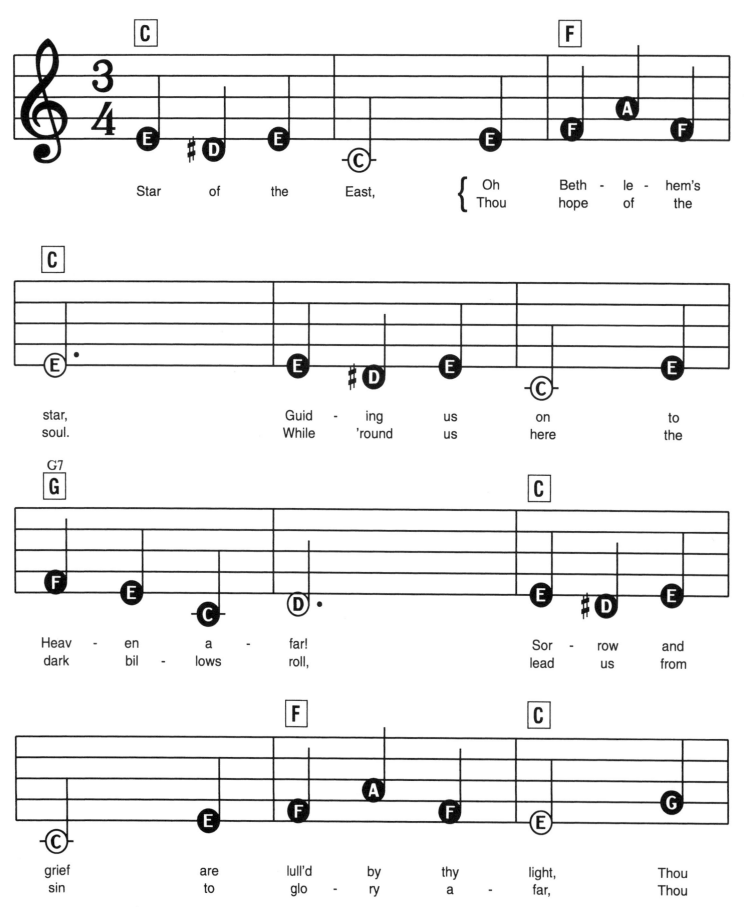

227

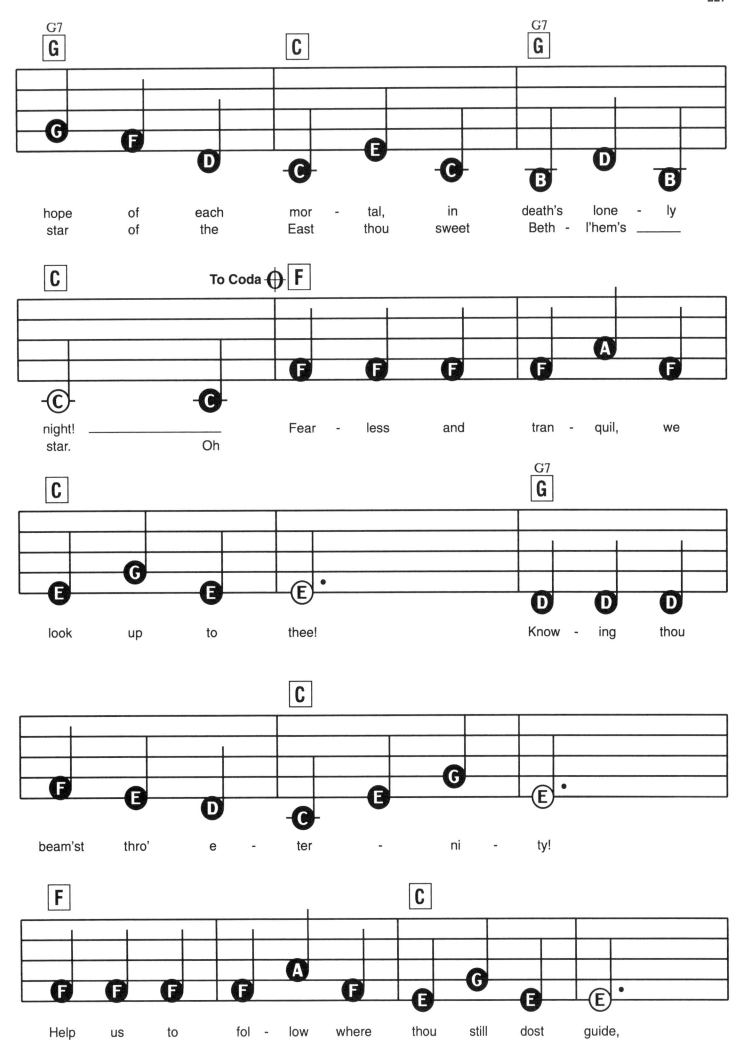

228

D.C. al Coda
(Return to beginning
Play to ✣ and
Skip to Coda)

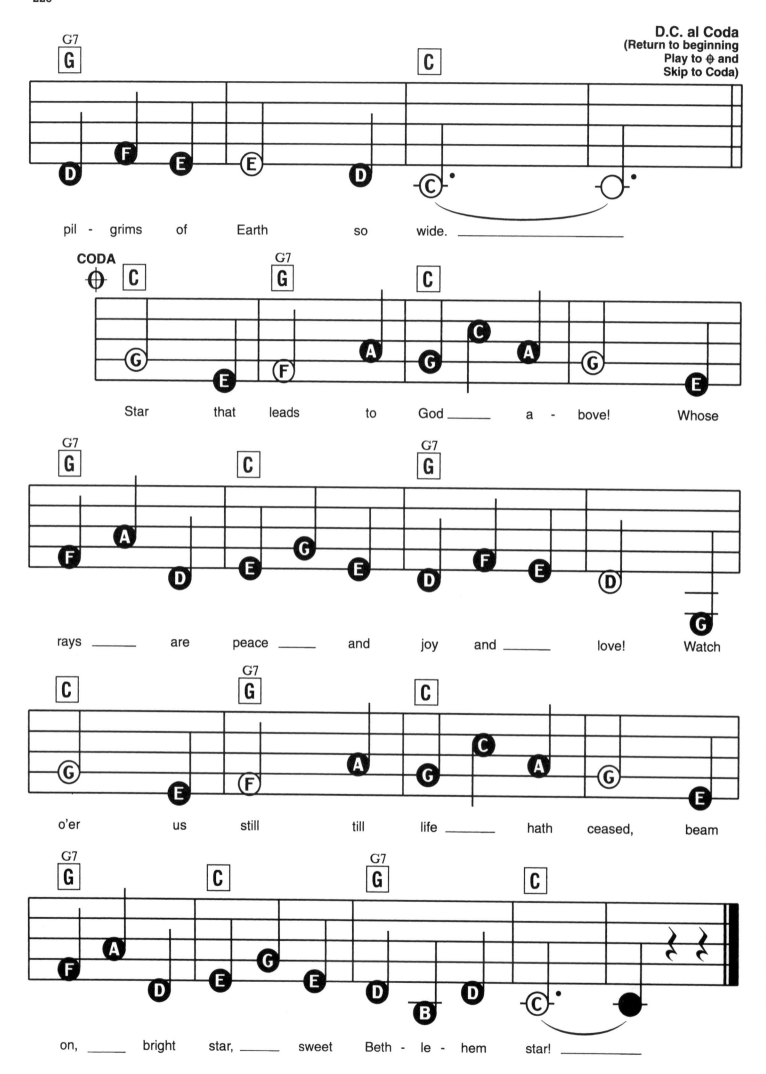

Still, Still, Still

Registration 5
Rhythm: None

Salzburg Melody, c.1819
Traditional Austrian Text

There's a Song in the Air

Registration 9
Rhythm: Waltz

Words and Music by Josiah G. Holland
and Karl P. Harrington

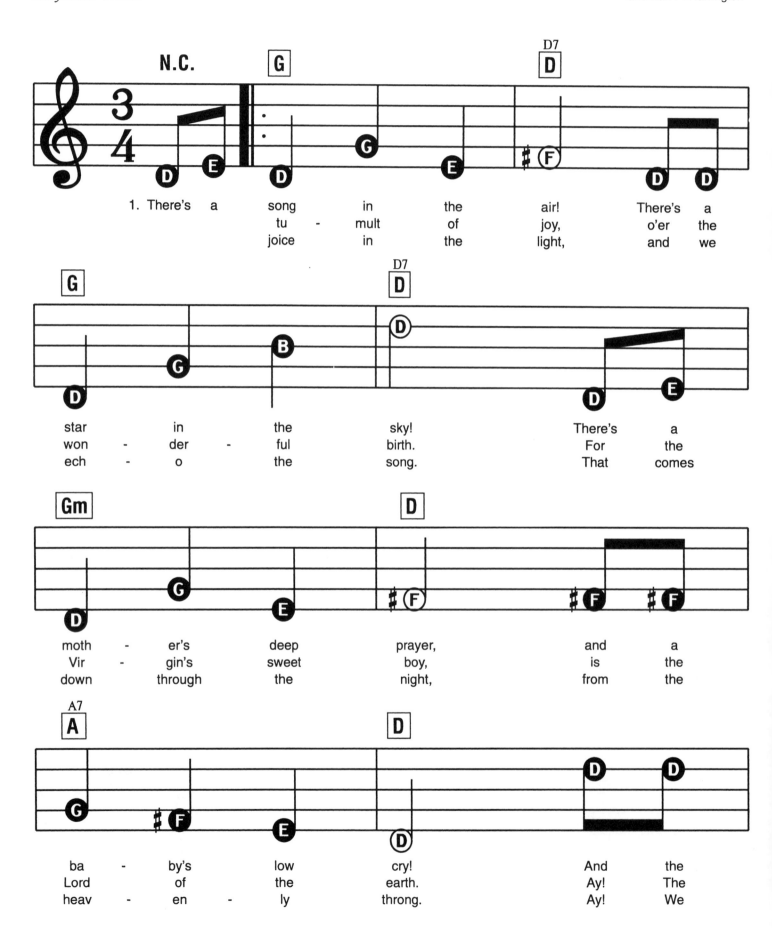

231

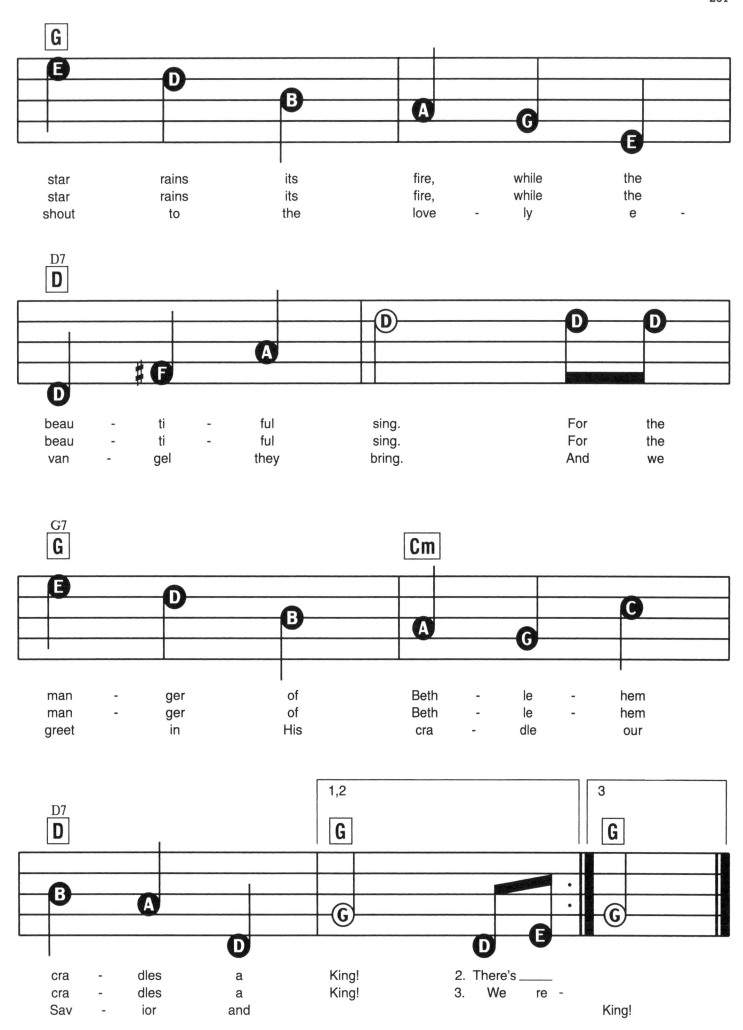

Toyland
from BABES IN TOYLAND

Registration 4
Rhythm: Waltz

Words by Glen MacDonough
Music by Victor Herbert

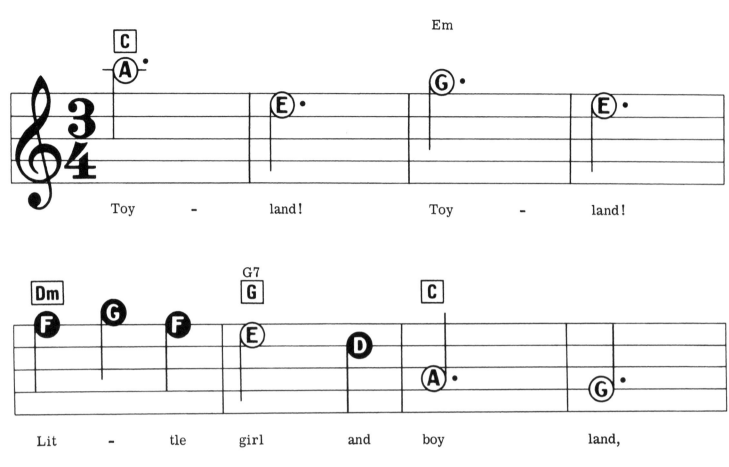

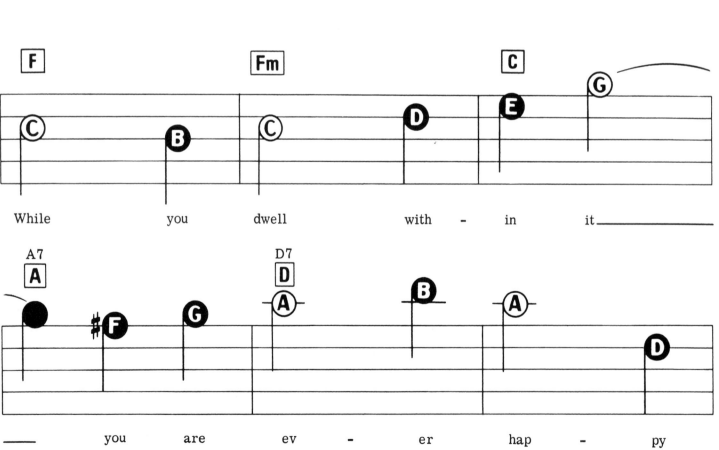

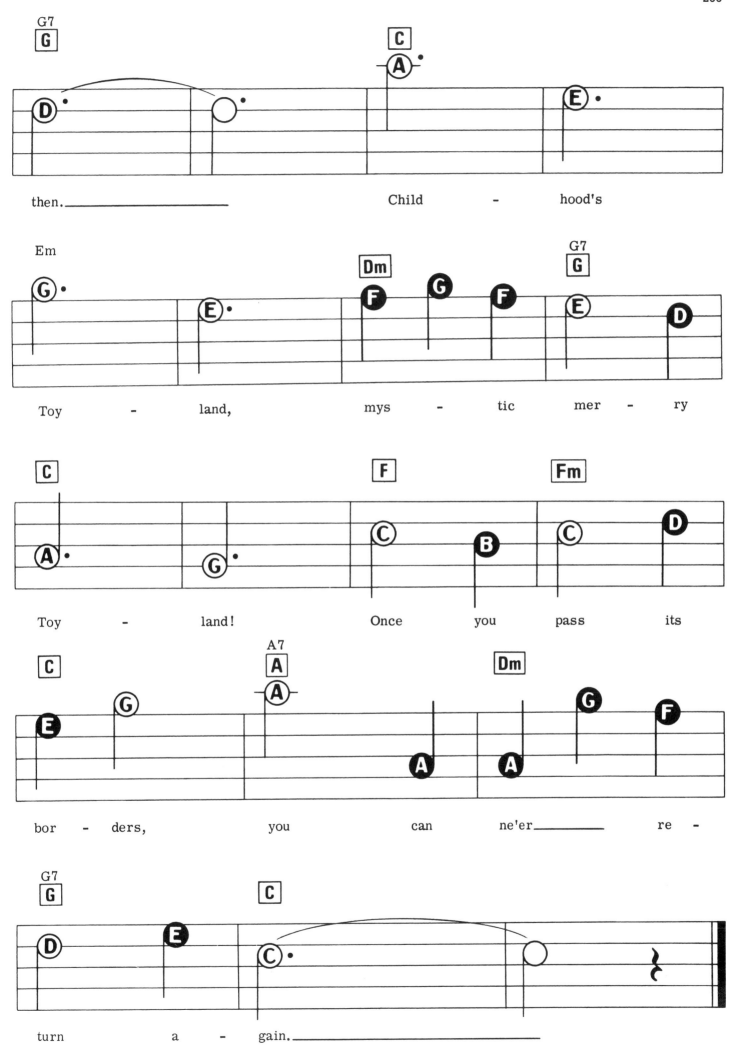

Winds Through the Olive Trees

Registration 2
Rhythm: Waltz

19th Century American Carol

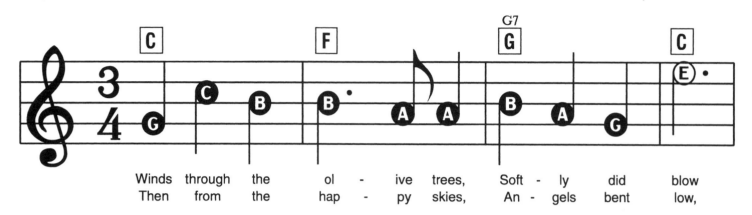

Winds through the ol - ive trees, Soft - ly did blow
Then from the hap - py skies, An - gels bent low,

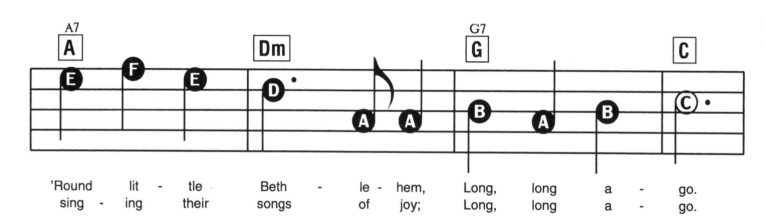

'Round lit - tle Beth - le - hem, Long, long a - go.
sing - ing their songs of joy; Long, long a - go.

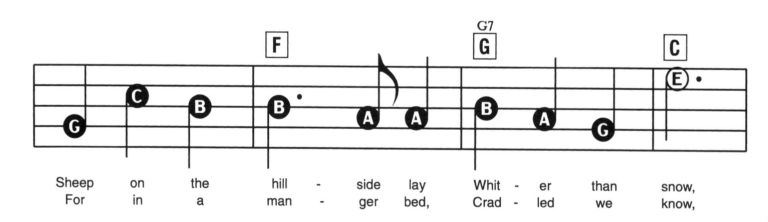

Sheep on the hill - side lay Whit - er than snow,
For in a man - ger bed, Crad - led we know,

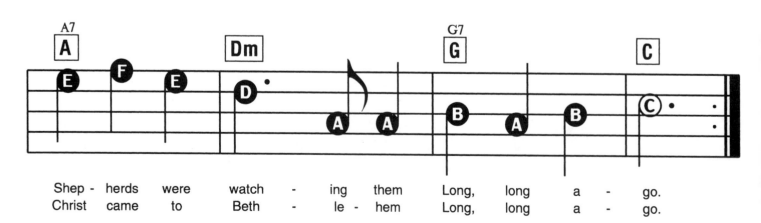

Shep - herds were watch - ing them Long, long a - go.
Christ came to Beth - le - hem Long, long a - go.

'Twas the Night Before Christmas

Registration 9
Rhythm: Swing

Words by Clement Clark Moore
Music by F. Henri Klickman

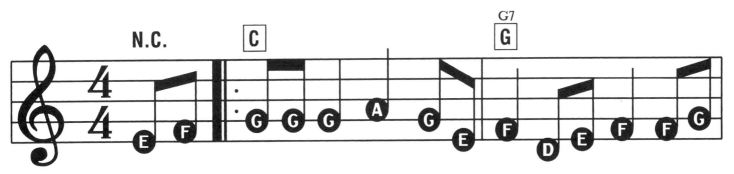

1. 'Twas the night be-fore Christ-mas when all thru the house, not a
2.-7. *(See additional lyrics)*

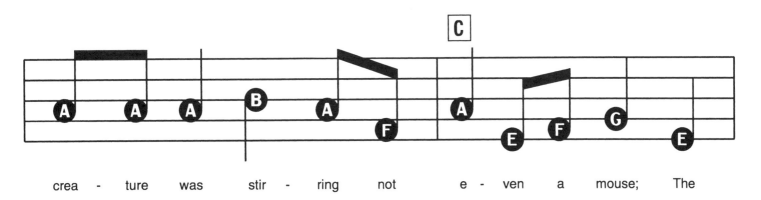

crea - ture was stir - ring not e - ven a mouse; The

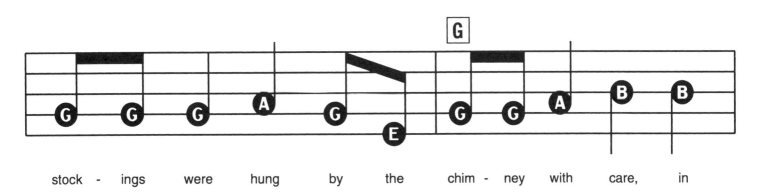

stock - ings were hung by the chim - ney with care, in

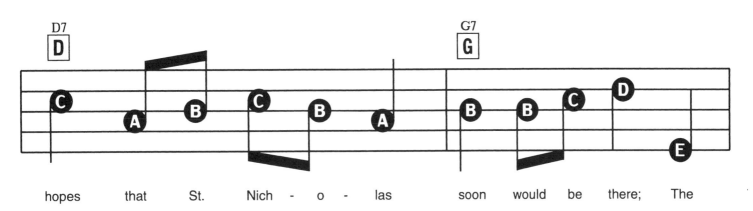

hopes that St. Nich - o - las soon would be there; The

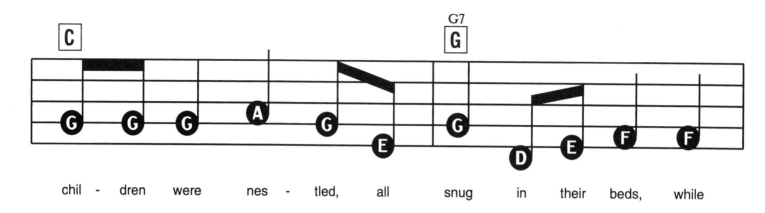

chil - dren were nes - tled, all snug in their beds, while

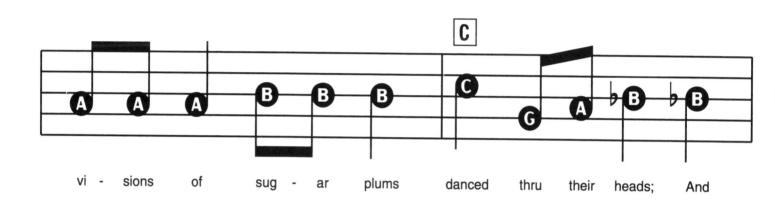

vi - sions of sug - ar plums danced thru their heads; And

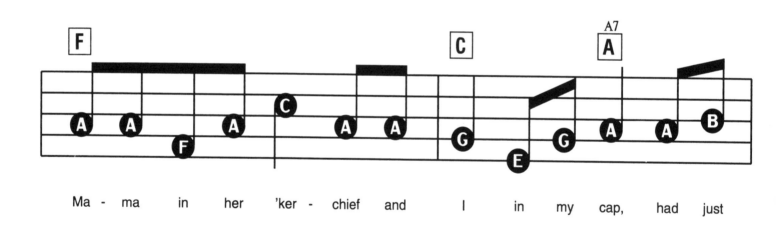

Ma - ma in her 'ker - chief and I in my cap, had just

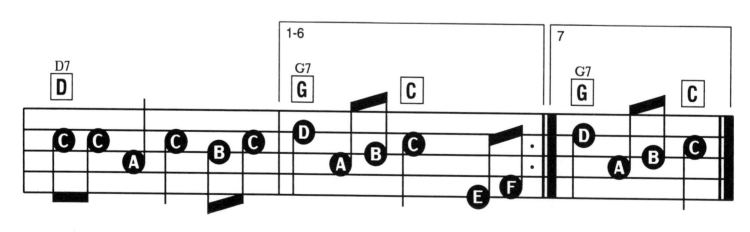

set - tled our brains for a long win - ter's nap. 2. When out all a good - night!"

2. When out on the lawn there arose such a clatter,
   I sprang from my bed to see what was the matter.
   Away to the window I flew like a flash,
   Tore open the shutters and threw up the sash.
   The moon, on the breast of the new-fallen snow,
   Gave a lustre of midday to objects below;
   When what to my wondering eyes should appear
   But a miniature sleigh and eight tiny Reindeer.

3. With a little old driver, so lively and quick,
   I knew in a moment it must be St. Nick.
   More rapid than eagles his coursers they came,
   And he whistled and shouted, and called them by name:
   "Now, Dasher! Now, Dancer! Now, Prancer! Now, Vixen!
   On, Comet! On, Cupid! On, Donner and Blitzen!
   To the top of the porch, to the top of the wall!
   Now dash away, dash away, dash away all."

4. As dry leaves that before the wild hurricane fly,
   When they meet with an obstacle, mount to the sky,
   So up to the house-top the coursers they flew,
   With the sleigh full toys, and St. Nicholas, too.
   And then in a twinkling I heard on the roof
   The prancing and pawing of each little hoof.
   As I drew in my head, and was turning around,
   Down the chimney St. Nicholas came with a bound.

5. He was dressed all in fur from his head to his foot,
   And his clothes were all tarnished with ashes and soot;
   A bundle of toys he had flung on his back,
   And he looked like a peddler just opening his pack.
   His eyes how they twinkled! His dimples how merry!
   His cheeks were like roses, his nose like a cherry,
   His droll little mouth was drawn up like a bow,
   And the beard of his chin was as white as the snow.

6. The stump of a pipe he held tight in his teeth,
   And the smoke, it encircled his head like a wreath.
   He had a broad face, and a round little belly
   That shook, when he laughed, like a bowl full of jelly.
   He was chubby and plump – a right jolly old elf –
   And I laughed when I saw him, in spite of myself.
   A wink of his eye, and a twist of his head,
   Soon gave me to know I had nothing to dread.

7. He spoke not a word, but went straight to his work,
   And filled all the stockings; Then turned with a jerk,
   And laying his finger aside of his nose,
   And giving a nod up the chimney he rose.
   He sprang to his sleigh, to his team gave a whistle,
   And away they all fled like the down of a thistle;
   But I heard him exclaim, ere he drove out of sight –
   "Happy Christmas to all, And to all a good-night."

The Twelve Days of Christmas

Registration 5
Rhythm: None

Traditional English Carol

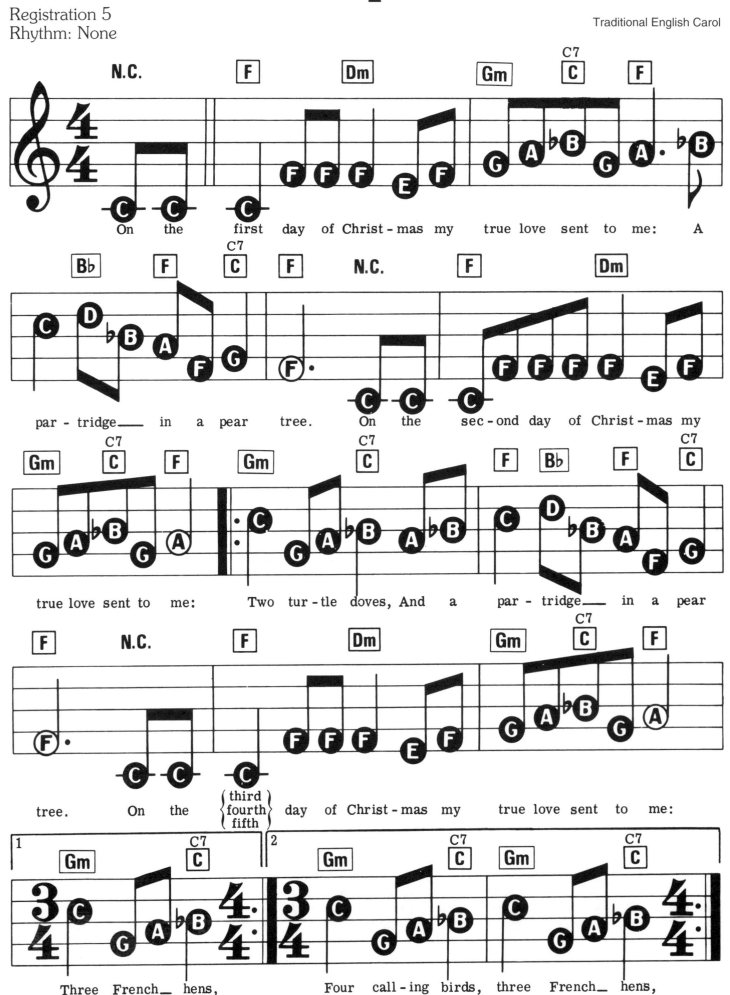

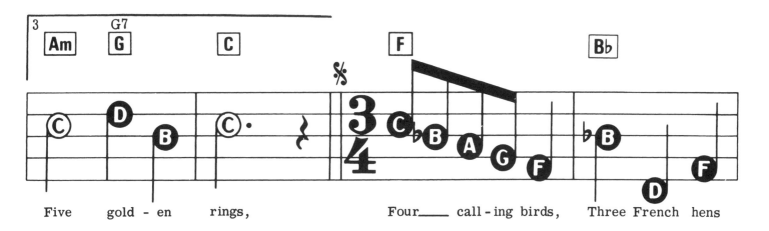

Five gold - en rings,   Four____ call - ing birds,   Three French hens

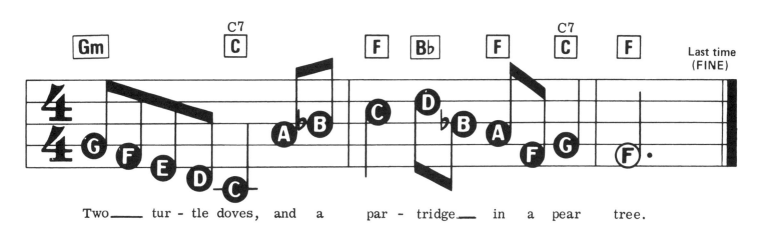

Last time
(FINE)

Two____ tur - tle doves, and a   par - tridge__ in a pear tree.

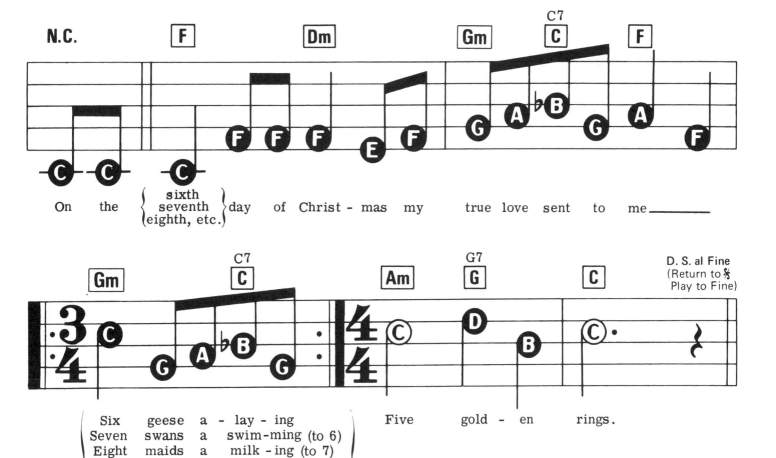

N.C.

On the ⎰ sixth ⎱ day of Christ - mas my   true love sent to me_____
       ⎱ seventh ⎰
       ⎰ eighth, etc. ⎱

D. S. al Fine
(Return to ℅
Play to Fine)

Five gold - en rings.

Six geese a - lay - ing
Seven swans a swim-ming (to 6)
Eight maids a milk - ing (to 7)
Nine la - dies danc - ing (to 8)
Ten lords a leap - ing (to 9)
Eleven pi - pers pip - ing (to 10)
Twelve drum-mers drum-ming (to 11)

While Shepherds Watched Their Flocks

Registration 1
Rhythm: 8 Beat or Pops

Words by Nahum Tate
Music from Easte's *Psalmes*, 1592

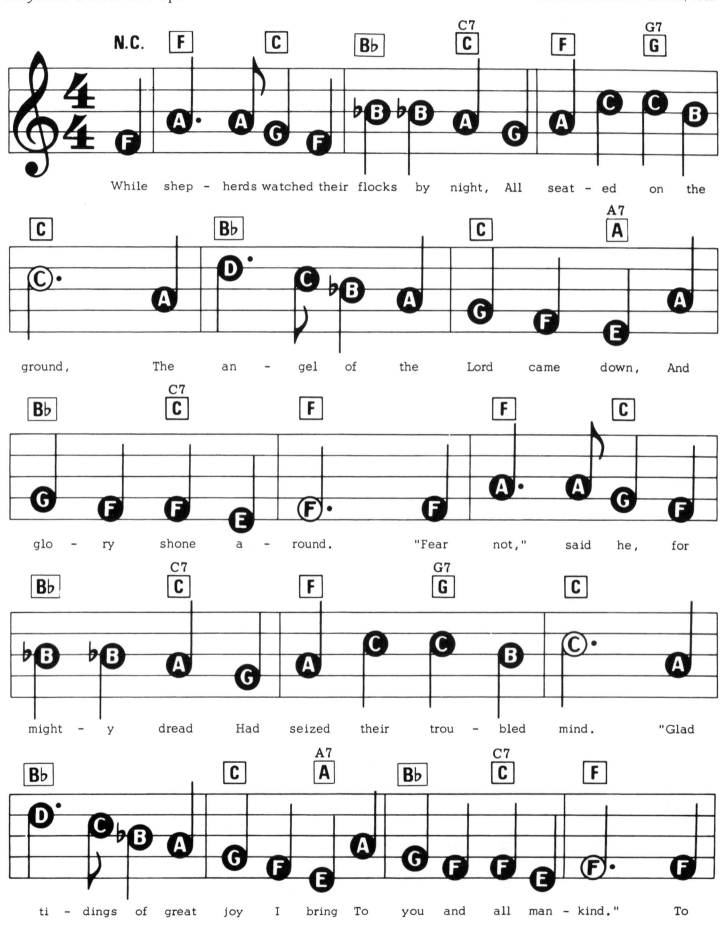

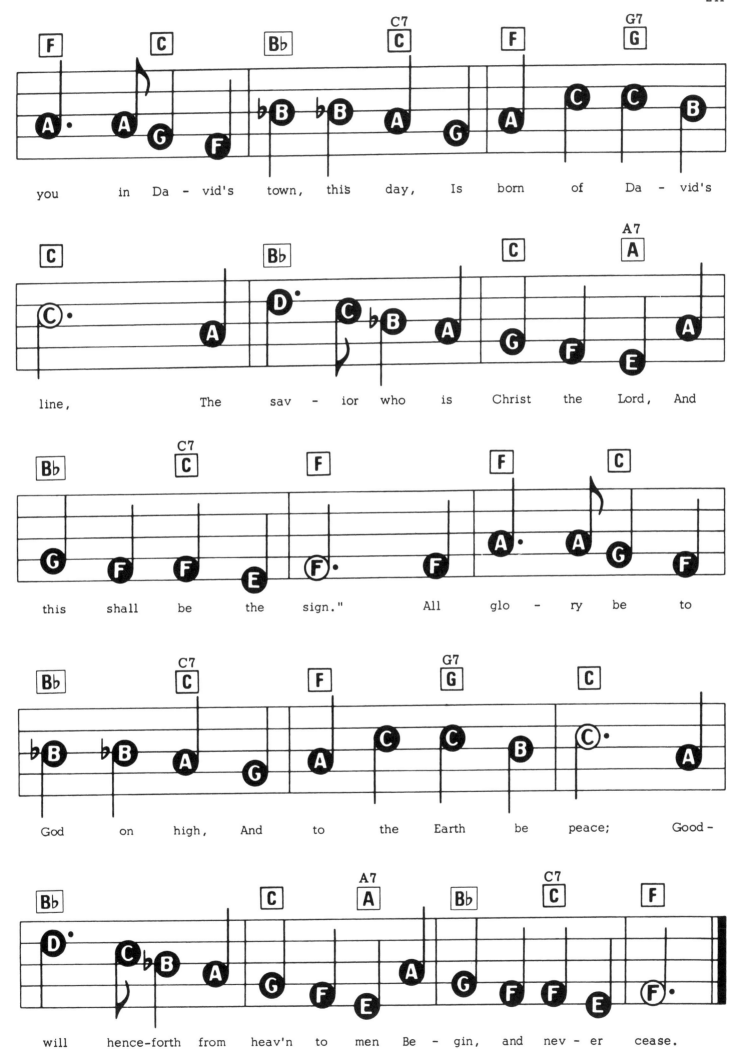

A Virgin Unspotted

Registration 9
Rhythm: None

Traditional English Carol

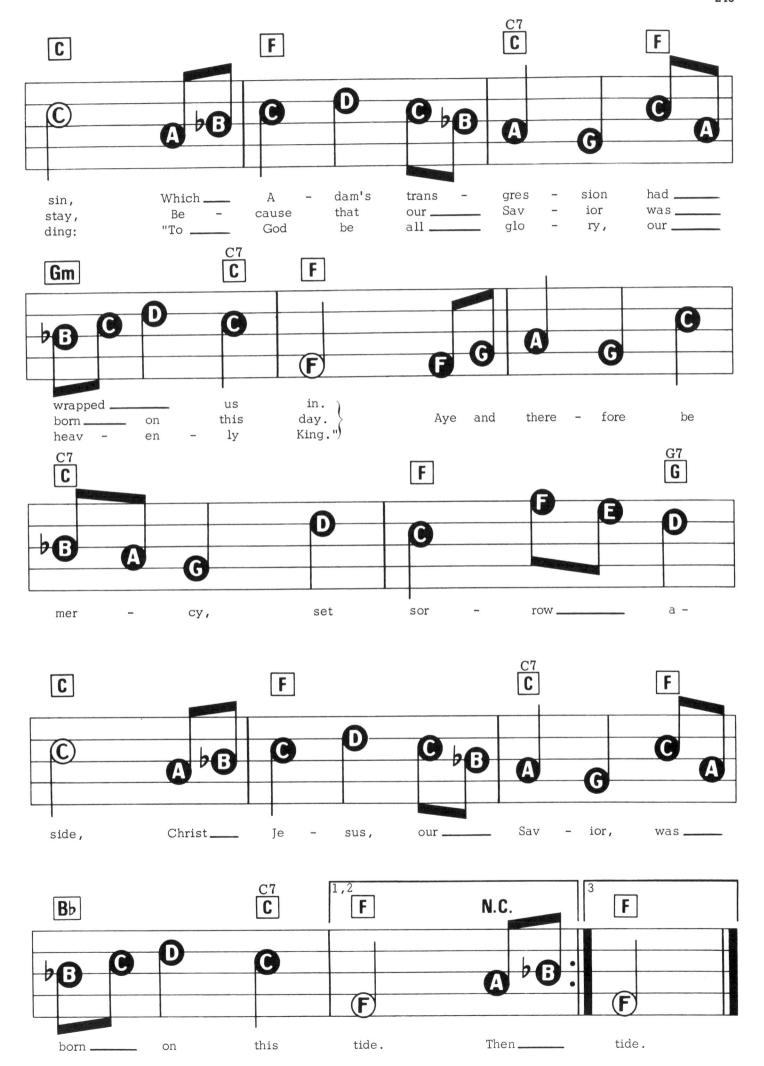

Watchman, Tell Us of the Night

Registration 9
Rhythm: None

Words by John Bowring
Music by George Job Elvey

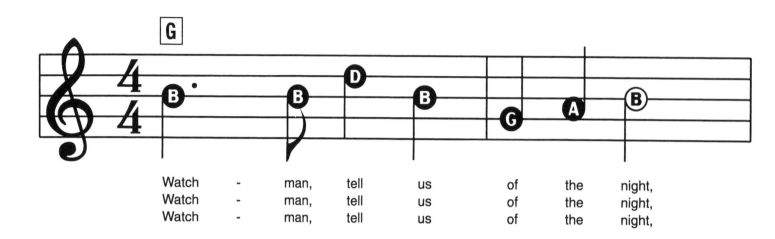

Watch - man, tell us of the night,
Watch - man, tell us of the night,
Watch - man, tell us of the night,

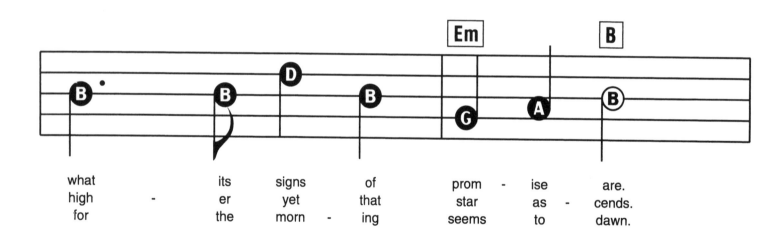

what its signs of prom - ise are.
high - er signs yet of that star as - cends.
for the morn - ing seems to dawn.

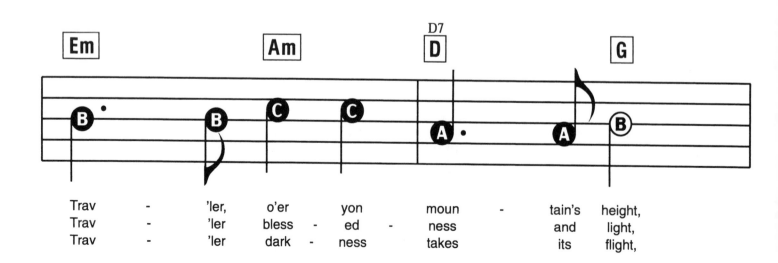

Trav - 'ler, o'er yon moun - tain's height,
Trav - 'ler bless - ed - ness and light,
Trav - 'ler dark - ness takes its flight,

245

We Three Kings of Orient Are

Registration 9
Rhythm: Waltz

Words and Music by
John H. Hopkins, Jr.

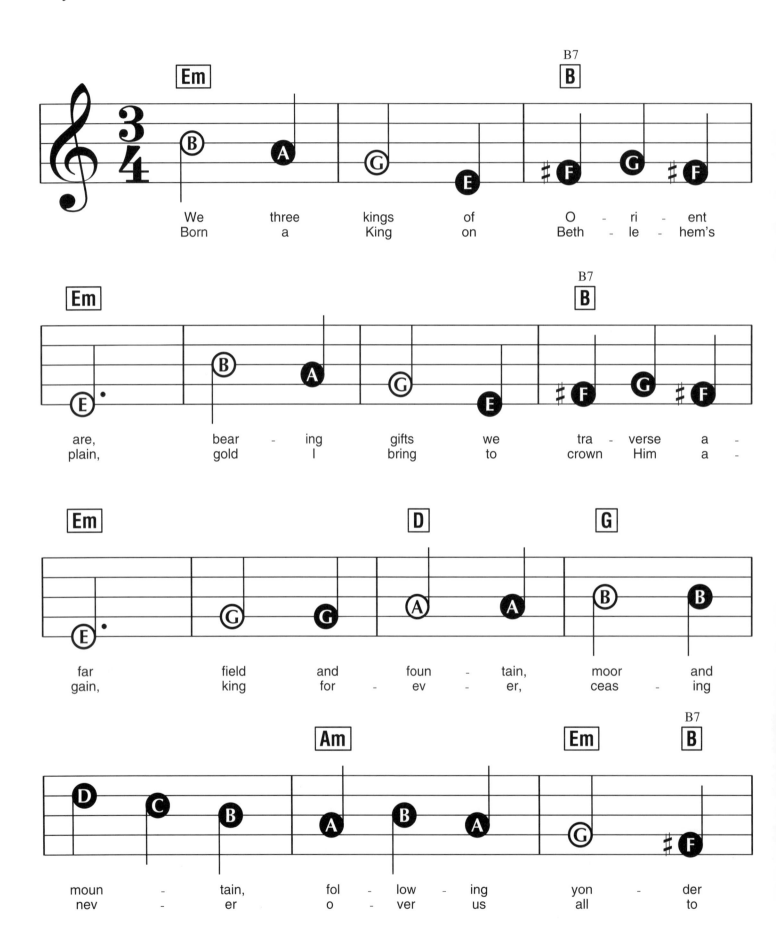

247

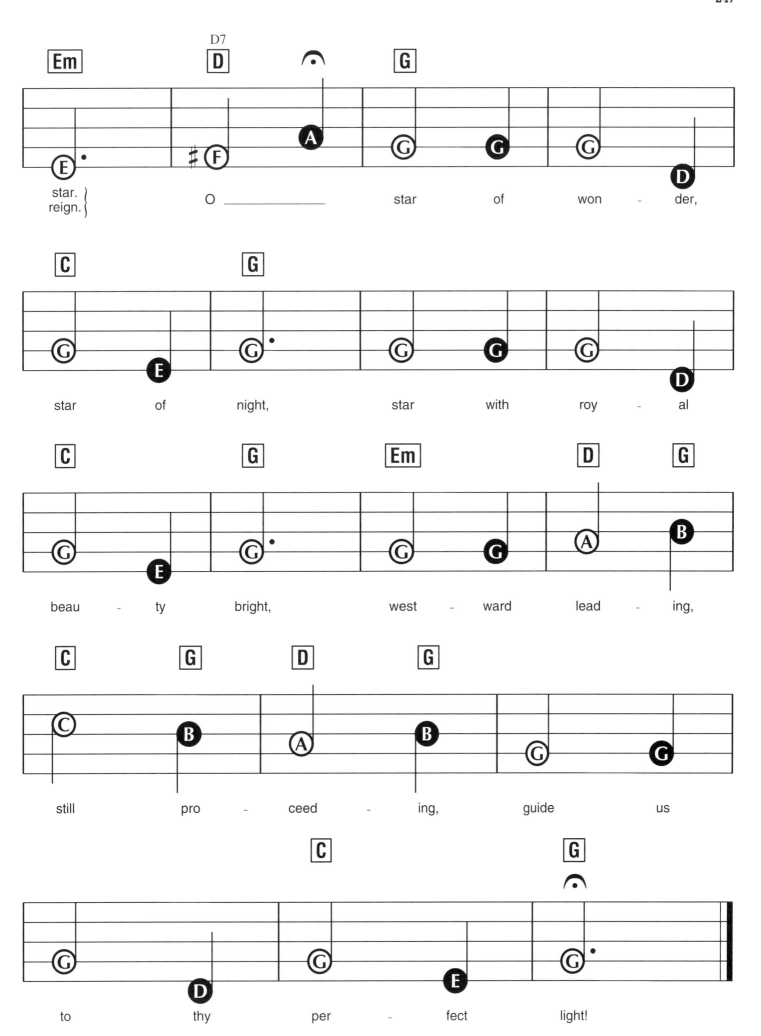

We Wish You a Merry Christmas

Registration 4
Rhythm: None

Traditional English Folksong

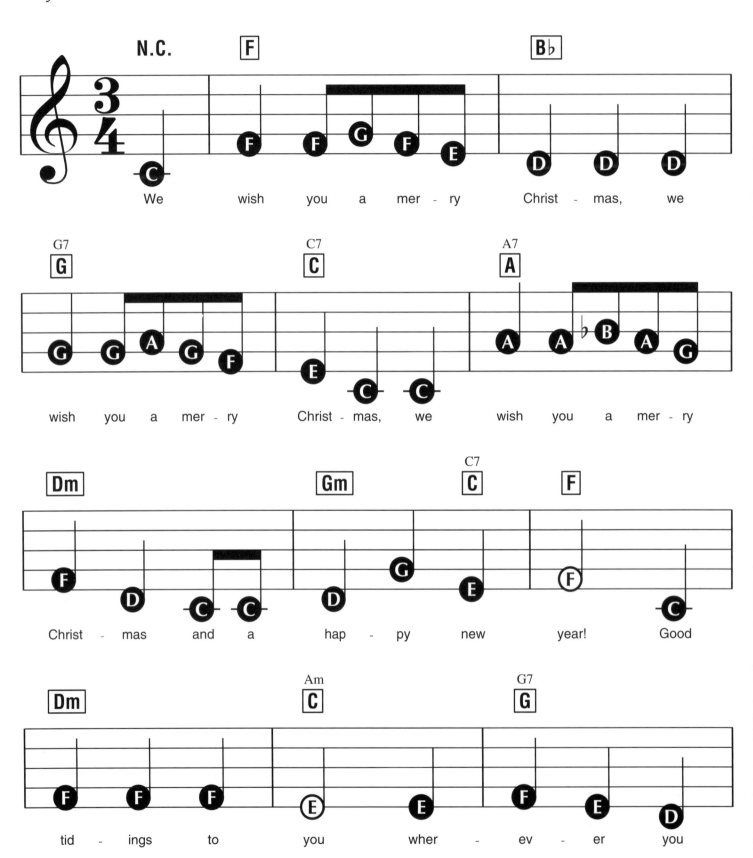

249

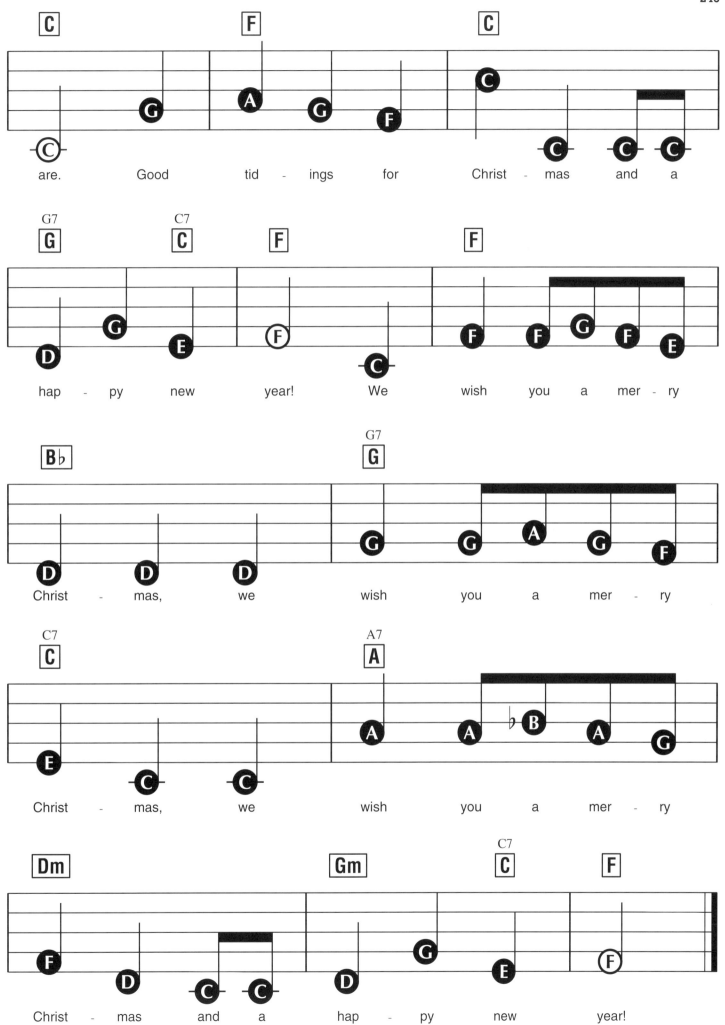

Wexford Carol

Registration 4
Rhythm: Waltz

Traditional Irish Carol

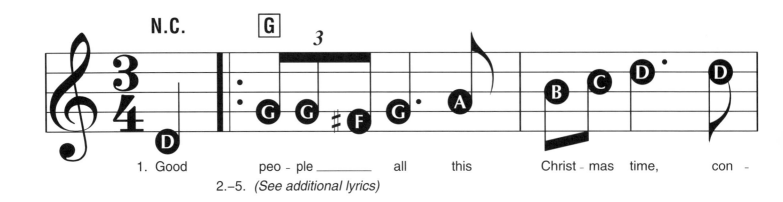

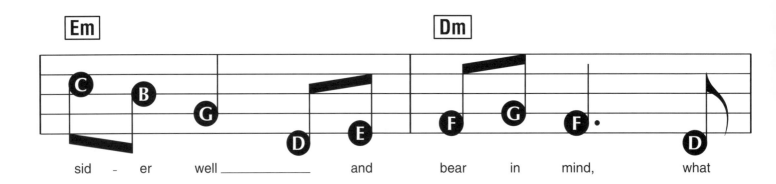

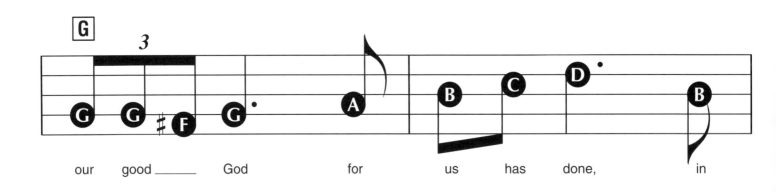

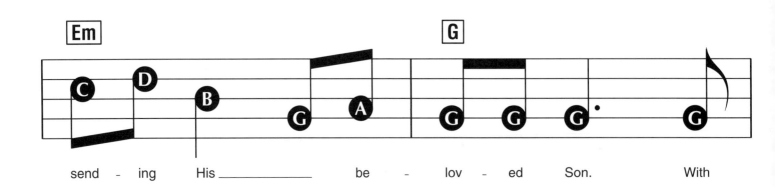

251

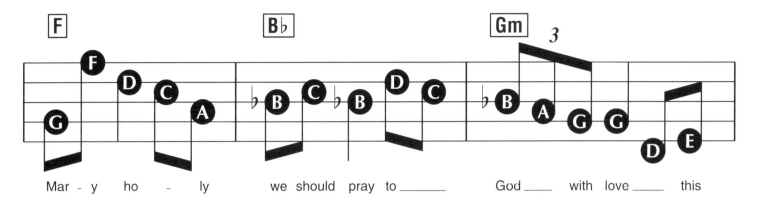

Mar - y ho - ly we should pray to _____ God ____ with love ____ this

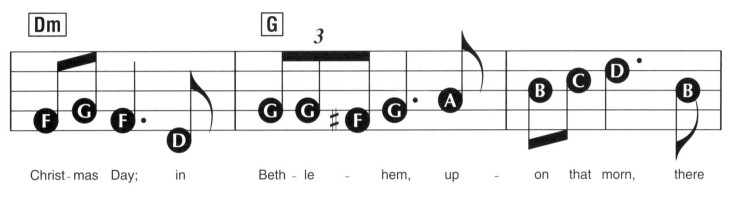

Christ - mas Day; in Beth - le - hem, up - on that morn, there

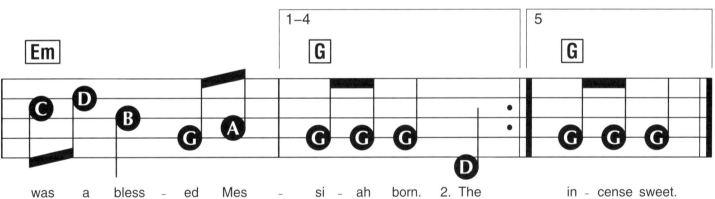

was a bless - ed Mes - si - ah born. 2. The in - cense sweet.

Additional Lyrics

2. The night before that happy tide, the noble Virgin and her guide
   Were long time seeking up and down to find a lodging in the town.
   But mark how all things come to pass: from ev'ry door repell'd, alas!
   As long foretold, their refuge all was but an humble ox's stall.

3. Near Bethlehem did shepherds keep their flocks of lambs and feeding sheep;
   To whom God's angels did appear, which put the shepherds in great fear.
   "Prepare and go," the angels said, "to Bethlehem, be not afraid;
   For there you'll find, this happy morn, a princely babe, sweet Jesus born."

4. With thankful heart and joyful mind, the shepherds went the babe to find,
   And as God's angel had foretold, they did our Saviour Christ behold.
   Within a manger He was laid, and by His side the virgin maid,
   Attending on the Lord of life, who came on earth to end all strife.

5. There were three wise men from afar directed by a glorious star,
   And on they wandered night and day, until they came where Jesus lay.
   And when they came unto that place where our beloved Messiah was,
   They humbly cast them at His feet, with gifts of gold and incense sweet.

What Child Is This?

Registration 10
Rhythm: Waltz

Words by William C. Dix
16th Century English Melody

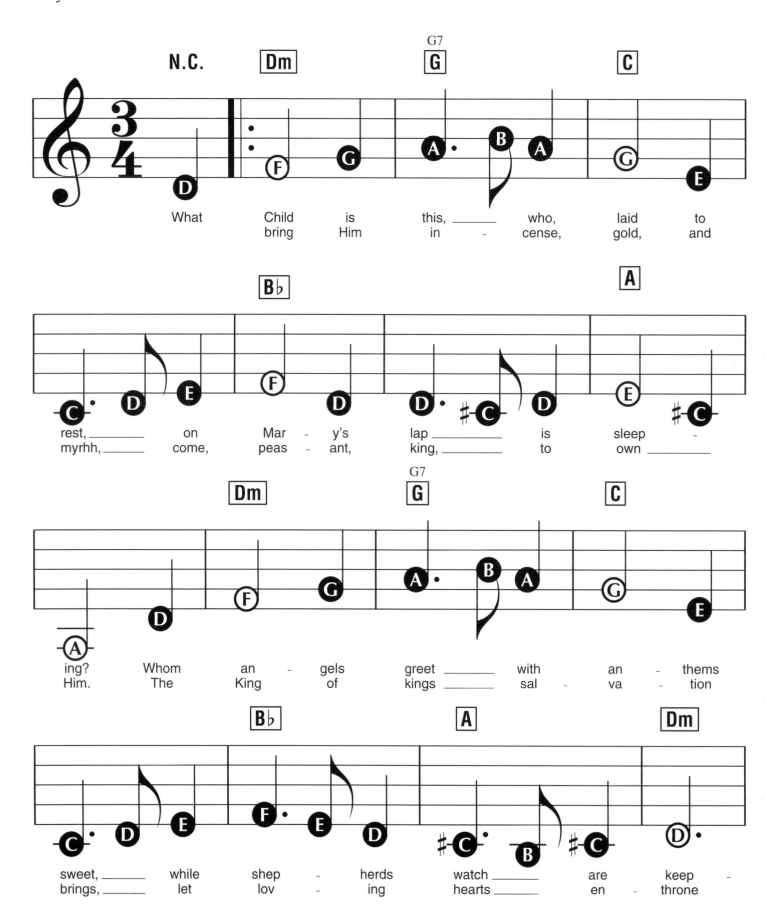

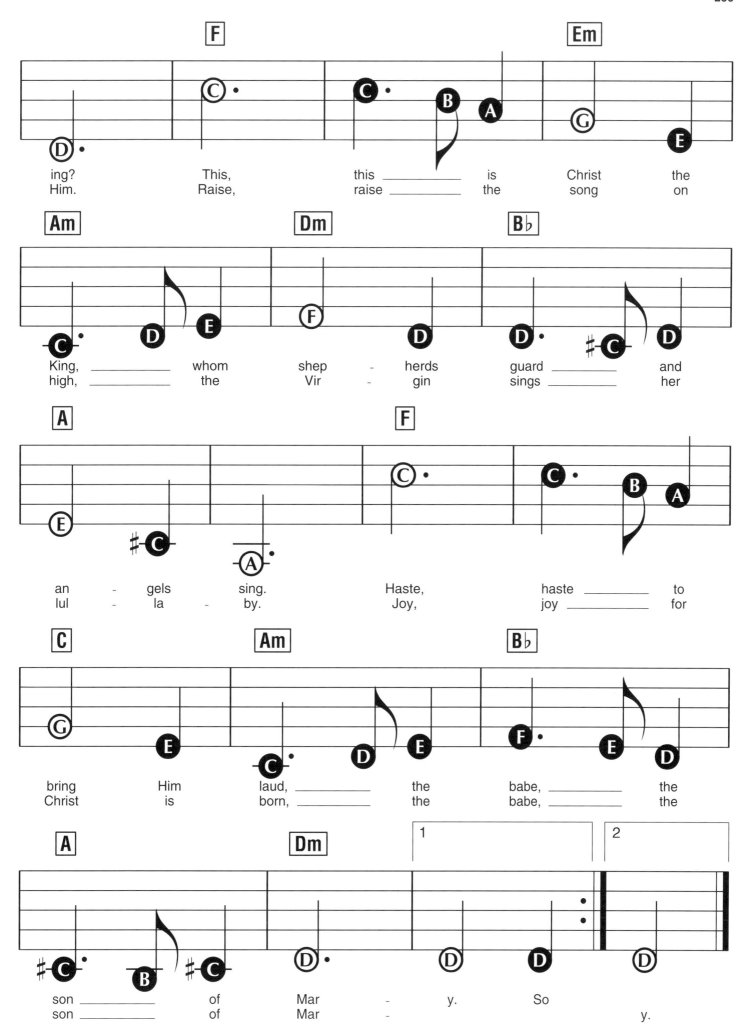

When Christ Was Born of Mary Free

Registration 9
Rhythm: None

Traditional English Carol

1. When Christ was born of
2. herds be - held those
3.,4. *(See additional lyrics)*

Ma - ry _____ free, In Beth - le - hem that
an - gels _____ bright, to them ap - pear - ing

fair ci - ty, an - gels did sing with
with great _____ light and said, 'God's Son is

mirth and glee; In ex - cel - sis _____
born this night,' In ex - cel - sis _____

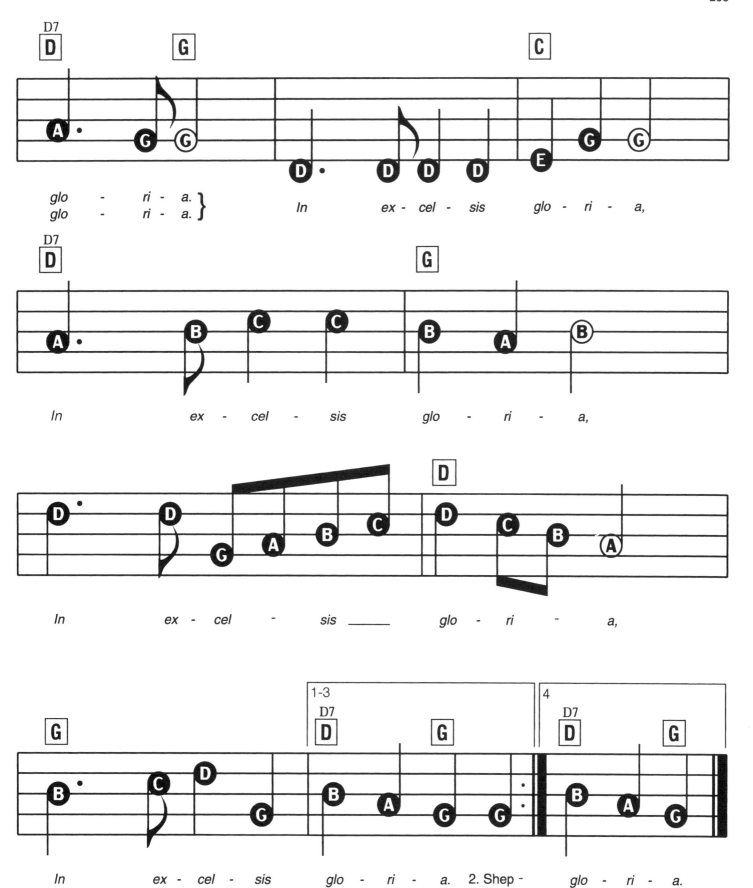

glo - ri - a.
glo - ri - a.
In ex - cel - sis glo - ri - a,

In ex - cel - sis glo - ri - a,

In ex - cel - sis _____ glo - ri - a,

In ex - cel - sis glo - ri - a. 2. Shep - glo - ri - a.

Additional Lyrics

3. This King is come to save mankind,
   As in the scriptures we do find;
   Therefore this song have we in mind;
   In excelsis gloria:
   Chorus

4. Then, O Lord, for Thy great grace,
   Grant us the bliss to see Thy face,
   That we may sing to Thy solace;
   In excelsis gloria:
   Chorus

When Christmas Morn Is Dawning

Registration 7
Rhythm: 8 Beat

Traditional Swedish

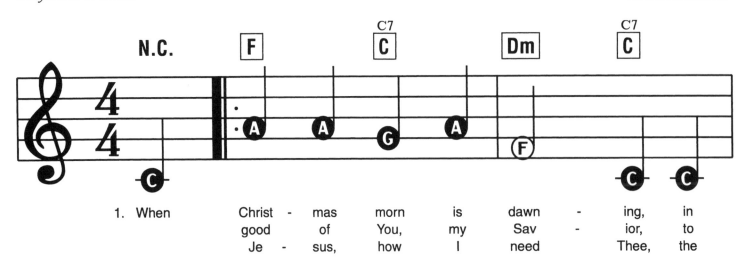

1. When   Christ - mas   morn   is   dawn -   ing,   in
   good   of   You,   my   Sav -   ior,   to
   Je -   sus,   how   I   need   Thee,   the

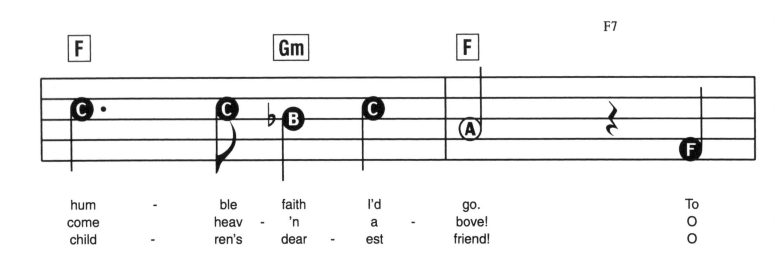

hum -   ble   faith   I'd   go.   To
come   heav - 'n   a - bove!   O
child - ren's   dear - est   friend!   O

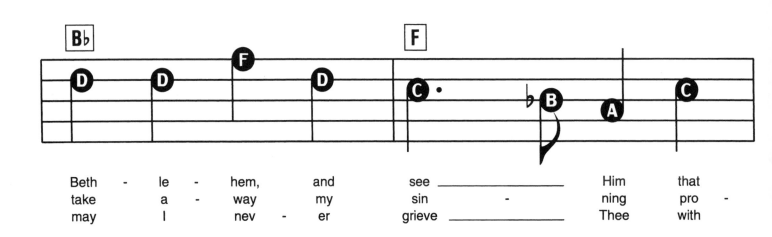

Beth - le - hem,   and   see _____   Him   that
take   a - way   my   sin -   ning   pro -
may   I   nev - er   grieve _____   Thee   with

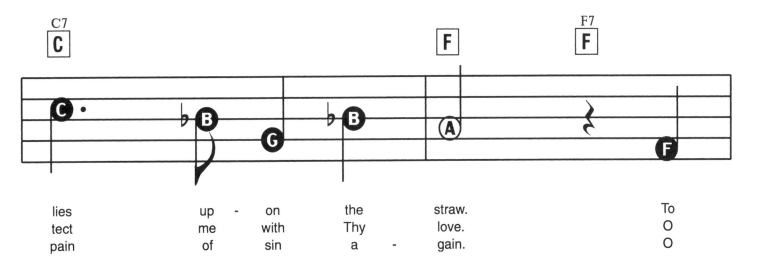

lies		up	-	on	the		straw.		To
tect		me		with	Thy		love.		O
pain		of		sin	a	-	gain.		O

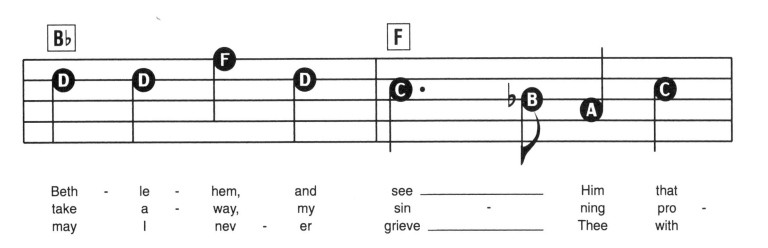

Beth	-	le	-	hem,		and		see _____		Him	that
take		a	-	way,		my		sin _____		ning	pro	-
may		I		nev	-	er		grieve _____		Thee	with

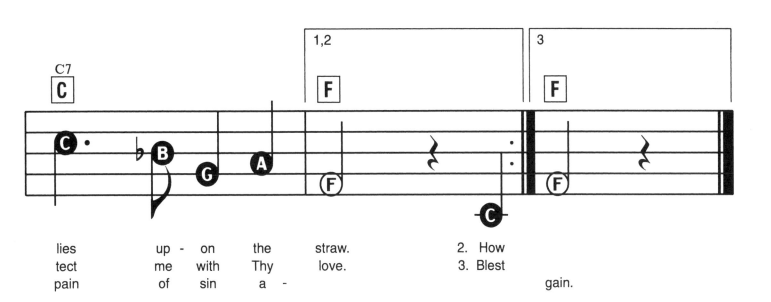

lies		up	-	on	the	straw.	2. How
tect		me		with	Thy	love.	3. Blest
pain		of		sin	a	-		gain.

While by My Sheep

Registration 3
Rhythm: None

Traditional German Carol

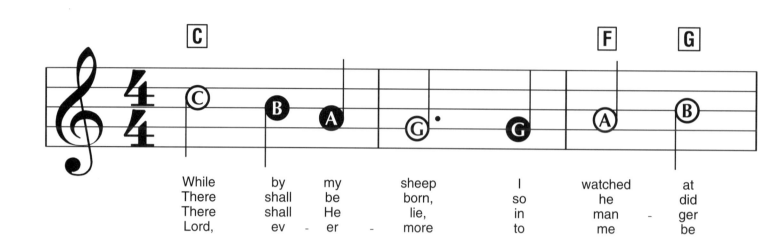

While by my sheep I watched at
There shall be born, so he did
There shall be He lie, in man - ger
Lord, ev - er - more to me be

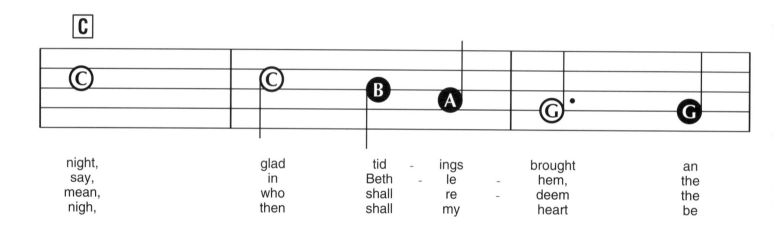

night, glad tid - ings brought an
say, in Beth - le - hem, the
mean, who shall re - deem the
nigh, then shall my heart be

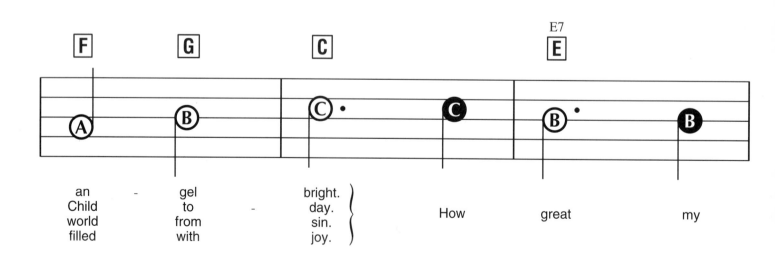

an - gel bright.
Child to day.
world from sin.
filled with joy.

How great my

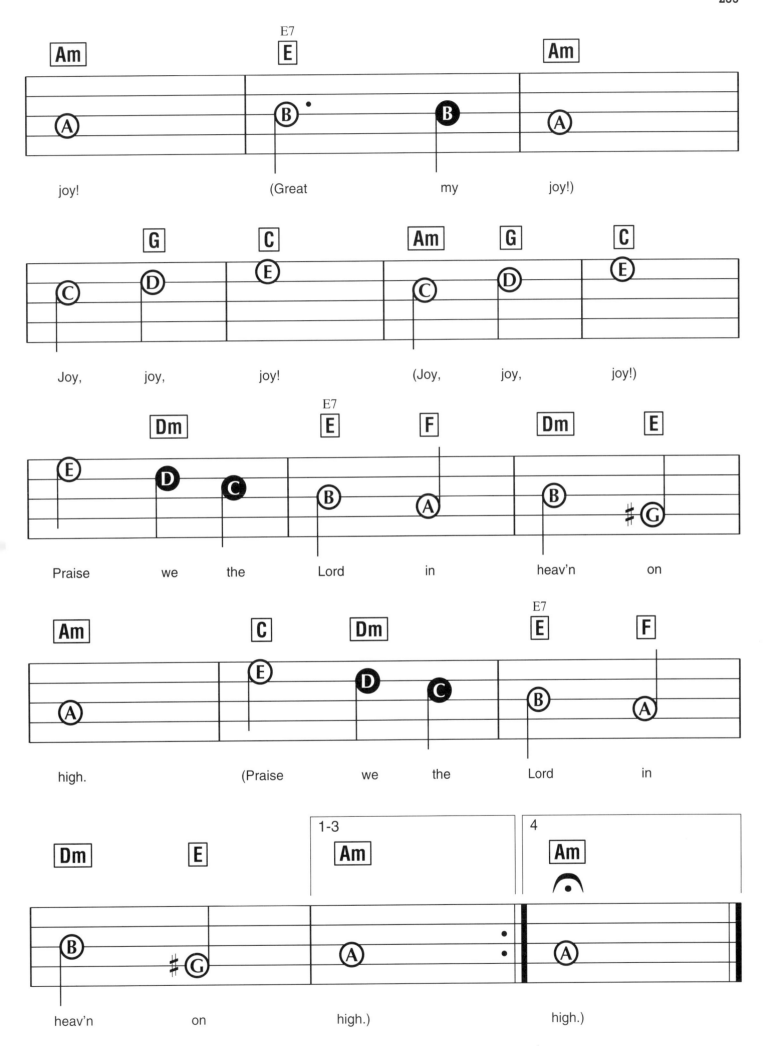

Up on the Housetop

Registration 5
Rhythm: Fox Trot or Swing

Words and Music by
B.R. Handy

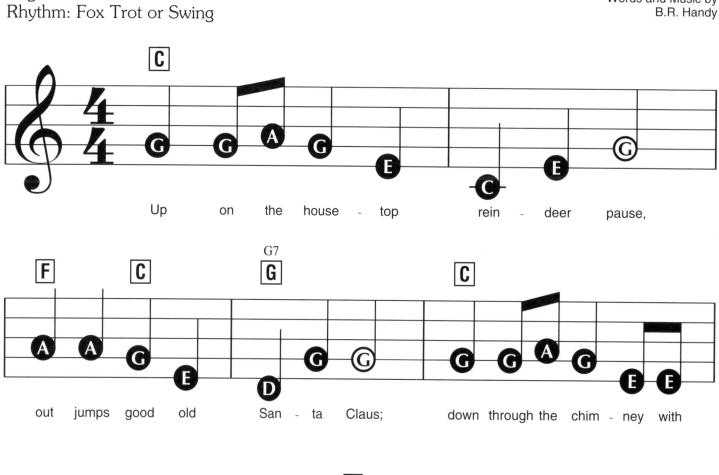

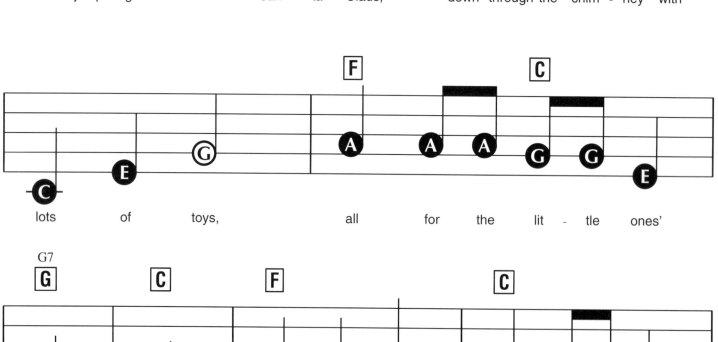

261

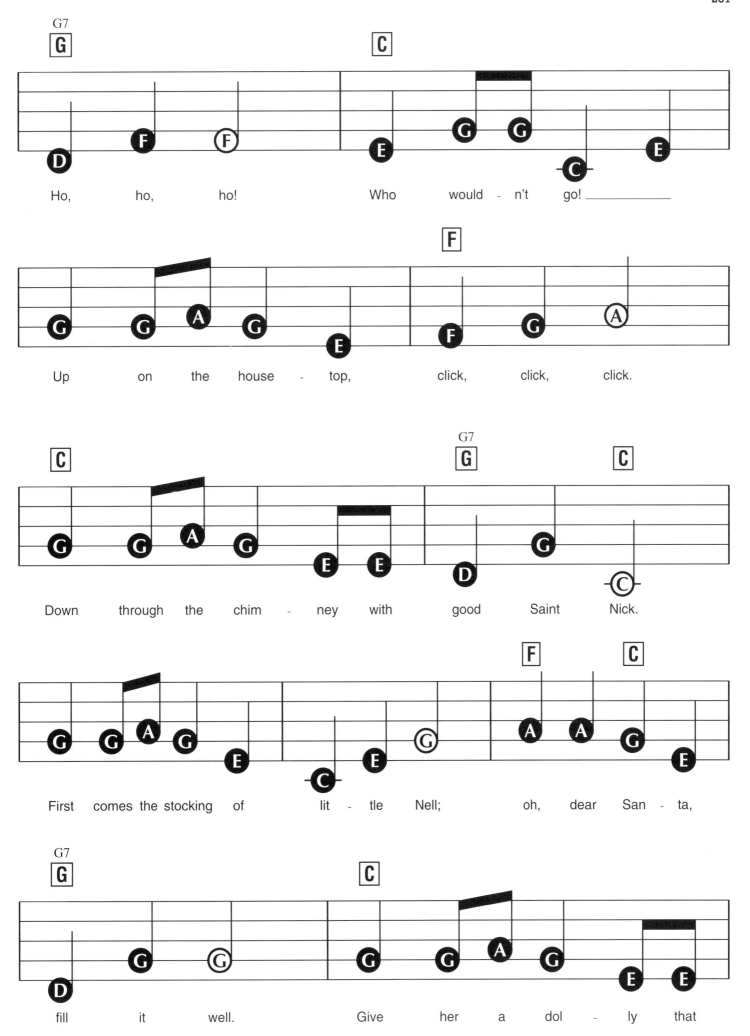

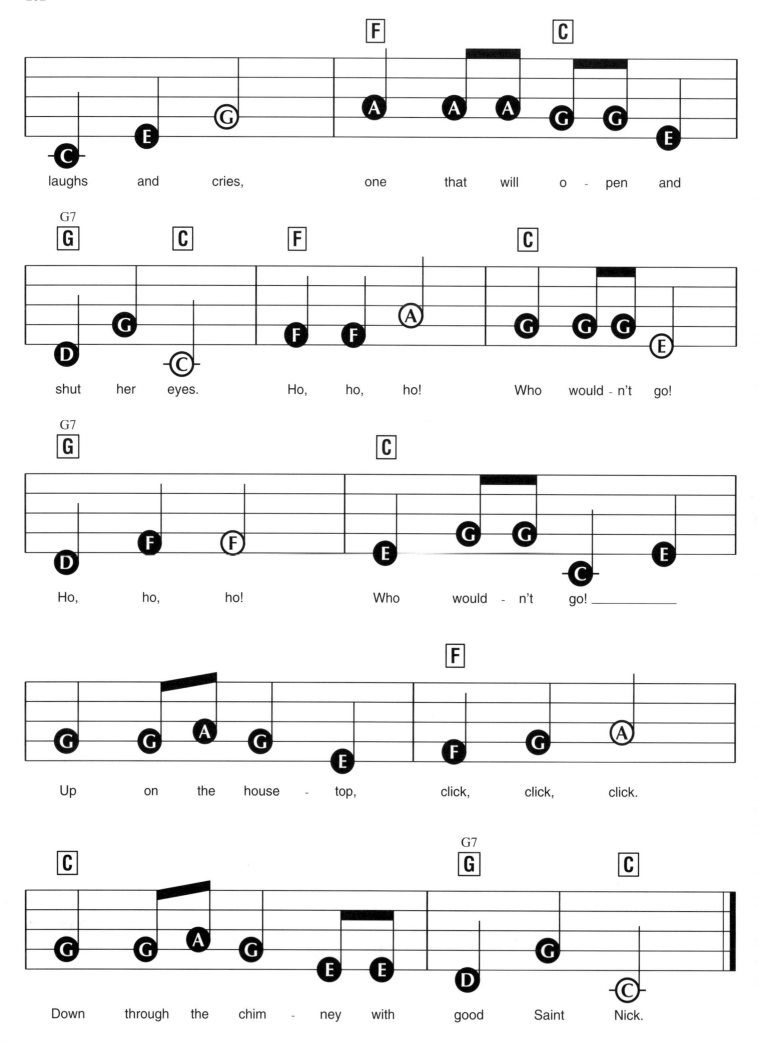

 **Registration Guide**

- Match the Registration number on the song to the corresponding numbered category below. Select and activate an instrumental sound available on your instrument.

- Choose an automatic rhythm appropriate to the mood and style of the song. (Consult your Owner's Guide for proper operation of automatic rhythm features.)

- Adjust the tempo and volume controls to comfortable settings.

Registration

1	Mellow	Flutes, Clarinet, Oboe, Flugel Horn, Trombone, French Horn, Organ Flutes
2	Ensemble	Brass Section, Sax Section, Wind Ensemble, Full Organ, Theater Organ
3	Strings	Violin, Viola, Cello, Fiddle, String Ensemble, Pizzicato, Organ Strings
4	Guitars	Acoustic/Electric Guitars, Banjo, Mandolin, Dulcimer, Ukulele, Hawaiian Guitar
5	Mallets	Vibraphone, Marimba, Xylophone, Steel Drums, Bells, Celesta, Chimes
6	Liturgical	Pipe Organ, Hand Bells, Vocal Ensemble, Choir, Organ Flutes
7	Bright	Saxophones, Trumpet, Mute Trumpet, Synth Leads, Jazz/Gospel Organs
8	Piano	Piano, Electric Piano, Honky Tonk Piano, Harpsichord, Clavi
9	Novelty	Melodic Percussion, Wah Trumpet, Synth, Whistle, Kazoo, Perc. Organ
10	Bellows	Accordion, French Accordion, Mussette, Harmonica, Pump Organ, Bagpipes

E-Z PLAY® TODAY PUBLICATIONS

The E-Z Play® Today songbook series is the shortest distance between beginning music and playing fun! It features full-size 9" x 12" books with patented easy-to-read, easy-to-play notation. The accurate arrangements are simple enough for the beginner, but with authentic-sounding chord and melody lines. The books also include a registration guide for choosing appropriate keyboard sounds.

FOR MORE INFORMATION, SEE YOUR LOCAL MUSIC DEALER,
OR WRITE TO:

HAL•LEONARD® CORPORATION

7777 W. BLUEMOUND RD. P.O. BOX 13819 MILWAUKEE, WI 53213

Songlists and more titles available at **www.halleonard.com**
Prices, contents, and availability subject to change without notice.